# THE PROTECTORS

The Heroic Story of the
in Their Unending, Unsung Battles
and Abroad. **by**

*Former United States Commissioner*

NEW YORK

# The Protectors

Narcotics Agents, Citizens and Officials

Against Organized Crime in America

## Harry J. Anslinger

of Narcotics, with J. DENNIS GREGORY

Farrar, Straus and Company

*The White House*

*To*

*Harry Jacob Anslinger*
*Distinguished Citizen*

In recognition of an outstanding record of achievement.

In your dedicated efforts to combat the illegal traffic in narcotic drugs, you have applied unparalleled knowledge, skill, perseverance and ingenuity and have fashioned an effective organization to pursue this objective.

Your noteworthy achievements in this field have earned for you the respect, gratitude and admiration, not only of your own country, but also of the world community.

*John F. Kennedy*

September 27, 1962

# INTRODUCTION

I have worked with or known intimately some of the bravest people in the world. This book is my personal tribute to them, and my thanks to them for having made my life richer. They have made living safer and the nation stronger.

But many of them are dead. Agent Moore, gunned down in a New Orleans street; Lieutenant Petrosino, a Mafia hunter who was executed by that infamous mob; Supervisor Bangs, blasted to death in Minneapolis. Their names mean little to the average citizen, but they guarded property and life in this land beleaguered with crime. They fought the hot war. No level of our society escapes it. It jumps on all fronts—espionage, narcotics, murder, white slavery, gambling. prostitution, extortion—they've fought in all phases. The battles aren't easy, for within the framework of the law itself there are weaknesses and weak people.

Organized crime wears no uniform, and its contempt for the uniform of the law is supreme. In order to smash criminal combines and bring gangsters to justice, we've had to step out of familiar uniforms into theirs—plain clothes. The criminal must always move in the shadows, in the underworld. It is our job to follow him there, but at the moment of truth the agent must expose himself as a representative of law and order so the criminal will know that, however deeply he has burrowed, he has been followed and caught.

The dangers to the undercover agent are many; one mistake can mean his finish. Therefore the agent must be tough, resourceful, and honest. Honesty cannot be taken for granted; the underworld controls millions of dollars; and in the criminal's view, the cop, unless he quickly proves otherwise, is always for hire. Because criminals come in all sizes, shapes and colors, so also do our agents. An agent must be a better actor than an Academy Award winner, quick on his feet, even faster with his hands, and ten times as fast with his mind. Even so, we seldom permit an agent to take on a job without "cover"—protection from other nearby agents who have both the operating agent and the criminal under surveillance. Unlike the crime dramas on television, the majority of criminal apprehensions are a matter of strict and smooth teamwork.

Undercover detection work is accepted police practice in many countries. In Mexico an agent who induces a criminal to perpetrate still another crime, has a difficult time of it in court. A number of judges in the United States also hold this view of the agent provocateur. However, we act within the law.

Sometimes our men find themselves outside the law. For example, while on an assignment, an agent may be picked up by local police. In such a situation he cannot tell the nearest cop who he is. He is jailed until we can get the ear of the judge after he has been bailed out by a local attorney. But before this happens, depending upon the seriousness of the charge or the urgency of the need to establish the identity of the prisoner, our man is quite likely, in more cities than I care to name, to be kicked and beaten, in violation of his elementary rights. I need not comment any further on this; the ramifications should be obvious to every citizen.

To be sure, most of the people in this book are agents, but many are not; many are criminals, some are plain citizens, and some are prosecutors or judges. A couple are espionage agents. Except for the criminals, they are Protectors all.

H. J. A.

# CONTENTS

# THE PROTECTORS

# I ACES BACK TO BACK

I began my government career as a member of the efficiency board of the Ordnance Division, War Department, in Washington in 1917. One year later, however, I found myself attached to the American Legation at The Hague, Netherlands; it was there that I met Julius A. Van Hee.

Dapper and always immaculately dressed, Van was born of American parents in Ghent, Belgium. He smoked cigarettes out of the left corner of his mouth. When he spoke, his words came like bursts of machine-gun fire. The American Vice-Consul at Ghent, Van knew the territory and the temper of the European people, and this was invaluable since we had been at war with Germany since April 6, 1917. Under the direction of Ambassador Brand Whitlock and Hugh Gibson, Counselor of the Embassy, Van had provided accurate information on German offensive actions even before we entered the conflict.

Van was directly responsible for saving thousands of Allied lives. Through a German contact he secured a model of a German

3

gas mask and smuggled it to his superiors between the legs of a young lady who wore it as a sanitary napkin. The model enabled the Allies to anticipate the possibility of gas attacks and to start a crash program to manufacture their own masks.

When he was not gracing the drawing rooms, Van spent his time around Schiedemskidyck, the skid row of Rotterdam. Rotterdam was filled with German officers who had been repatriated from England, and Van surmised that they would be in possession of a lot of information. On the docks he befriended a Dutch barge captain who, once joyous at the early German successes, had become disenchanted with them because they controlled the Dutch waterways with a stiff hand. The captain ran his barge between Terneuzen, Holland, and Ghent. It was through this disgruntled captain that Van met a German sergeant who hated his superiors. The sergeant worked in the office of General Moritz Ferdinand von Bissing. Bissing had been a cavalry general of the 7th Army Corps from 1901 to 1907 and Governor-General of Belgium from 1914 to 1917. All of his family, the sergeant confided to Van in a Ghent restaurant, had been destroyed by the Prussian warmongers. They kicked him; they cuffed him; they treated him like a dog. The sergeant was seeking revenge and Van was aware of it. A few days later he contacted the sergeant. Could the sergeant give him any information on the morale of the German army? What was the weather like along the Somme? These were vague questions, of course, but the answers came back with such accuracy and speed that Van was sure the sergeant could be developed into an important source of information.

Even as he was cultivating the German sergeant, Van had another task on his hands—keeping the Dutch out of the war. Although professing neutrality, the Dutch were strongly pro-German. When there was an Allied gain in the south, the Dutch were glum; when the Germans were winning, they cheered. The Duke of Mecklenburg, Queen Wilhelmina's consort, was a German. He had a small band of cavalry which he kept trying to enlist on the German side. It was all the Queen could do to keep him from dashing off to the front. One night in a restaurant where Van and I had gone for a decent meal—the food wasn't very good at this time—the Duke came in and loudly voiced pro-German sentiments. A young Dutch officer walked up to him and said, "Can't you understand, the Queen is trying to keep us neutral!" The young officer let fly and the Duke wound up on the seat of his pants.

Van had a knack for getting along with people on all levels and this led him into a meeting with a young attractive English girl who later became famous as a novelist and playwright. She had heard so much about him that she came to him for help in getting through the German lines to Brussels. Most of her luggage was still in her hotel room there and rumor had it that the city was due for a plundering by the Germans any day. With American flags flying from his speeding car, Van drove her to the Hotel DeVille. The Palais des Justice and the Cathedral had already been taken over by the Germans. The great square of the Gare du Nord was being used as a barracks and was guarded by sentries. It was Sunday when Van drove up with his attractive guest, leaped out of the car and, with his customary courtesy, helped her out. They had not moved more than a dozen steps before a sentry leveled his rifle at them and ordered them to get back into the car.

"Go to hell," Van said, "and don't point that goddam gun at me or I'll break your head for you."

The sentry lowered his rifle; Van had talked to him like a German officer. The girl secured all her luggage and she and Van drove back to safety.

On another occasion, he sped from Ghent to Brussels to get some vaccine that would help avert a possible epidemic. In the car he took a package of letters from German officers who had been captured and imprisoned at Bruges. As he expected, he ran smack into trouble getting back. He promptly called General von Ludewitz, the commander, and asked for safe conduct to Ghent.

Brusquely, von Ludewitz said, "I am sorry, Mr. Van Hee, but there is nothing I can do. Perhaps in a few days."

"Oh, General, that won't do at all," Van said. "I intend to get back today."

Ludewitz coughed impatiently into the phone.

"It happens," Van went on, "that I have with me a great number of letters from the German officer prisoners at Bruges. They would do wonders for the morale of your men. No pass, General, no letters. . . ."

Van got his pass.

Van Hee was joined in his work by Charlie Dyar. Dyar worked out of The Hague and was so good at his job that he was considered the unofficial ambassador. Van, meanwhile, had been getting important information from his German sergeant. German attacks were blunted mysteriously or feinted out of position; the Allies counterattacked with success after success. The German General Staff was in an uproar; von Bissing shook up his staff and an intensive hunt for Allied espionage agents began. Van went to The Hague, waiting for things to cool off. There he helped Charlie Dyar card some 13,000 German spies for French Army Intelligence; most of the spies were Belgian.

Charlie was so astute an analyst of the war that President Wilson ordered and received his report of current situations in Europe the very first thing each and every morning. After digesting Charlie's notes, the President could then interpret the progress of the war. Charlie Dyar was just the opposite of Van; he was a Harvard man, tall, well-groomed, taciturn, with remarkable composure. He looked a little like Gary Cooper and was called "The Sphinx." He almost never smiled. Behind this cool façade Charlie was very retiring and often downright shy. But with his thirteen years as a Foreign Service officer in Berlin, he knew the Germans as no one else. The Germans greatly respected him and for a time he was kept under as much surveillance as Julius Van Hee.

By now, with some of the heat off, Van had returnd to his post at Ghent. He resumed contact with the sergeant, but that relationship was coming to an end. The German U-boats had played havoc with shipping and the Allied High Command decided that one way to insure shipping was to blockade the U-boat fleet.

So, on a fog-shrouded night, the British cruiser Vindictive, her ancient screws turning with much effort and noise, her crew tense, joined in a raid upon the German submarine base in the Zeebrugge Canal. The base, near the North Sea, was the largest of the German fleet. The Vindictive and her crew had but one objective—to place the weary old cruiser across the Canal and scuttle her. This was a volunteer mission for the crew. Gunfire was heavy; spotlights swept the area, but the raiders steamed in, firing back. The Vindictive maneuvered into position and explosives were set and the sea cocks opened. Her survivors were swept from the sea by a gallant destroyer assigned to the task of picking up whatever crew remained alive.

The Allies didn't know how successful the mission of the Vindictive was until Van's sergeant stole photographs that showed the old cruiser in place across the Channel. The Germans had been thoroughly bottled up. Now they bent every effort to keep the Allies from knowing how well they had succeeded. The pilfered photographs gave away the answer.

So dramatic had been the role of the Vindictive that the British had the battle scene painted on the walls of the Pantheon where they record great British sea battles. King George unveiled the painting—and the Germans knew that Allied espionage had discovered the extent of the damage caused by the raid. German intelligence tracked the theft of the photo from the desk of von Bissing to the sergeant and finally to the Allies. Of course, Julius A. Van Hee had been behind it all.

The sergeant was sentenced to die by firing squad. I was told that he went to his death bravely, not regretting for a minute his stand against the Prussian masters.

When, late in 1918, it became apparent that the Germans had lost the war, Van was rushed to the border, assigned to get through the lines and pinpoint the bridges over which the Germans were retreating. The information was telegraphed to London, and within hours the British Royal Air Force had bombed the escape routes. The Germans, who by this time were in full retreat, were forced to cross a narrow sector in the province of Limburg. That strip juts from Holland into Belgium. The Germans requested permission to use the strip to permit the escape of thousands of troops. Immediately the Dutch Foreign Minister gathered the Allied ambassadors and ministers in The Hague and bluntly told them that he would give Germans permission to use the corridor, and thus violated Dutch neutrality. The Duke of Mecklenburg may also have cast his weight in favor of the German request.

The Allies never forgave the Dutch this partisan act and they shifted the League of Nations headquarters from The Hague's Peace Palace (which had been built with funds from America's Andrew Carnegie) to Geneva, Switzerland. Had it not been for that breach, today's disarmament talks might now be going on in Holland instead of Switzerland.

Tough and relentless during the war, Charlie Dyar was one of the first to let his hair down when the Armistice came. Plastered to his chops, Charlie and Lou Wilson, an American bartender, rushed through the streets shouting and singing, leading Dutchmen by the hundreds in wild, rollicking song. The Dutch didn't understand Charlie. He was sailing through "Bless 'em All," substituting a four-letter word for "bless."

President Wilson sent Charlie on an interim appointment to begin peace negotiations with the Germans. Ellis Dressel took over soon after with Allen Dulles, then a twenty-five-year-old boy wonder, as first secretary.

Van turned his many talents to helping distribute food supplies to the Belgians under Herbert Hoover's American Relief Administration. This vast organization provided food and other urgently needed items to sixteen million people in eighteen European countries between 1918 and 1923. In the middle of this mighty mercy mission was Van.

Among the pro-German Belgians particularly, he had created

some enemies. When he finally left Foreign Service to go into a private export business, they charged him with having been a German spy. In spite of the great work he had done to help the Belgians, the charge stuck and Van, who had been made a kind of knight and presented a decoration by the King of Belgium, was brought to trial. "Sir" Van, as we called him when we stopped by to drink up his champagne, was in trouble.

But sentiment reversed itself and when his trial was held in Brussels, he was soon acquitted. His enemies left the country. At the trial Van requested permission to speak. This granted, he arose, took out his decoration, slammed it on the judge's table and said in a ringing voice, "Please return this to the King with my compliments." And Van went on to tell the judge what the King could do with the medal.

Van became a successful importer and exporter. He visited America only once, to my knowledge, spending a couple of days in New York, which frightened the hell out of him. He took the next ship back to Ghent.

As for chess-playing, multilingual Charlie Dyar, there were many things in the postwar period that would require immediate attention; his services would be invaluable.

# 2 DRY AMERICA

On December 18, 1917, the United States 65th Congress had sent to all states a proposed amendment prohibiting the sale of intoxicants, defined as "containing one half of one per cent of alcohol by volume." By January 16, 1919, the measure was approved by three-fourths of the states and it became Article 18 of the Constitution. The law, which had been introduced by Congressman Andrew J. Volstead, became effective January 16, 1920. It was passed over President Wilson's veto.

At last the Prohibition party, whose platform was that the federal and state governments forbid the "manufacture, sale, importation, exportation or transportation of alcoholic liquors for beverage purposes," had achieved its aim. Organized in 1868, the Prohibition party has nominated a candidate for the Presidency in every national election since 1872.

Prohibition, conceived as a moral attempt to improve the American way of life, would ultimately cast the nation into a turmoil. One cannot help but think in retrospect that Prohibition, by depriving Americans of their "vices," only created the avenues through which organized crime gained its firm foothold.

As first attaché to the American Legation at The Hague and then vice-consul at Hamburg, I was not involved in anti-Prohibition activities. But as consul in La Guairia, Venezuela, during 1923–1925, and consul at Nassau, the Bahamas, in 1926, I came closer to seeing the spread of smuggling activities.

In 1926, as chief of the Division of Foreign Control in the Treasury Department, charged with halting the flow of illegal liquor from foreign ports into the U.S., I needed help, good help, and I requested Charlie Dyar, "The Sphinx," to augment our existing forces.

Sent to Halifax, St. Pierre Miquelon, and many ports in the maritime provinces of Canada, he soon was able to name every important vessel in the bootlegging trade, the owners of the ships and the types of whisky they carried. He was part of the "Flying Squad" which was assigned to dig up evidence against the big smugglers in Canada who were smuggling booze across the borders into America.

Hunter T. Nugent, Garland H. Williams, Malachi Harney, and Bill Harmon were four of many agents combating not only the whisky mobs, but citizen complacency as well. Harney would become my assistant in 1936.

Nugent was also a member of the Flying Squad. Tough and honest, you couldn't get the time of day from him if he wasn't in a good mood. He was a handsome man, big and blond, with a stomach as flat as a board; he looked like a Viking. He had been among the first men selected when the Pennsylvania State Police were organized. I used him to good advantage while I was in Nassau; there, he worked his way into the "Black Dan" mob, a gang of bootleggers, and broke it up.

Bill Harmon and Garland Williams were stationed in the South, Bill along the Florida coasts, and Garland along the shorelines of Texas, Mississippi and Alabama.

Part Cherokee, Bill Harmon never smiled, he went after everything in deadly, quiet earnest. Perhaps the only incident that ever got under his skin had to do with the *I'm Alone* and her skipper, John T. Randall.

One of our informers (we call them "special employees" now) had tipped Bill off on the activities of the *I'm Alone*; she took aboard whisky at St. Pierre Miquelon, cruised down to Belize, British Honduras, for rum, and then slipped along the Louisiana and Florida coasts to rendezvous with shore launches.

The voyages of the *I'm Alone* were remarkably successful because of Randall. He would have made a good cop. A huge, broad man, he was every inch an adventurer and fighter. He came from a seagoing Newfoundland family and shipped to sea at sixteen. A few years later he was at the front in the Boer War where his service was distinguished. In World War I, as captain of a British trawler in the North Sea, he won decorations from the French as well as the British. At the time Bill Harmon was riding herd on him, Randall held a commission as a lieutenant commander in the British Royal Naval Reserves. All this meant that he was also an accomplished navigator. He would nose his fully loaded vessel in toward the American shores and, at the first sign of Coast Guard cutters, turn his vessel and streak for the high seas, outside the 12-mile limit. Later, probing through the darkness of night, he found his launches. The British jack flying from the *I'm Alone* soon came to resemble the Jolly Roger to Bill Harmon and the Coast Guard.

The Coast Guard got its present name in 1915, when the Revenue Cutter Service was merged with the Life Saving Service. The Coast Guard had to expand in the twenties and early thirties to stifle the smuggling of illegal whisky into the States. Two Coast Guard cutters finally brought a halt to the arrogant John T. Randall.

Bill Harmon had received word that the *I'm Alone* was heading for a Louisiana rendezvous. He immediately radioed the Coast Guard, and on a stormy March day, the cutters *Walcutt* and *Dexter* surprised Randall inside the 12-mile limit, his vessel loaded to the gunwales with booze. He turned, and with the sea boiling over his bows, made for the south and the open sea.

Under the legal doctrine of "hot pursuit" a ship apprehended inside the 12-mile limit may be followed, boarded and searched on the high seas, if under continuous chase. The *Dexter* and the *Walcutt* overhauled the *I'm Alone* in the Gulf of Mexico. They signaled for Randall to stop, but he pressed on over the swells. The Coast Guard fired blanks, but Randall continued. Finally pulling alongside, the Coast Guardsmen hailed Randall through a megaphone: "Stand by. Stand by to take on a boarding party."

Randall answered that they could sink the damned ship; he wasn't going to surrender. Captains Paul of the *Walcutt* and Powell of the *Dexter* had no choice; this time live shells were used and within minutes the *I'm Alone* was going down by her bows and her crew floundering in choppy seas. Coast Guardsmen rescued them; Randall himself was pulled from the sea. Two Canadian seamen died in the incident.

Canadian officials were incensed that a Royal Naval officer flying the Union Jack on his ship had been fired upon. It took an international commission of Canadians and Americans six years to settle the grievances; it found the sinking of the *I'm Alone* unjustifiable and found that behind the scenes the people involved in whisky smuggling were nearly all Americans. The U.S. Treasury Department (the Coast Guard is under the Treasury Department) had to pay Randall, his crew and their families a sum of $50,000. But Bill Harmon was happy; he wasn't plagued any more by John T. Randall and the *I'm Alone*.

Some of Bill's later achievements came with the help of an old and shrewd bootlegger, Captain Eddie. Harmon had had good luck breaking up Dwyer's operations and Eddie, believing that the hoodoo sign was on him, decided that if he couldn't beat the federals, he would join them. The Harmon-Eddie combination nailed over 150 boats of all sizes, and made a lasting dent in the ship-to-shore operations of the bootleggers.

Harmon often worked with other agents, but Garland Williams preferred to work alone. He haunted the bays and inlets of three states, sitting in a small boat waiting for the bootleggers to make their runs in from Mexico, British Honduras, and Cuba. He always rented a boat and lugged his Coast Guard radio equipment. As soon as he saw fleets of small boats putting out to sea, as if to fish, he hit his radio and within minutes cutters were steaming in to ambush the incoming ships. The work was so demanding that he fell ill in Belize, a port that even today is one of the most racket-ridden in the world. The doctors there and in Tampico and Mexico City gave him a short time to live; fevers from the mosquitoes and poor food seemed to have done the damage.

But Williams recovered. He returned to work on the largest smuggling conspiracy at the time, a plot hatched and headed by Marvin James (Big Jim) Clark. Big Jim ran the most extensive small boat and big ship whisky ring in bootlegging history; the *I'm Alone* had been one of his vessels. Like John T. Randall, Big Jim had spent many years in the Navy, but his success was due to his organizational ability. He induced hundreds of poor fishermen along the southern coasts to make their boats available to meet his incoming ships, unload the contraband whisky and move it stealthily into the cities. The fishermen saw this as a way to increase their meager incomes. But the sinking of the *I'm Alone* began the downfall of Big Jim. His gigantic conspiracy was ended with the helpful testimony of many of the fishermen who, for various reasons, had fallen out with Clark.

Most of Clark's booze found its way to New York City where it was distributed to the local speakeasies and the Eastern seaboard by Daniel (Danny) Hogan. When Clark was indicted, Danny went into hiding. Williams had returned to Washington to clear up odd ends of the case and to get a line on Hogan. A tip came in: Danny Hogan was holed up with a lovely redhead in New York. She had her hair done at a very exclusive East Side shop. If Williams hung around there, he might be able to follow her home to Hogan. Williams hustled himself aboard a train, determined to stay in New York until he had Hogan behind bars. Then and only then could the Clark ring be smashed for good. If Hogan remained free, some other fleet owner would contact him and soon trucks, cars and even fleets of freight cars would be running booze into New York again.

After weeks of waiting, Williams found the girl. He caught fleet-

ing glimpses of her rushing into cabs, down into the subway, leap-
ing aboard buses. Finally, he managed to trail her to her apartment
building where he learned that Danny was living under the name
of Hill.

"Mr. Hill" emerged from the apartment on a gray Sunday morning, on his way to the corner newsstand. Williams fell in behind
him and when Hogan turned, Williams smiled sweetly and said,
"Good morning, Danny." Hogan gathered himself for a sprint, but
before he could pull away, Williams closed in, pushing him into
his car. Hogan shouted his innocence all the way down to the old
Post Office and the U.S. Attorney's office. Halfway up in the elevator, the cable on the old chain-lift broke and the car plummeted.
Later Hogan said that even as they were falling he was thinking of
how to get away. But when the elevator hit bottom, he found himself wrapped in Williams' arms, cables and chains falling all over
them. Neither was hurt. Hogan was convicted and sentenced to a
long term in jail.

Williams was also engaged in crushing the last major whisky-
smuggling group during and shortly after the repeal of Prohibition.
A group headed by Adam Smith was buying legal alcohol in Mexico and smuggling it into the U.S. along the southern coasts from
San Diego to New Orleans. Like Big Jim Clark, Smith owned a
fleet of boats as well as a fleet of high-powered cars. Treasury dispatched Williams to Mexico. The plan was to secure the cooperation of Mexican officials, from President Cardenas on down, in
stopping the traffic. Cardenas, after a great many discussions and
considerations, signed a decree which placed an export tax on alcohol. Additional provisions allowed arresting officers to share lib-
erally in any recoveries. The night the law was signed, a large force
of soldiers standing by at Tampico captured seven schooners
owned by Smith, and a few days later, Smith himself was in a
Mexican jail, his organization completely destroyed.

# 3 *THE BIRTH OF A BUREAU*

While Chief of the Division of Foreign Control, I served two years running as the U.S. Delegate to the Conference on the Suppression of Smuggling at London and at Paris. In 1929, four years before the repeal of Prohibition, I was appointed Assistant Commissioner of Prohibition, which had a unit of the Treasury Department directly concerned with the mushrooming narcotics traffic into and throughout the nation. In that same year federal funds were allocated for two "farms" designated for the use of drug addicts. The first was at Lexington, Ky., and the other was to be located "in a section comprised by the states of Oklahoma, Arkansas, the southern portion of Missouri, the southeastern portion of Kansas, and the northeastern portion of Texas."

Narcotics gangs were already forming in the West and East, where the large seaport cities could receive and distribute drugs sent from overseas. Congress first provided regulations governing traffic in narcotics in 1890; the Act of 1890 imposed a tax on the importation of opium and morphine and on the manufacture of

16

smoking opium in the United States. By 1909 legislation prohibited the entrance of opium and its derivatives into the U.S.
except for medicinal purposes. In 1914 Congress followed up these
early measures with the Harrison Narcotics Act, which provided for
strict regulation and control of drugs and also called for stiff penalties. Other acts, treaties or obligations to control and provide
penalties were established in 1931, 1937, 1939, 1942, 1948, 1956
and 1960.

On June 14, 1930, a federal law provided for the establishment
of the Bureau of Narcotics, effective July 1 the same year. The old
Prohibition unit was completely reorganized; the Bureau would
concern itself not only with enforcement on a local basis, but with
a broad national and international policy to control and limit the
drug traffic from abroad and within the continental United States.

Many attempts have been made down through the years to
transfer the Narcotics Bureau out of Treasury Department, with
no success. Because of the law enforcement nature of many offices
and bureaus under the jurisdiction of the Treasury, the Bureau has
proved to be in the best position. This because of the fine teamwork that goes on, that must go on among these particular bureaus.
Narcotics, for example, has worked with the Coast Guard, Customs, Secret Service, Internal Revenue and its adjunct, the Alcohol
and Tobacco Tax division. We exchange information, we create
teams of specialists drawn from each of these bureaus and services,
if the need warrants. In addition, these close-knit operations have
been of immense value to the Justice Department. Finally, treaty
obligations required, when it was established, that the Bureau of
Narcotics possess a single administration.

But let me take you back to the beginning.

I was appointed Commissioner of the newly formed Bureau of
Narcotics September 25, 1930, and immediately looked with trepi-
dation toward the day when Elizabeth Washburn Wright would
call on me; she was one person I didn't want to meet, not right
away.

Attractive and refined, Mrs. Hamilton Wright was by every

standard an aristocrat. The daughter of a former Ambassador to France, she married Dr. Hamilton Wright, a missionary in the Far East. Dr. and Mrs. Wright and Bishop Charles H. Brent combined their energies to rid China of her opium problem. It was because of these three vigorous persons that President Theodore Roosevelt had convened the first meeting of the International Opium Conference in Shanghai during the early 1900's. Bishop Brent and Dr. Wright were the U.S. delegates; they urged the other representatives to limit the production of opium to world medical needs. Eventually that principle came to be the guiding force behind the production of the drug.

A second conference with essentially the same nations attending took place at The Hague in 1912 and again Bishop Brent and Dr. Wright were delegates. Mrs. Wright was also in attendance. Brent and Wright tried to persuade Great Britain, France, the Netherlands, Japan and Portugal to abandon smoking monopolies which made the drug available to their populations for about eight cents per day. Although many high-sounding phrases were offered, this was not done. Most delegates favored a gradualistic approach to the suppression of the opium traffic.

Traveling with the sanction of the U.S. State Department, Dr. Wright was killed in an automobile accident in France. Mrs. Wright took on by herself the crusade against narcotics.

The Geneva Conference of 1925 followed, and another was held in the Orient. At a second Geneva conference Mrs. Hamilton Wright attended as an alternate delegate. Summoned by the League of Nations, the Convention, with forty-one nations participating, established a routine for permits and records for transactions involving the importation and exportation of narcotic drugs. Further, each signatory nation was to report statistics to a central international authority. Finally the Convention also established an independent Permanent Control Board to examine the figures on cultivation, manufacture, import and export, stockpiling and seizures of illegal narcotics within the borders of each member nation. But these, for Mrs. Wright, were not enough; she had seen first-hand the widespread terrible effects of opium, and she wanted more stringent controls. It was apparent to her—and to other observers—that those nations which controlled large amounts of opium were opposed to any hard and fast line advanced by Mrs. Wright and the regular U.S. delegate, Congressman Stephen Porter of Pittsburgh. Porter, Chairman of the House Foreign Relations Committee, had also spent a large part of his life fighting the illegal opium traffic. The British pressed for easy regulations, but Porter took their delegation to task and rendered their position indefensible, until Lord Robert Cecil was hastily summoned. He took the floor against the Americans and battered them away from their rigid stand. Mrs. Wright and Porter saw that the Convention was going to the side of Lord Robert, and they gathered their papers and left the floor, determined to show the body that the United States was committed completely to the proposition that opium smoking be altogether outlawed.

After the convention, the famous cartoonist Derso lampooned Lord Robert. Called before the "Almighty" in Derso's sketch, Lord Robert is asked, "Who sent you to Geneva to defend *that* cause?" It would take until 1959 for Mrs. Wright's dream to come true; then it was announced in the United Nations that Thailand, the last nation remaining with no ban on opium smoking, had finally complied with world demand. It was also noted that continued United States support for the ban had made Thailand's compliance possible.

Years after that memorable convention, Mrs. Wright received the decoration she so richly deserved for her long years of service. The presentation was made in Washington by the Chinese government. If onlookers thought she was just going to accept with a few token words of thanks, they were sadly mistaken. Mrs. Wright gave everyone hell; she lashed out at all the great powers for failing to outlaw opium traffic—including the United States. The ears of the dignitaries burned, but they had to stand and take it until she was through with what she had to say.

It was this unrelenting, restless spirit, this surging drive that in great part helped to establish the Federal Bureau of Narcotics under the Treasury Department. Mrs. Wright had earmarked as her own choice for Commissioner, Admiral Mark Bristol, then the High Commissioner to Turkey. But Bristol had drawn the wrath of President Hoover for testimony given before a congressional committee and the President was not about to appoint him to any position. I was appointed instead. And soon after, I sat in my office waiting for Mrs. Wright, a woman with great power—power enough to lift a telephone and secure an immediate audience with any Cabinet officer. She had the ear of the President himself.

I had appeared before many government investigating bodies and been questioned by the best, but no questioning could begin to compare with what Mrs. Wright put me through that afternoon. When she left, I knew she was not satisfied with me; she had worked a long, long time and wanted all the assurance in the world that the best man was in the chair I sat in. She came over to my side during the 1931 Geneva Conference for the Limitation of the Manufacture of Narcotic Drugs. It was good to have her on the team. Treaties and protocols, successfully signed, followed our new liaison. When it became necessary to tighten national controls, Mrs. Wright, with her access to Capitol Hill, would buttonhole every Senator and Congressman who was in Washington. Sometimes her pressure was so intense that they called me to ask if I couldn't influence her to go a little easier. But our goals were set; my answer always was that the only way Mrs. Wright would stop her pressure was by their passing stiffer legislation against the illegal drug traffic.

Supporting Mrs. Wright in her grim battle were Mrs. Helen Howell Moorhead and Miss Ellen N. LaMotte. Like Mrs. Wright, they were wealthy; they traveled around the world attending conferences. Sometimes their methods were a little different, and that caused some friction. I was lucky, for somehow I always managed to straighten out their differences. I had to; we needed people like that. We could use more of them today.

It was predictable that after the repeal of Prohibition, in 1933, the gangs would convert to the procurement and sale of illegal drugs; they had the organizations, the contacts, the personnel. In fact, the Parmagini and Balestreri mobs were but two of several gangs already engaged in illicit narcotics traffic before repeal. The second year after the Bureau was created, some fifteen ships, many of them American, were discovered transporting drugs into the States. Some 15,000 ounces of morphine were captured that year along with 134,847 pounds of opium and almost half a million pounds of coca leaves.

Yes, the traffickers also had the market—the users, the addicts; one out of every five hundred persons was addicted at this time, many because of unwise medical practices common before the Harrison Narcotics Act of 1914. Addiction was on the rise again, not because of doctors who didn't know their business, but through the activities of uncaring, unscrupulous dope peddlers. Many people became addicted unknowingly as they were being introduced into criminal circles. This was especially true of young girls drawn into prostitution through the widespread white-slavery rackets. Made dependent upon drugs which would then be withheld until the victim complied with the wishes of the pusher— often a pimp and a very small cog in a larger organization—the women acquiesed and became whores. Prostitution is a historical adjunct of crime. Both Al Capone and Lucky Luciano and others before them ran red light districts which they pumped full of illegal drugs. The most pitiful prostitutes were those who worked only to be able to buy enough drugs to satisfy their craving. They gave themselves away for nothing. But the profit for the big man of any mob is almost 200 per cent.

Even without subsidiary ventures, the profit in illicit drugs is astronomical. The ordinary table salt shaker probably holds an ounce. If it were heroin it might be worth $600. When cut with milk sugar or theobromine and sold retail in "pieces"— also called capsules, "caps" or "things"—the peddler grosses about $40,000. In no other trade can so large a profit be turned so quickly, not even by rigging stocks, and that is why there are so many traffickers. They consider themselves businessmen.

Where does most of this business take place?

In New York, greatest port city in the world. There, over 20,000 *known* drug addicts spend around a quarter of a billion dollars annually on heroin; most are in their teens or early twenties. New York is also where at least one death per day, every day in the year, is caused by an overdose, faulty mixture, or too potent a shot of heroin. (We suspect that the death of football star Eugene [Big Daddy] Lipscomb on May 10, 1963, may have been a result of a shot of heroin handled by an inexperienced pusher who didn't know how to cut it.) Outside of New York City, from 20,000 to 35,000 addicts range through the country. These are the known; the unknown, usually of the upper classes, have the means—money—and professional contacts which very often permit addiction without danger.

For some, narcotics block out the sights and sounds of poverty and inequity, the rapid pace at which we move in today's world, the constant trembling on the brink of disaster. For others, the reason for taking drugs has been forgotten; narcotics has become their way of life.

For a long time the Orient provided a continuous flow of illicit opium into the United States. Opium, *Papaver somniferum*, "the flower of sleep," is the source for morphine, heroin, Dilaudid, dionin, laudanum, thebaine and papaverine. Largely controlled and distributed by criminal tong groups, opium soon found its way to all the large and many small cities in America. But it had come farther in history than in miles.

The cuneiform tablets of the ancient Sumerians record that *gil*, the juice of the poppy, was collected in the morning. The Sumerians, who lived in what is now Iraq, believed that *gil*, so painstakingly gathered, gave great joy to the person who tasted it. The rampaging Babylonians, who inherited the Sumerian civilization, carried knowledge of the poppy—as a medicine—to Persia and Egypt, where it was in widespread use as a remedy during the reign of the Hyksos kings, who thrived during the 18th century B.C.

The ancient Greeks called the juice of the poppy *opion* before Homer sat down to pen the *Iliad*. The "Father of Medicine," Hippocrates of Kos, recommended a dram or two of the juice of the white poppy "mixed with the seed of the nettle." When the Moslems swept into Europe in 700 A.D., their doctors carried with them the knowledge of the benefits of opium as a medicine. This information greatly aided in the advance of surgical techniques for which the Arabs were famous at an early time in history. Until the 12th century the drug was largely confined to medical uses.

Two centuries earlier, Arab traders and physicians had carried their famous Arabic Pharmacopoeia to China where, as in the past, opium was found to be an effective remedy for dysentery. The "flower of sleep" journeyed through Persia and India, the explorer Magellan noting in 1511 that the "Moors" and "Indians" ate it. Already involved in African slave trade, the Portuguese embarked upon the transportation and sale of opium to the Chinese. By 1729 they were selling more than a thousand great chests of opium of undetermined weights annually in China. The British East India Company, as infamous as the Portuguese East India Company, for more than 275 years sold opium in wholesale lots to Chinese merchants.

Wars, corruption in high places, collusion, the dependence of western European countries on the profits derived from opium sales, all combined to make China and the rest of the Orient the hell hole Elizabeth Washburn Wright called attention to. The Opium War of 1840, which lasted two years, was won by the British, and the humbled Chinese emperors could no longer oppose the opium traffic.

With the native leaders beaten in their efforts to stem the flow of opium that was decimating their populations, even Americans joined in the traffic. Visiting Hong Kong in 1842, Commodore Kearney found evidence of extensive American participation. Notorious among the American firms were Russel & Company and Augustine Heard & Company, both of Boston. So debilitating were the effects of opium, that when the Japanese invaded China during the 1930's, the narcotic was distributed in advance of the troop movements to render the populations useless or uncaring.

In America we eventually faced up to the inglorious history of the poppy when the Harrison Act was passed. The Federal Bureau of Narcotics absorbed the old Prohibition Unit, providing this country with a staff of men who could devote full time to the war against illicit traffic in narcotics.

Among the 284 agents (our total force was 424 people) were Charlie Dyar; he would uncover startling tie-ins between American criminals and Elie Eliopoulos, the "Drug Baron" of Europe, who controlled and operated factories which supplied illicit narcotics. Through Elie, Dyar would learn of the criminals in our own back yard; Legs Diamond, Dutch Schultz, Little Augie Del Gracio, Al Spitzer, Abe Stein, the Louis Adelman mob, the Newman brothers, and "Big Nose" Fleishman. Charlie would also learn of connections between Eliopoulos and his brother and persons in the French government.

Hunter T. Nugent, a man with a violent temper, was in our new Bureau. I often sent him around to our district offices to see how things were coming on. When the secretaries in these offices learned that Mr. Nugent was coming, they all ran out and bought new dresses. Nugent always got what I wanted; he had little time for the adulation of the girls. Nugent was good anywhere. Under cover, he would burrow down so deep that he couldn't be found. He had a peculiar tic—when you saw his neck twitch, the best thing was to stay away from him; you didn't want to tangle with him. When his neck jerked, he was angry. A meticulous man, Nugent always took good care of government cars; he was just as thorough with his investigatory work.

Garland H. Williams was another good man. It seems fitting that at this writing the former New York City District Supervisor, a man with the poise of a diplomat and one of the most proficient law enforcement officers I have ever met, is helping some of the new nations in Africa set up police and intelligence departments. Williams would become chief of the wartime Counter-Intelligence Corps and Director of Special Training for the OSS. Like Bill Harmon, Williams' government career began in the United States Customs Agency during the very early Prohibition days.

# 4 TRAFFIC ON THE BARBARY COAST

Elizabeth Wright's attention had been focused on the broad international evils of illegal narcotics traffic and lack of controls. Even as she girded for her first fights, even as the Prohibition unit sought to do a job which was, at that time, highly ineffectual, Antone (Black Tony) Parmagini reigned as a dictator of the West Coast underworld. When, through the singular efforts of Agent Lovejoy, a member of the small Prohibition unit, we arrested Parmagini, panic seized the narcotics racket, and scores of addicts in several Western states checked into hospitals for cures because they could no longer obtain their dosages. Black Tony was one of the first big-time violators. Mrs. Wright would have been dismayed to learn that, even though the world community was moving toward some international agreements and checks, the U.S. was battling to the death to cut down addiction caused by illegal traffic.

Smuggling was rife in the days of Black Tony, and almost unlimited quantities of drugs were available to those who needed or wanted them. At the time Black Tony was convicted in 1930—the same year the Bureau was created—morphine seizures had amounted to 27,000 ounces for the previous ten years; for 1930 alone the amount captured was 119,587 *pounds* of opium, coming in from nine different foreign countries on eleven ships. Black Tony's associates included, at one time or another, Arnold Rothstein, Legs Diamond, Waxey Gordon, Dutch Schultz and Baby Face Nelson. The lesser criminals he knew in the hundreds.

Parmagini lived in a luxurious hotel in downtown San Francisco. His fortune was counted in the millions of dollars. By the back path he had come a long way. The son of poor parents, Parmagini quickly became a clever, quick boy of the streets. He knew the infamous Barbary Coast better than any ten policemen; he rolled drunks regularly and found it profitable. At fourteen he was an accomplished pickpocket. Also at that age, he was able to secure morphine, opium and cocaine for the addicts so far gone that they couldn't move out of their places in the alleys. A breeder of intense loyalties, Black Tony, with his daring and left-handed skills, became the leader of the Rock Rollers, a tough gang from North Beach. The Rock Rollers got their name because they dislodged huge boulders on Telegraph Hill and sent them crashing down upon either police or rival gang members. Parmagini got his name, Black Tony, because of his raven hair and swarthy skin.

Unlike the other small-time hoods, Tony was friendly and even accommodating to the police—until their backs were turned. His thefts provided enough money for him to buy a small café and some interests in a few whorehouses. In the process of growing up, Tony had learned that dabbling in politics could be profitable, and he worked unstintingly to help the "right" candidates get elected to office. During one election, in order to insure a heavy vote for his candidate, he hired every dance hall in his district, announcing that he was having a vast pre-victory celebration. The voters were escorted to the halls in droves. Entertainment was lavish and free. Liquor—for this was before Prohibition—flowed freely. Late in the evening, when it began to look as if the guests were thinking of going home, Tony ordered the doors to the halls bolted. "No one gets out until the polls open in the morning," he said. Then each "guest" was given a card upon which was printed the name of Tony's candidate. By the time the polls shut the next night, that candidate had won by an overwhelming vote.

The café Tony used as his personal headquarters became a hang-out for bandits, smugglers, kidnappers, dope addicts. Bank robbers brought "hot" money and bonds there for cashing, for less than their actual value, for Tony was a businessman.

One day a police officer dropped into Tony's for a drink and found, standing beside him at the bar, a wanted criminal. The officer took him to the station.

"Why didn't you arrest Tony too?" his captain shouted angrily. "For aiding and abetting. He knew we wanted this man. In fact, he promised to let me know if he ever came to the café!"

With great reluctance the officer told the captain why he had not brought Tony in: "I knew it, sir, but I told you about my little girl, Elsie, breaking her leg and the bone not knitting. I spent all the dough I had and got nowhere. Then Tony found out about it a couple of months ago. He came to my house and said he'd have her all fixed up. What could I do? The kid needed help and we were broke. Tony could help her. He told me it wouldn't mean anything between us; it would be between him and Elsie. He got the best doctors he could find. Elsie's all healed and walking again. It never would have happened if it hadn't been for Tony. So how could I take him in?"

Yes, Tony had become a big-hearted fellow, a charitable guy, but always for a reason. His motto was, "Any guy's crazy who don't spend one buck to make two."

Before he was thirty, Tony was known as everyone's friend. If a cop needed help—and their salaries then weren't anywhere near what they are today—Tony gave it. At Christmastime he played Santa Claus and distributed large amounts of food, candy and clothing. For the underworld he offered more help and protection as well.

With the advent of Prohibition, Tony Parmagini started toward another million dollars. He bought four big ships and they transported liquor from Shanghai to San Francisco. The liquor had come a long way: Canada had furnished some; Europe had provided some. At Shanghai the booze was transferred to Tony's ships. Tony was one of the major suppliers of illegal whisky for the West Coast, if not the biggest. And he increased his narcotics trade with a vengeance. He was under suspicion, yes, but the PU (Prohibition Unit) could fasten nothing on him. He was helpful, however, giving us from time to time small bits of information that enabled us to crack a competing ring. When we questioned Tony about his own activities he would say, "I'm not distributing narcotic drugs. I'm in another game."

That game was financing narcotics peddlers. Two of those peddlers grew wealthy in the racket. They became theatrical agents in Hollywood and later married film stars. One who had become one of the most powerful men in the movie industry later went to Europe and, because we suspected that he was making European narcotics contacts, we shadowed him there and back. We finally secured the evidence we needed against him, but the statute of limitations stymied our efforts to prosecute.

At that time one of our agents was a fellow named Lovejoy; he had perfected some of the undercover techniques we later would use on a large scale. He was a dark-complexioned, medium-sized man, quiet, with a secretive air. We sent Lovejoy to worm his way into the Parmagini mob. He succeeded. After a time Tony and his army of peddlers came to know and trust Lovejoy, unaware that he was quietly making arrests of some of the smaller fry. Then he pushed for a head-to-head contact with Tony; if a personal transaction took place, Tony would be "made." Lovejoy indicated that he had a big deal on the fire; it was so big that he wasn't going to buy from anyone but Tony himself.

Although Tony himself avoided selling, this deal was so big that he agreed to a "meet" with Lovejoy on the condition that the agent come alone. Tony, however, brought with him Bill Levin, a henchman who was reputed to know the face of every federal lawman. Levin was satisfied that Lovejoy was not a PU agent and the deal was completed.

Within a few hours Parmagini and Levin were arrested. Tony denied that Lovejoy had bought any drugs from him and that money had changed hands. The marked bills, however, were already tagged as evidence.

"This will end satisfactorily for me," Tony proclaimed. "The law can't touch me." He was wrong. He could not fix the government as he had done with local agencies; his money and political influences were useless. Antone Parmagini, alias "Black Tony," and Bill Levin were convicted on all counts, fined $17,000, and sentenced to seventeen years in prison.

Tony spent vast sums fighting the case. Appeals followed, but the verdict of the lower court was affirmed. Knowing now that he had to go to jail, Tony, while he was out on bond, contacted persons of considerable influence in an attempt to be incarcerated in the Carson City, Nevada, penitentiary, a local jail. But Tony had committed federal crimes and was bound for Leavenworth, failing in his efforts to manipulate the degree of his punishment. At our insistence, an application for parole was denied. Tony had so much money and influence that it was almost as difficult to keep him in prison as it was getting him there.

While he was in the federal penitentiary at Leavenworth, nearly everything he owned was confiscated by the government for income tax evasion. Tony was penniless and without a friend. "What's become of all them guys I used to know?" he would ask. "I never hear from none of 'em. A lot of 'em owe me money. A hundred thousand bucks some of them guys owe me."

And then Black Tony fell ill—cancer. His days were wracked with pain. Only morphine gave him any ease—morphine, the drug he had used to destroy thousands of lives, that had made him the richest dope peddler on the West Coast. "Imagine me having to depend on that stuff," he gasped, "what a laugh!"

At the end Black Tony Parmagini was screaming for more morphine, like the thousands of addicts he had so cruelly serviced.

Just before Parmagini reached the terminal stage of cancer he met Mario Balestreri, who had been in four federal prisons and as many state jails, and had just succeeded in getting a twelve-year sentence reduced to five; he wasn't yet forty years old. Then a parole came through for him and he went to say good-bye to Black Tony. "The trouble with our racket, boy," Parmagini said, "is that after you get to the top, they're after you from both sides; if the law don't get you, some lousy hophead will give you the double-cross. You never got real friends."

Balestreri should have listened, but he didn't. It was a warm June day when he hurried out of Leavenworth, intent upon getting to the Coast and gathering under his personal wing all the under-world power which once had belonged to Tony.

Like Tony, Balestreri set himself up through partnerships in several dance halls and night clubs. The latter were called "John joints" because the gullible came in by accident or on slumming expeditions and were expeditiously taken. Balestreri also had pieces of several waterfront dives and package liquor stores; the sale of alcohol was now legal. His best known club was the Redwood Village Restaurant; his partner in that operation was Johnny Provanzale, or Johnny "Bananas," as the underworld called him. Salvatore Taranto was a silent partner and supervisor of the counterfeit racket division; Gaston (Frenchie) Quillet, the Redwood Village floor manager, usually handled the heroin traffic.

Redwood Village was also a haven for many a notorious criminal on the run. Harry Edwards, just out of prison, loitered here; he was one of the best "pen off" artists in the counterfeit racket. Pete Dallas, an ex-convict and confidence man, liked to drop in for a drink and bat the breeze and look over the "Johns." Phil Gargano, a blackmailer, came in between jobs. Guiseppi Sylvestri with the blessing of Frenchie Quillet, peddled heroin; sometimes they worked together. And Mario Carelli and his woman could be seen there after their frequent white-slave junkets throughout the Southwest.

For Balestreri business couldn't have been better. He owned

three high-powered automobiles; he set his mother up in a luxurious home; he had funds unlimited. His empire extended down into Mexico and up into British Columbia. Big Bill Hildebrandt, the powerful Minneapolis drug trafficker who would be nailed in 1937, was an acquaintance of Balestreri's. The San Francisco gangster looked forward to the day when he might penetrate New York City.

Not content with his Mexican and Canadian sources, Balestreri started bringing opium, morphine and heroin from the Orient. He became a part of an international dope-smuggling ring which ranged from Kobe, Japan, and Shanghai, to San Francisco. Further emulating Parmagini, Balestreri never carried drugs on his person; he supervised delivery and collected money. If the local police nabbed him or tried to implicate him, he bought his way out with a minimum of difficulty and a stooge took the rap.

We were aware of the Balestreri operations, but were unable to secure the evidence needed to bring him to trial. Ironically, it was not dope but counterfeit money that gave us the leads to Balestreri in the first place. Like all who deal in bogus bills, he couldn't resist the temptation of passing the "queer" himself. Just for kicks. Shortly after he paid off his musicians with "bad bread" a phoney $20 reserve note turned up in a bookie's office. One week later the Secret Service, also under the Treasury Department and directly responsible for the apprehension of counterfeiters as well as other well-defined tasks, arrested a notorious counterfeit passer. He admitted that he was obtaining the bad money from the Balestreri-Provenzale-Taranto combine.

Still later, a Mr. and Mrs. Harry Graham registered at the Olympic Hotel in San Francisco. Mr. Graham was an undercover agent on assignment from his Middle West office. His wife was to make the cover secure. (We seldom use agents' wives any more.) With the Grahams were Mr. and Mrs. Billy Charles. Charles was an addict; together with his wife, he had turned to the Bureau for assistance in breaking his habit. Lexington was recommended; the institution had been completed in 1932. Another hospital at Fort

Worth was still under construction. Mrs. Charles agreed with us that the surest way to halt the spreading addiction was by breaking up the gangs. Since Charles was familiar with Balestreri's district, he volunteered to help us set up a deal. Within a half hour after they had checked in, Charles had made contact. "I've talked to Balestreri," he advised Graham. "Said he'd be glad to see us tonight at Redwood Village."

Graham's report follows:

"On February 2 about 8:30 P.M., I went to Redwood Village, located at 150 Mason Street, San Francisco, accompanied by Billy Charles, his wife and Mrs. Graham. As we entered, Mario [Balestreri] was seated at the top of the stairs leading to the bar, talking to a man. He arose and we were introduced. He excused himself, saying he was busy but would be with us in a few minutes.

[At this point all Balestreri knew was that Charles was acting as a go-between to set up a big buy between himself and Graham.]

"Mario returned to our table about 10:30 P.M. When he returned the ladies left, leaving Mario, Charles and myself at the table. Mario opened the conversation by asking us what we had been doing.

"Charles asked him how the dope racket was and he said we could get all we wanted, provided we were willing to pay the price. We told him we wanted morphine, but he suggested opium. I told him it was harder to handle than morphine, but he insisted it was always good and the price did not fluctuate as with morphine. He said if he had the money to lay out, he would buy all he could and hold it for a price. I said that if things were so tight now due to waterfront strikes, I couldn't see how prices would get better later on. I agreed to take five 5-tael tins of opium at $97.50 a tin. Balestreri would not transact business that night or the next day."

Balestreri wanted time to check out Graham. He sent out orders that every gangster known to his combine should give the once over to Graham and his wife either at the club or while they were in their hotel. Graham got the okay and he duly reported the next meeting:

"We stopped by the checkroom when Mario called me aside. 'I know how you feel about having that money on you,' he said. I told him my wife had it. I then called her and told her to give me $500. She went to the ladies' rest room and returned, handing me the money. I told Mario I had the money but would have to get a $20 bill changed in order to make the deal. He took me to the bar and while the bartender was changing the bill, explained that if I got in any kind of jam while I was out here, I should tell him, Mario, immediately, and he would have his lawyer take care of everything for me. He said his lawyer was hooked up with every big mobster in the country and could get me fixed up with no matter what. By this time I had the change and we went to his office. I purposely left the door open and told my wife to watch me give him the money. While the door was open I started to count the money on top of the safe in piles of $100. I had counted out two or three piles, which Mrs. Graham saw me do, when Mario said, 'You'd better close that door!' I did.

"Mario asked me if I wanted the stuff delivered to Charles or me. I said to me. We then left Redwood Village. The next day I answered the phone and Mario asked me if I could be in Charles's room at the Continental Hotel at 4:45. I told him I would be in room 328. He said, 'All right.'

"At 4:45 Mario entered Charles's room. The ladies left immediately. Mario said he too would have to leave right away. But before he left he said he had gotten us a price on the white stuff, which was the same as the opium cost us, and that it was the best he could do for us at the time. I asked Mario if he could ship the stuff East for me. He refused. He left and was gone perhaps four or five minutes. When he returned, he was carrying a yellow paper sack. He only came inside the door three or four feet, placed the sack on the dresser and said, 'There it is. You boys be sure and come over tonight and see me.' Before I could open the package he closed the door and left. Upon opening the package I found five cans, each with the figure 55 stamped on one side and Chinese lettering on the other."

Elated that Balestreri himself had made the delivery, Graham, Charles and their wives left San Francisco, presumably to unload the "mud" or brown heroin they had bought. We decided that if Balestreri could so easily be involved, the other members of the combine could also be made. As a result, Graham's group returned to San Francisco one week later and met Balestreri. His report continues:

"The four of us were sitting at the bar in the Redwood Village when Mario entered. He walked over to us. I called him aside and asked how soon he could score for me, saying I wanted to leave town early the next morning. I said Charles was having a hard time getting straightened out and that if he didn't get on his feet I was going to take him away for a week or so and get someone else to work with me. He said he thought that was a good idea. I suggested that Charles was on a drunk and my whole conversation relative to getting him straightened out was to make another quick buy. Mario thought it was a good idea and left. He returned in ten minutes."

Billy Charles and his wife had played their parts well; now they could be moved out of the picture to safety. Graham himself was doing all the talking and setting up the buy on the basis of his earlier contact with Balestreri. Ten days passed. Graham was joined by another agent, James Nash, who posed as Charles' replacement. Together the agents made a purchase, not from Balestreri but from one of his aides. Still another agent, on an independent assignment, bought six ounces of morphine from Joseph (Mope) Alliottos and Joseph Spinoza in the Broadway district of San Francisco. They proved to be part of the Balestreri mob.

For Balestreri, a certain uneasiness about Graham prevailed. He was not completely satisfied with his credentials, nor with those of Jim Nash. To put a final check on Graham, he issued word through the grapevine that he wanted to see Graham right away; he made sure that this word reached the ears of an informer who, it was expected, would feed it to Graham. If the agent answered the summons, which would have come to him only through the informer, then Balestreri would know that Graham was a federal agent; Balestreri was prepared to kill him. Graham did get the word, but knew it exactly for what it was. The time had come for direct action.

The Secret Service, working on the counterfeiting activities of the mob and narcotics agents, posing as customers in another of Balestreri's clubs, the Silver Bowl, watched a transaction involving bogus money. Balestreri, Taranto and Provenzale were picked up and found to be in possession of phoney $20 bills. Narcotics agents then swept to Redwood Village and picked up a mixed bag of racketeers.

Balestreri received sentences totaling twenty-seven years—fifteen for counterfeiting, five for violation of the Harrison Narcotics Act, and seven for violating his parole. He had been out of Leavenworth just a little under four years. Black Tony's observation that "they get you from both sides," proved true with a twist. One side was the Secret Service and the other the Narcotics Bureau. Balistreri was sent to the federal penitentiary at McNeil's Island, Washington. Like Black Tony, he would impart words of wisdom to another young hood going out on parole, but they never listen; they have to learn the hard way.

# 5 A PEEK AT A PIMP

Big Time Charlie Allen, a contemporary of Black Tony Parmagini, lived in Denver. Although he was an active criminal before the 1920's, he eventually arrived at a prominent position in the advertising industry, contributed heavily to both political parties, and at least on one occasion had a box at an Inaugural Ball.

Eight shapely girls hustled for Charlie Allen when he settled in Denver. He had been a boisterous soldier of fortune, running guns for Latin American revolutionaries, quartermastering on Pancho Villa's staff (where he taught Villa to make the revolution pay by selling the hides and meat from cattle they killed), making his way through gold camps in Alaska with a team of sled dogs. Back in America, he acquired a big Belgian police dog and equipped it with gold teeth, and traveled up and down the Pacific Coast matching his dog against the canine mascots of the U.S. Naval stations and fleets. By the time Big Time Charlie Allen settled down in Denver with his bevy of whores, he had gone through three fortunes.

Charlie was not an ordinary pimp; the average panderer takes good care of his girls (unless they have to be whipped back into line) on the theory that if they are taken care of they will earn his living for him. Not Charlie. He never paid his girls off with money in the first place; he gave them heroin. He didn't have to beat them, merely threaten to take away their drug. He wasn't very careful of the amount he gave one of his girls, and she began selling what she didn't require for herself. She sold some to one of our agents named Williamson, who was then a member of the old PU.

In July, 1919, Williamson led a raid on Charlie's home and found a large supply of morphine and cocaine stashed away inside a collection of Kewpie dolls. Heroin was found in the pipes under his sink, and in cans buried behind the brick and mortar walls of his cellar. On December 14, 1920, Big Time Charlie Allen was sentenced to five years in Leavenworth.

Charlie's time in Leavenworth overlapped that of Black Tony and Mario Balestreri, but it is not known whether he knew them. While in prison, Charlie met a wealthy businessman—let's call this man B. H. Mogul—president and owner of one of the largest advertising specialty companies in the world. He had been jailed for income tax evasion. For Charlie Allen, prison life was just another challenge, but for Mogul it was hell; he was used to finer things. Mogul had a rough time of it until Charlie befriended him and became his protector. The friendship grew firm. Mogul and Charlie had many talks and Mogul was convinced that with half a chance Charlie would become a good citizen.

Mogul got his attorney to plead parole for Charlie. When Mogul got out of prison Charlie was also released. Mogul put Charlie to work in one of his Midwestern plants. Soon Charlie worked his way up from laborer to vice-president of the plant.

Sometime later the two friends went on a fishing trip into wild territory that required the services of an Indian guide. Big Time Charlie was sole survivor of that trip. Neither Mogul nor the Indian was ever found. When Charlie reported, he said that their canoe had capsized; the current had been swift and it was each man for himself. When the last will and testament of Mogul was read, Charlie found himself with one third of Mogul's fortune, about $3,000,000, and an $80,000,000 business consisting of an advertising agency and several other corporations employing about six thousand people. Within two years Charlie had increased the agency's business more than 40 per cent.

All this did not satisfy him; he hankered for the civil rights he had lost as a result of his imprisonment. His application for the restoration of his rights had to go to the President of the United States. Before this happened, however, he had to pay the fines and court costs assessed against him in 1920. He promptly deposited with the clerk of the court at Denver $3,265 for payment to the Collector of Internal Revenue.

While waiting for action on his petition, Charlie undertook to give other ex-convicts a break; he hired them by the dozens. He employed so many that the parole board made it a condition that convicts could go free only if they went to another city and did not seek employment in Big Time Charlie's plants.

The former pimp lived on a vast estate. He liked to drive around in an armored car with holstered guns fastened to the doors. When he was not riding his bulletproof car, he raced high-spirited horses over his lands, dressed in a cowboy outfit studded with silver.

Now Charlie, in spite of having pleaded guilty to crimes for which he had served his time, repeatedly claimed that he had been framed. To make his petition easier to read, he contributed $80,000 to a presidential campaign; it was accepted without question. A governor and a senator visited me, in the hope that I would recommend a full pardon for Charlie; the recommendation would make it easier for the President to okay it. The governor came quickly and briskly to the point; he needed Charlie's support; it could mean the difference between defeat and re-election. The senator needed Charlie for the same reason. In fact, Charlie had already received fifty thousand blotters with the senator's picture on them to be used for the campaign.

"Charles Allen was framed," they told me.

I made no decision in the matter. Charlie got his presidential pardon, framed it and mounted it on the wall behind his desk. "See," he told his visitors, "I was framed and there's the pardon to prove it."

Then he would tell the story of his arrest. According to Charlie, when Williamson broke in on that morning long ago Charlie seized him by the seat of his pants and threw him out. Williamson was one of our best judo experts and could have broken Charlie's neck with a flip of his wrist. It was like Charlie to brag about his muscle, but there were things he never spoke of behind his big walnut desk: the whores who had worked for him, or the $100,000 in Liberty Bonds he sent to racketeer Bugsy Siegel, who later was killed by a bullet between the eyes in the Hollywood home of Virginia Hill. Nor did Charlie ever speak of Mogul and the Indian guide. Or how, each time he came to Washington, he planned to steal his dossier from our files. We always got word of these visits through an informer and took special pains to see that Mr. Allen never got near the evidence of his lurid past. He settled down in Advertising Alley in New York and died peacefully only a couple of years ago, leaving behind him a score of unanswered questions.

In the early thirties Big Time Charlie Allen would have fitted in well in Washington, D.C.; it was filled with con men and fakers. Glibness was a social grace. One of the saving things was the presence of Elmer Irey, whom I met at about the time Mrs. Wright had the residents of Capitol Hill hiding under their desks. Elmer, as the chief of the Intelligence Unit of the Bureau of Internal Revenue, was clearing both sides of the street. Elmer's task in Intelligence was to investigate cases involving Treasury Department personnel and to crack major conspiracies to avoid payment of income tax. Elmer was instrumental in helping us to break up the major Canadian combines which smuggled liquor into the States during Prohibition. He was also responsible for getting a ruling from the U.S. Supreme Court which stated that if a ship was beyond the 12-mile limit and small boats were un-loading it and ferrying the cargo to the shore, that a ship-to-shore operation existed, putting the large vessel technically within the 12-mile limit. Primarily, Elmer and his unit worked on the account books of those suspected of avoiding the payment of taxes; they were as effective with the books and pencils as they were with guns—which they often had to use.

The arresting officers came in for more credit than Irey's men who, through careful checking and double checking, managed to pull in Al Capone, Waxey Gordon, Tom Pendergast, Johnny Torrio and others on charges of income tax evasion, when other crimes could not be proved. Later Elmer was to disclose that he had been on the track of Huey Long for nonpayment of taxes when the Louisiana demagogue was shot to death in 1935.

Elmer started as a clerk stenographer in the Bureau of Internal Revenue and worked his way to the top as one of the nation's most important criminal investigators. Although he was a big man, his thick-lensed glasses and mild voice softened the impression. Elmer was always plagued by a slight heart condition, but that didn't slow him down; he went on to become "The Giant Killer."

Our first job together was a big one involving President Hoover, Vice President Curtis and Secretary of the Treasury Andrew Mellon. We had received word from a group of extortionists that these officials were alleged to be implicated in a bootlegging conspiracy worth millions of dollars. The disclosure, the blackmailers told us, would "blow the lid" off the White House. Telegrams, one allegedly from Al Smith, and documents from government officials who knew about the deal, were in their hands, the blackmailers said.

I was ordered to make contact with them and see how much they wanted. Curtis, mindful of the scandals common during the Harding administration, wanted to protect the present administration from any hint of scandal. "If it's to save the administration, go ahead and pay," he said. After examining the documents, which had been given to me, Elmer and I decided they were phoney; we took them to Secretary Mellon. He said, "The first and last pages look authentic. But look what's between—all those signatures—'this is a true copy' and all that sort of thing. I'm inclined to agree with you and Elmer, Harry; this is a fraud." He leaned back in his chair and lit up one of his Between the Acts cigarettes. Elmer and I believed the Secretary to be completely innocent of any wrongdoing; that went for the President and Vice President also. Exhaling smoke, Mellon happened to glance at my socks. "What do you pay for those?" he asked.

"About a dollar and a half, sir," I answered.

He made a face and said, "I get mine at the five and dime."

Then we returned to business. Elmer and I agreed to meet the extortionists. One of us would be a corroborating witness.

When we met the boss of the blackmailers at the appointed place, I said, "We don't think you have a damned thing. Your documents are phoney. We are not paying you one red cent."

"Okay, okay," the boss said. "Now we are going to move into the White House." They all got up to go, looking very sure of themselves.

"Why don't you give it up?" I asked.

They stopped. "We'll let you off the hook for three thousand bucks," the boss said. "Take it to the men's toilet and put it in the first room. We'll pick it up from there and leave these documents."

I had returned the papers to him, after making sure that several copies had been made. "I'm not going to argue with you," I said. "You can burn those papers." That ended the extortion attempt.

The man who tried to engineer it was a distinguished-looking ex-criminal who had served time for murder in Kentucky. Through powerful connections, he later was able to cull thousands of dollars from gullible senators and congressmen and many others, with the promise that he was about to sell Muscle Shoals to Henry Ford at an enormous profit. That plot also failed.

Elmer was involved in many exciting cases, but the Enoch L.
(Nucky) Johnson case was one close to me because a dear friend
of mine, a judge who later died of a heart attack, had got himself
entangled in it. I suppose I also choose this case to illustrate how
crime can enmesh the respectable and use them for its own ends
and, in fact, try to assume a posture of respectability.

I first heard about Nucky through Charlie Root, Chief Intelligence Officer of the U.S. Coast Guard, who was fuming because
Nucky couldn't be stopped by local, state or federal law enforcement agencies; he ran Atlantic City and ran it wide open. Nucky
was also running booze; it was close to repeal and he was making
all the money he could while the getting was good.

"Just give me a high-powered rifle. I'll stop the bastard," Charlie
Root said, when I discussed Nucky with him.

Sometimes in this business you get to feeling that way.

Nucky had a piece of everything. No one drew breath in Atlantic City unless they first got Nucky's permission. Finally Elmer
Irey's Intelligence Unit was called in; perhaps there was a question
of income tax evasion.

Elmer sent his men to a well-known house of prostitution in
Nucky's bailiwick; he was sure that for the madam to operate she
had to pay Nucky. But the madam, a very chic woman—for she
ran a high-class place—refused to tell Intelligence anything.

Then Elmer had an inspiration. He next sent his men to several
laundries in town and eventually got hold of the madam's towel-
cleaning bill. Every customer of any self-respecting house is given
a clean towel. Elmer's men found themselves knee-deep in soiled
towels, but when they were through, they had an accurate idea
of how many tricks the girls had turned during a given period of
time. The number was huge. Atlantic City at that time was perhaps the biggest resort town in the East.

While a part of Elmer's unit was counting towels, the other
had been tracking down the political partnership of Nucky and
my friend the judge. The judge and Nucky had collaborated to
see that a certain railroad company got a much wanted right of

way; they had been well paid for their efforts, but neither had entered these monies on their tax returns. The judge came to me distraught. "I'll be destroyed," he said, "ruined, ruined. What can I do?"

"Get a good lawyer and resign from the bench," I advised.

But he wouldn't step down and was eventually indicted. He got off without going to trial. He would not testify against Nucky. At first I thought it was because of fear of a reprisal from the gang lord, but this was not so. I was astounded to hear the judge say, "I'm one thousand per cent behind Nucky." But was Nucky one thousand per cent behind the judge? He was not. The judge went on the stand to make his defense without any aid whatsoever from Nucky Johnson.

However, the judge's testimony against Johnson was not needed. A connection was shown between the madame's towels, which represented an incredible amount of business, and Nucky Johnson. The madam had come forward to save her own pretty neck, and testified against Nucky, who drew eleven years for income tax evasion, thus breaking up the rackets in Atlantic City.

Elmer Irey was fortunate to have Henry Morgenthau, Jr., as his boss. Morgenthau had been Undersecretary of the Treasury for two months in 1933 and then Secretary. Although his experience had been in conservation, agriculture and banking, he made a fine law enforcement official. He brooked no political interference. When he said a thing, he damn well meant it. Mr. Morgenthau and I didn't always see eye to eye, but he doted on Elmer; Elmer was his boy, and he gave him all the support and encouragement Irey needed. There had been a hiatus when people in the administration felt that collecting taxes was more necessary than catching the hoods, who owed the government untold millions which they never declared. It was felt that the criminals should be convicted on criminal charges and not for tax evasion. But with Morgenthau's blessing, Elmer took off the wraps; it was all right to pursue these people by any means possible.

His men dogged the giants of crime and made them realize that the federal government had some sharp teeth indeed. Guy Helvering, Commissioner of the Bureau of Internal Revenue, sided with Morgenthau and urged Elmer to get the big ones. Senator Carter Glass, one of the sponsors of the Federal Deposit Insurance Corporation, was also in favor of knocking over the big boys. His statement was simple and succinct and completely befitting a former old-school newspaper man, which he was. When an imposing criminal was marked for investigation, he said, *"Get that son of a bitch!"*

Now, a good cop always finds himself under pressure from various sources, low and high, to ease up on investigations. Irey was no exception. Handed a list of his men who were Democrats and/or Catholics and told to get rid of them, he ignored the order. He let it be known that he would hire anybody he damn well pleased, come hell or high water. The pressure didn't come again, on that score or any other.

Gangland set up elaborate plans to frame him. They employed beautiful women and they offered money—on one occasion a million and half dollars, from a crime leader about to be sent to jail; he supposed that Irey would take the money and pull strings to keep him out. He served his time.

Undoubtedly much of Elmer's success was due to his ability to organize. He put this ability to the test in 1934 when the son of Charles A. Lindbergh was kidnapped and killed at Hopewell, New Jersey. That was the most publicized and muddled crime of the century. The police of New York and New Jersey were conducting aimless investigations. Irey helped straighten out this waste of time and manpower. Bruno Richard Hauptmann was later arrested, convicted and executed for the crime.

The great bulk of Irey's work was done inside, with pencil and paper. His men would go over columns of figures endless times, and always they came up with the key to a set of juggled books. Sometimes the marrow of a case involved a little black book that could have disrupted a thousand respectable homes. The Intelligence Unit also uncovered tax frauds implicating disk jockeys who took payola and didn't report it; filling-station operators who ran illegal lotteries, the more obvious examples of the padded expense account, head waiters who received huge undeclared tips, and even fishermen who would not work unless their skippers understated their earnings.

Elmer was highly regarded by people on both sides of the law. For example, the notorious racketeer Johnny Torrio bumped into Irey in Penn Station and said, "Hello, Mr. Irey, how're things going?"

Adjusting his glasses, Irey turned and answered, "Pretty good, but I'm sorry, I didn't catch your name."

"I'm Johnny Torrio," the Al Capone henchman said with a smile.

Not taken aback, Irey said, "Johnny, nice of you to stop and chat with me. I appreciate it."

"My pleasure, Mr. Irey."

Irey's Intelligence Unit was decentralized, and some of the chiefs who followed Irey disliked book work; they wanted to be in the field with gun and siren. But Irey proved beyond a doubt that pen and paper are mightier than the sword.

# 6 THE BUREAU
ON THE MOVE

The activities of Irey's Intelligence Unit were exciting to watch, but the flow of illegal drugs throughout America claimed most of our time and energy. Quantities of illicit narcotics from Europe were passing through the port of New York, and in an attempt to combat this traffic I organized a secret panel of narcotics law enforcement officers from Canada, the United Kingdom, Holland, Germany, Switzerland and France. To handle the home front, I called in Garland Williams. Our conversation was brief. "You go to New York as District Supervisor," I said. "Here's your list of targets. I expect you to break every one of these gangs. Ask for whatever you need and we'll get it for you."

Williams took the list and headed for New York. First he took on the Polakewitz mob. When he got through cleaning house the members of that gang were in jail from Shanghai to Berlin. Williams went overseas to nail Jack Katzenberg's group, traveling to Athens, Marseilles and Vienna to gather the evidence. Katzenberg himself was allowed to languish in a Greek jail while Williams tied up loose ends; an American jail cell is the next thing to a Betty Furness kitchen compared to its Greek counterpart. The Katzenberg mob had shipped tons of opium into America in trunks along with hundreds of kilograms of heroin.

Williams had a brush—his second—with Louis (Lepke) Buchalter and Jack Shapiro. His first had occurred in the twenties when Lepke was earning his reputation for brutality. Now Lepke was wheeling and dealing with at least one prominent labor leader as he forced his protection racket throughout the garment industry in New York. When the occasion demanded it, Lepke became a strikebreaker. He was also involved in dope peddling, although we were unable to prove it. We thought Lepke ran his own mob, but it later turned out that he was an important cog in the Mafia and subject to the orders of the big boys of that organization. With the help of brilliant undercover man Andy Koehn, Lepke was later arrested and electrocuted for murder.

Williams moved once more against "Little Augie" Del Gracio, who had connections with the Eliopoulos ring of Europe. But some of his toughest battles were against the mobs of the Brooklyn waterfront and the 107th Street gang on the upper East Side of Manhattan. Both areas, even when crippled by frequent raids and arrests, seemed able to continue to spawn long lists of major and minor dope racketeers.

Opium was becoming obsolete in New York because of its bulk and telltale odor. Williams used German shepherd dogs and fox terriers to help detect buildings and rooms where the drug was being used or stored. However, opium remained a preferred drug in the Midwest, largely because of the Hip Sing Tong in Minneapolis. This criminal group attracted the attention of Malachi Harney and the dean of narcotics supervisors, Joseph Bransky. The case was Harney's introduction to organized crime. Narcotics was much more satisfying than the old bootlegging trade, because transporting and concealing opium was easier than bothering with cases and bottles of whisky which not only weighed a great deal but took considerable storage space as well.

The presence of many minority group members in gangs at this time may have been due in part to their exclusion from the mainstream of the national economy because of race prejudice, forcing them in their desperate circumstances to earn their bread illegally. But even among the "socially deprived" there were great numbers who did not fall prey to the axiom that crime is man's left-handed endeavor to be successful. I have in mind, among several others, Joseph Bransky.

A man with immense courage and skill, Bransky could have passed as a rabbi. To him I assigned many cases that required the utmost discretion; I knew few men I could trust so well. As a licensed pharmacist, he was particularly adept at investigating the records of drug manufacturers under question. Wholesale and retail dealers and the medical profession itself were well within the scope and understanding of Bransky when it came to illegal deals. When he was assigned to one district, the state pharmacists association asked me to transfer him. I wanted to know why, suspecting that there was some bigotry at work here. I was told that as a Jew, Bransky favored Jewish pharmacists, that he overlooked the faults of the Jews and pounced on the non-Jews. Besides, the complaint went on, Bransky hustled drinks.

"Oh, yes?" I said. "What does Bransky drink?"

"Scotch, always scotch."

"Oh hell," I said, "Joe Bransky's never taken a drink in his life. What're you pulling?"

A year later, when I assigned Joe to a new post, the same officials of the association returned and asked me not to take him away. "He's a great supervisor," they said.

During the twenties narcotic drugs were being dispensed free or at low cost in some forty clinics throughout the country. This was when the Prohibition Unit was active. Growing concern for the increasing crime rate, which seems to attend many addicts, forced the closing of these institutions. The American Medical Association was one of the many prominent organizations which brought pressure to bear for the closings. Bransky was charged with shutting the places in the South. While he was there, he noticed and passed along to PU the information that a great deal of morphine was showing up in Dixie. Since Bransky was still busy with the clinics, we sent down an undercover man who in six months could discover nothing. We put Bransky on the case. It turned out to be a pretty fantastic one.

Two unattractive sisters, in charge of the narcotics section of the manufacturing plant to which we had traced the origin of the illicit morphine, had got involved with some good-looking thugs. The men set up a cottage on a lakefront. The girls, who had never before been involved with men, found life beautiful indeed; there were several fellows around to meet their demands. The girls rushed to the cottage from work every night, and were reluctant to leave it in the morning. The hoods planned for them to fall in love, which they did. Once the girls were hooked by the heartstrings, they were told that if they wanted things to continue, they would have to obtain morphine tablets for the boys every day. "No morphine, baby, no love," was the way they put it.

For the girls, the choice was simple: morphine it was. Each night, their ample bosoms concealing bottles of 100 half-grain tablets of morphine, they met their lovers who were waiting in parked cars, and were whisked away. Love would come after the hoods took the morphine and passed it on to traffickers, getting a large cut themselves. The girls had done away with the records of the morphine they stole. No one in the plant knew what was going on until Bransky cracked the case for us. The people directly involved were arrested. The owners and supervisory personnel of the plant were severely admonished and warned to keep a close check on their records.

Working in the North, Harney clinched a case against an obscure pickpocket and dope peddler named Irving Wexler. The evidence against Wexler was not conclusive and he was released. Harney and the Bureau would have another crack at him later, after he had changed his name to Waxey Gordon and had become the beer baron of New York City.

As a supervisor in the Intelligence Unit under Elmer Irey, Harney often handled charges lodged against our agents, for that too was a function of the IU. Sometimes charges were instituted by criminals out of revenge, or defense attorneys brought charges in an attempt to discredit agent witnesses. The IU acted as a neutral court which heard the charges and determined the facts. Harney was in on one hearing alleging misconduct on the part of a Chicago supervisor and his agents. It was charged that the agents were furnishing narcotics to informers for leads. (Agents supplying narcotics to informers for the purpose of obtaining information have been, and always will be, vigorously prosecuted.) Other irregularities were also charged. When Harney's investigation was over, the allegations were substantiated; the supervisor was dismissed and indicted. Although acquitted by a jury, he was not reinstated. The agents were convicted. This case was one of our earliest and largest and is worth noting because charges are still occasionally filed against our agents; some are proved, but the great majority are not.

Harney stayed on in Chicago and for a time supervised the activities of Frank Wilson and Elliot Ness, along with many other fine agents. Elliot Ness was a bright, tough and resourceful agent, but not the one-man scourge depicted on television. No successful law enforcement venture can be a one-man job; I believe Ness would be the first to back me up on this. He went from government service to the position of Safety Commissioner of Cleveland. His record for establishing effective law enforcement there was remarkable; he sent twelve corrupt police captains of that city to prison shortly after assuming his duties.

Frank Wilson, who later was to become Chief of the United States Secret Service, was appointed a Special Agent in the Intelligence Unit in 1920. It was Frank who, ten years later, suggested to Chief Elmer Irey that two men infiltrate the Al Capone gang. While this was being done, Frank sat down to study the accounts of the Capone enterprises, a task which kept him engaged sixteen to twenty hours a day. Frank Wilson personally handled more than a million checks cleared by Capone men. Somehow Capone got wind of Wilson's efforts. One of the undercover men called Wilson and warned him that the very next day he was to be killed by gunmen brought in from Brooklyn on Capone's orders. Wilson checked into another hotel and continued his work while Capone issued orders to his entire criminal network to get him.

But Al wasn't closing in on Wilson; Wilson was closing in on Al. He had come upon a ledger from a gambling casino in Cicero, Ill., a Chicago suburb practically owned by Capone. From the ledger, Wilson traced leads to Gary, Indiana and then to Miami, Florida. At Miami he smuggled a Capone bookkeeper into custody and safekeeping. In alarm, Capone placed a price of $25,000 on the head of this key witness, but he never had an opportunity to pay. In October, 1931, Capone was indicted for failure to pay over $200,000 in back taxes. (His take for 1927 alone was estimated at $105,000,000.) He wanted to settle out of court for one and a half million dollars, but his offer was refused; too many law enforcement people, local, state and federal, wanted Capone off the streets. He was sentenced and later sent to that formidable, renovated military prison, Alcatraz, for ten years. He was to be released in 1939, a victim of paresis, as was Elie Eliopoulos. Eight years later he was dead.

In the Southwest, opium was pouring in across the Mexican border. Phlegmatic Bill Harmon, who also had been taken off booze and put on junk, was working on one case after another almost without respite.

The Woody Wilson case called for Harmon to act out of character. Playing the part of a flashy gangster, Harmon blew into Yuma with a sexy-looking doll on his arm—Miss Norma Bacon, a secretary from Harmon's Nogales office. After several weeks of posing as an easy come, easy go pair from New York, Harmon finally met Woody Wilson, who was peddling bulk opium and heroin. Wilson was married to a former actress.

Several meetings between Harmon and Wilson took place before the agent dropped the hint that he was interested in picking up some junk. Wilson agreed to deliver two ounces of heroin to him, but Harmon said that he wasn't a piker; he didn't want to deal in small amounts. He was looking for big bundles. But to keep Wilson happy and unsuspecting, Harmon bought several small amounts.

Later, during a conversation in Harmon's room (with Miss Bacon and another agent concealed in the closet), Wilson agreed to deliver 20 ounces of heroin. Woody Wilson's demands for the transaction left Harmon little opportunity to get the required cash from government sources. He knew that if he didn't come up with the money at the appointed time, he would lose Wilson. Thinking fast, Harmon went to the Valley National Bank of Yuma. There he discussed the problem with Mr. Oliver, the president of the bank. Oliver checked Harmon's identification. Bill Harmon wrote out an IOU for the amount required in the transaction—$9,200—and Oliver counted out ninety-two hundred-dollar bills. You don't get that kind of cooperation from banks today.

With the money Harmon baited the trap. When the 20 ounces of heroin was delivered, Woody Wilson and seven other persons were caught. Woody posted bond and fled to California where he was later caught again, this time for armed robbery, and sentenced to ten years. A hold order was placed on him so that when he was released from San Quentin, he could be charged for violation of the narcotics laws.

From the Woody Wilson case, Harmon went on to the Miguel Brey border case which involved the transportation of opium from Mexico to the United States. With the cooperation of the Mexican police, Brey and an accomplice were convicted. The Alfonso Montoya case was next for Bill, and he cracked it by seizing thirty cans of smoking opium en route by car from Mexico to El Paso. Also operating out of El Paso, Bill closed the Jim King Wong and Lung Wuen cases, which choked off other sources of opium.

Seeking a well-earned rest from his labors, Harmon was sitting at the desk of his El Paso office one day when an informer called and told him that two girls, one of whom was named Hortencia Diaz, were carrying a suitcase filled with opium to New York City. Harmon got this information ten hours after the girls had left the city. He took a full description of them and forwarded it to the New York office, asking agents to meet the train, find the point of delivery, and arrest the girls and the persons to whom the drug was being delivered.

But the girls got off the train in New Jersey. They took a taxi to New York, delivered the drug, collected $24,000 and put up at a hotel. After we caught up with them we found out that they had also gone ice skating. We wondered what they had done with the money while they were on the rink. They said they had put it in their skating shoes.

The girls agreed to cooperate with the Bureau, and after an exchange of calls between Harmon and the New York agents, it was decided to let them return to El Paso accompanied by an agent and a woman inspector. The boss of the operation, we learned, was a fellow named Pan Yee who lived in Mexico. The girls crossed the border with $24,000 in their shirtwaists and fingered Pan Yee, who was subsequently arrested and convicted. He died in the late fifties after his release from prison.

In the meantime, Malachi Harney and Hunter T. Nugent were chasing women, Harney in Chicago and Nugent in Nevada. Both chases, however, were quite legal and defined as work. Harney was breaking the case, which had been hanging for some time, against the notorious Kitty Gilhooley, Dope Queen of Chicago. Kitty was the undisputed narcotics boss of the Windy City until Harney ran her in.

Nugent was involved with a woman who had earned the picturesque name, "The Lady in Red." She was not John Dillinger's lady. Divorced several times, Red had been jailed for forging checks to meet her Reno gambling losses. While in jail she learned from her cellmate, a chick from Los Angeles who was an addict, that she regularly received morphine from one of our agents. Red gave us the tip and Nugent baited a trap for our erring young man. When he made his next delivery, Nugent stepped out of the jail shadows and nailed him; the crooked agent had had several ounces of morphine on his person. He drew twelve years. The crooked agent had been one of our best known and liked agents in the West. But like a few other men in the Bureau, he got stardust in his eyes and went "Hollywood." The Lady in Red, on the basis of her help, got a lot of publicity and she turned writer, producing many magazine articles.

While in prison, The Lady in Red became great friends with the sheriff. I'm not suggesting that the prison was run somewhat irregularly, but I later got word that the sheriff and Red had gotten married.

Another woman was now capturing national headlines. Before she was to be relegated to the back pages of the newspapers, agents Garland Williams, Andy Koehn, Malachi Harney and others would have been directly or indirectly involved with her. U.S. prosecutors Thomas E. Dewey and Skelly Wright would render decisions of concern to her.

The woman was "The Million Dollar Girl"—Lady Margaret Burton, granddaughter of the Earl of Wakefield, niece of the African explorer and translator of the *Arabian Nights*, Sir Richard Burton, and protégé of Sir James Barrie, author of *Peter Pan*. She said she had discussed with King Edward his romance with Wallis Warfield Simpson; she assured the American press that whatever Edward did—for he had not yet abdicated—the British people were behind him. All this made up her pedigree. In England where she'd been acclaimed a beauty queen, she was called the "Pocket Venus"; she stood only five feet tall.

Within two days of her arrival in Hollywood, she secured a six months' contract at $150 per week. Before long she was making pictures with Hoot Gibson, the cowboy hero; Paul Lukas, Betty Compton and Norman Kerry. Her studio launched a million-dollar publicity campaign, which earned her the name, "The Million Dollar Girl." Lady Margaret Burton was then selected to play the lead in the film version of Sir James Barrie's *The Boy*

*David*. The film was just going into production when a studio head, browsing around the dressing rooms, came upon her sniffing cocaine.

Hollywood was no longer risking its image for drug addicts. The experiences with Alma Rubens and Wallace Reid had taught Hollywood a grim lesson. Production on *The Boy David* was stopped. Lady Margaret went to a rest home for treatment. By the time she announced her cure, however, her part in the film had been assigned to someone else.

Margaret Burton was no lady of nobility; she had never seen King Edward VIII and she was related to no one of great importance. But for cocaine she might have been able to carry off her grand masquerade. She was born plain Margaret Burton in a Yorkshire slum. She had to leave school early in order to help her mother sell flowers and oranges in the streets. At sixteen she was a beauty and a friend suggested that she enter a beauty contest; she did—and won. She moved on as a chorus girl at the London Hippodrome where she met Nicholas McCormack, alias "Red Lewis." Miss Burton had already been through four relationships, some of them marriages, some of them not. It was believed that McCormack may have been responsible for Miss Burton's addiction; love at first shot was the way one agent put it.

McCormack made good use of Margaret's beauty. He headed a blackmail ring, carefully schooling several women, grooming them, and then setting them up as members of European aristocracy or society matrons. They mixed in the finest circles, on the watch for likely victims. The men they attracted found them a little stand-offish at first. But soon, very soon, the girls would pretend they had been swept off their feet by the "Johns." Glorious conquest! The relationships would continue with mounting intensity until a male member of the ring or McCormack himself would break into the apartment at the moment of compromise. A photographer would be on hand. Margaret Burton was charged with being involved in this ring before she came to Hollywood.

Margaret also stated that a big producer-director first "turned her on," gave her the first narcotics she ever received, which had caused her addiction. Not even the presence of McCormack in Hollywood helped her rescue her career. McCormack, himself an addict for some thirty years, posed as an assistant film director, managing in the meantime to gather some experience at directing. When he was later picked up in New Orleans on a charge of mailing narcotics, his address book contained the names and numbers of known narcotics users and peddlers, movie stars, pickpockets, a countess, and Margaret's London address. She had returned to England, despairing of success in American movies. Once she ventured a return to America in a vain attempt to triumph over her past, but she could not get past New York. In England she wrote:

I landed in America a complete mental and physical wreck. Some friends took me at once to a shabby hotel on 72nd Street. That place was the headquarters of a dope ring. You just walked in, paid your money, told them the drug you wanted, and a nurse gave you a jolt of the stuff in your arm.

It was because of Margaret that McCormack was arrested and convicted; he had been mailing narcotics to her in magazines. Scotland Yard and the Bureau of Narcotics cooperated in his arrest. Without Nicholas McCormack to supply her drugs, "The Million Dollar Girl" wasn't worth a penny.

The first Roosevelt administration brought about a temporary reversion to the spoils system, and Malachi Harney was replaced at Chicago and returned to the Twin Cities, Minneapolis and St. Paul. Here the Hip Sing had been superseded by a hoodlum named William ("Big Bill") Hildebrandt. An even bigger man than John T. Randall of the *I'm Alone*, Hildebrandt stood six feet four inches and weighed about 260 pounds. He had fought all the way up—or down—the ladder of crime from street fighter and box car thief to bank robber, and he was a dangerous criminal. Hildebrandt tolerated no underworld competition. Had the tongs been in full swing at that time, a full-scale gang war would have broken out; now Big Bill operated openly and without friction. He had a record of apparent immunity from serious consequences when he collided with the law. Under Hildebrandt, the illicit drug traffic out of the Twin Cities was threatening to take over the near and far northwestern states as well as some of the Canadian provinces. Harney had his hands full.

The agent and the crook played a fascinating game of chess. When Harney moved, Hildebrandt had him checked; when Big Bill moved, he found that Harney had preceded him. Hildebrandt called in all his weapons—the underworld, the politicians, the "respectable" professionals. But Harney was determined either to make his own break or wait until Hildebrandt stumbled.

Even though Harney had manged to trace an illegal transaction through Big Bill, assistant U.S. Attorney George Heisey advised a delay in the all-out attempt to secure corroboration. Then the mistake occurred.

Certainly Hildebrandt knew we were after him. His error could only have come about because he was in the process of setting up something so big that he couldn't afford the possibility of Harney catching him in the middle of it. And so, when Assistant District Supervisor of the Bureau John Wall was approached by a discredited ex-chief of detectives of St. Paul with a proposition, he was stunned. Could Hildebrandt be that stupid, or was he desperate? This is what we were waiting for—that one slip. The man behind the former detective, of course, was Big Bill. What rankled was that if Hildebrandt thought he could buy the Bureau, he must have bought some pretty high local offices. Thinking quickly, Wall pretended to agree to the proposition and then reported it. It was then relatively simple to build a strong case against Hildebrandt and twenty of his aides. The crime czar of the Twin Cities stood trial and was convicted. Judge Gunnar Nordbye sentenced him to twenty years.

Before he was put away, Big Bill had chosen Thomas Nelson of St. Paul to handle his business during his absence. Nelson was not as clever as Hildebrandt, nor was he as adept at keeping the connections open. But Nelson thought he was a very clever man; we nailed him because of that notion.

We sent in a man to make a buy from him. This is the surest way to make a case. Very often the peddler approached will not sell until he knows the buyer, and then will let someone else deliver it, keeping his own hands clean. But Nelson liked to be one of the boys; he occasionally made his own sales. Each time our man approached him, however, Nelson turned him down. Whenever the agent was with Nelson, he purposely exposed a handful of bills folded in such a way that a $10 bill looked like a $100. Nelson knew the bills for what they were, but he admired the cockiness of the agent. After many months, while the agent was handling some bills, Nelson agreed to sell.

"What made you change your mind?" the agent asked. "I've been after you to sell and you've always said no."

Nelson grinned. "The gambler's crimp."

After the buy, Nelson was arrested and put away for fifteen years.

Almost at once the Minneapolis syndicate took up the slack and, even in spite of constant arrests, continues to operate. Attorney General Robert Kennedy mentioned this group not long ago. Although the syndicate had a reputation for bribery and intimidation (one of Harney's witnesses, a bookkeeper, was shot and killed by killers who were never identified before he could be placed on the stand), Harney and another agent were able to put together a case which resulted in one of the very rare prosecutions of this group.

# 7 FROM THE KALLIKAKS OF CRIME TO MURDER, INC.

Within only a few years after the Federal Bureau of Narcotics was established, it became apparent that the gangs were making still another conversion. From illicit whisky they had gone into opium traffic, and now in the thirties, the switch was to drugs of smaller bulk—cocaine, morphine, and especially heroin. Any of these drugs, and many others derived from them, could be concealed in the smallest conceivable space. Morphine and heroin require some minor preparation before taking; cocaine could be sniffed from a handkerchief without any preparation at all if an addict desired this rather than intravenous injections. Smoking opium, on the other hand, was rather bothersome; some cooking was required, and pots which left telltale evidence. Besides, opium smelled. A tin of it was the size of a can of pipe tobacco, ten or even twenty times as large as a capsule of heroin.

While heroin was expensive, the profits were larger. It could be moved quicker, sold without creating a lot of attention. Heroin was coming to be the drug most handled by dope peddlers.

How it got into the hands of Ma Booley and her family was not only a mystery but a disaster to nearly everyone who came in contact with this group, which could be called the Kallikaks of Crime. The last time Ma Booley appeared in court in the thirties, she was a haggard, detestable sort of vermin. She stood hunched before the bench in a federal court in Texas. Spectators found it impossible to believe that she was a member of the human race, much less a mother. She had borne six children. There motherhood stopped. Ma Booley's children and their husbands or consorts—ten persons altogether—by 1951 had served a total of 104 years in jail. Nonfamily members put up by Ma to serve her time for her, did over 200 years, a total of three centuries and more.

Ma was sixty-seven years old when she appeared before the judge in Texas; she had had only two previous convictions, being powerful enough in that region of the country to get patsies to do her time for her. When they refused, they had a way of turning up dead. No one dared turn her in. Not even her husband, who, a weak man, had looked on helplessly as Ma turned their daughters into street tarts.

In her youth Ma had taught her daughters to steal, and soon they became peddlers of dope. They weren't old enough to know that the cubes they were delivering were not sugar, but morphine. As soon as the three children reached puberty, she forced them into prostitution; when they found customers on the streets, they brought them home. Ma served as the madam and collected the money. One of the daughters was arrested at fifteen for hustling. She was committed to a local jail. The next morning she was found dead, victim of an overdose of heroin.

One of the remaining daughters described the nightly routine:

When we girls would go out to work the streets at night, Ma would parcel out the cubes of morphine for us to sell. Of course, now, we only do a wholesale business, because Ma kept her word to us. Just as soon as we had made a lot of customers, she moved out of the district and we girls got off the street.

After the girls and the narcotics started to bring in money regularly, Ma took a great fancy to clothes. And she went to beauty shops regularly. Her territory expanded from a shabby district in one city to an empire comprising six states. She possessed some not insignificant political power. Among the addicts she serviced she demanded loyalty or no drugs. Sometimes she ordered death.

With agents like Bill Harmon operating in the Southwest, her empire began to dwindle. Ma was apprehended in one of her last holdings, a package liquor store across from a tourist camp. Our agents had secured evidence that she was selling heroin as well as whisky and they pulled into the tourist camp one night. The camp itself was a sorry symbol of the times; farmers whose lands had turned to dust stopped there en route to California. Ma made her money from those occasional tourists who wanted to drink while they drove. When the agents entered the store, they found one of Ma's sons, Tom, behind the counter. The agents approached and asked him for heroin. Tom was a slow-witted boy, and he was taking too long to prepare the drug and get the money. From her peephole, Ma, assured that the visitors were genuine buyers, became impatient. Why was the boy taking so long? Greed made her impatient. Finally, she came out herself, took the powder from the boy, and with one hand passed over the drug while taking the money with the other. She was promptly arrested.

There was not much life left in Ma when she passed out of court, sentenced to two years because of her age. Behind her she left a shambles, a record that should never be forgotten. One child escaped the life of theft, the drug addiction, the utter depravity of the family, and it is because of this man and his family that I have changed the name of his mother. The son grew up to be a good man and to marry a fine woman. They put their children through college, and the grandchildren and the great-grandchildren know nothing of the Booleys.

While Ma Booley was serving her time, Nick Surrell, a full-blooded Cherokee who looked like an addict and who weighed a hundred pounds soaking wet, made a case against an Indian peddler named Red Cloud Fleetwood. With the oil discoveries in Oklahoma during the thirties, the Osage Indians had become rich. Red Cloud Fleetwood had been selling heroin to the sons of the chiefs. The chiefs themselves had come to Washington to ask me if there was some way Red Cloud could be stopped. With the cooperation of the chiefs, and with Surrell on the case, Red Cloud turned up within a week.

One of Surrell's most important cases, however, may have influenced the voting in Congress. This is the way it happened:

An attorney in a Western city was running for Congress. A case of armed robbery came up and the attorney, being a criminal lawyer, took the case. The gunman had specialized in knocking over banks and wholesale drug houses. The attorney lost the case, but sought to secure his fee while his client was in jail. The gunman had no money but suggested that the attorney take instead a bottle of a thousand half-grain tablets of morphine worth $5,000 on the illicit market. The attorney agreed and the robber told him where to find the valuable bottle.

Having innumerable underworld contacts, the attorney sent out word that he had narcotics for sale. Before long he found a buyer—Nick Surrell. Surrell made the preliminary arrangements with the local police, then went to the attorney with other agents covering and put down a "flash" roll—$100 bills on the outside and one-dollar bills in the center. The attorney snapped for the bait like a hungry rat and the transaction was completed. Surrell walked to a window and lowered a shade. That was the signal for which the other agents and police were waiting. When they came tramping through the door, the attorney turned twenty colors of brown. All this happened just a month before election day. The attorney's opponent didn't have to campaign a single day after that.

Not long ago a famous politician spoke with me at a dinner. "Do you remember the ——— case?" he asked.

"I certainly do," I answered and then, taking a closer look at him, I was startled to recognize the man who had come into Congress as an aftermath of Surrell's undercover work. The congressman had done a damned good job, too. But for Surrell we might have had the wrong man sitting in Congress today.

Another fine agent who worked in the West for a time was blond, rugged Andrew Koehn, one of the most successful undercover men of his day. Koehn acted as though clocks didn't exist. A working day to him consisted of up to eighteen hours. I've heard men complain about long hours, but Koehn was not one of them.

One of his many prominent investigations took place in Denver, the former home of Big Time Charlie Allen. Koehn was after Lou Blonger, a man who grew up in Canadian saloons, dance halls, and near gaming tables. At a very early age Blonger learned that there were law enforcement officials who could be bought, and he bought them. At one time he had a direct telephone line to the office of the Denver chief of police.

Boss of one of the shrewdest gangs in the West, Blonger, among many other things, ran phoney race horse rooms. The huge blackboards, the masses of clamoring telephones, the stacks of money flowing back and forth, were all props to part the poor yokel from his hard-earned money. Blonger also had a fake stock brokerage office complete with all the trimmings: calls from Wall Street, stock quotation figures always rising, ticker tape, and so on. Plants of this type proved to be too much for the hayseed, who would run to the bank and draw all his savings, or take a loan on his farm or home, come back and lose it in two hours. He wouldn't know he had lost it, for the show usually ran through the night with the hayseed scheduled to return next morning. When he did, the room would be vacant.

Blonger also fixed fights. But his downfall began when Phillip S. Van Cise was elected district attorney of the city and county of Denver. Van Cise went to the office of the new police chief, a man who was honest but helpless because of pressure from above. He told the new DA that every time he started to move against Blonger, the orders came to leave him and his growing group of drug addict associates alone.

Van Cise returned to his office and called the Federal Bureau of Narcotics. "I want Andy Koehn," he said. The use of narcotics by Blonger's men made Koehn's entrance into the case quite proper.

Sometime before, Koehn had made a con man who was an addict and had taken from him a small box such as carpenters carry for their best tools. In this box were seals and equipment for a notary public, stationery imprinted with the names of several phoney businessmen and fraternal organizations, envelopes, impressive red and gold seals, sheriffs' badges, letters of warning from brokerage houses, with buy and sell tickets on the international exchange, and bonding security company certificates. All this was the usual equipment of the con man. I think Andy sometimes had himself a ball with the kit.

Koehn, who spent a great part of his career doing surveillance, had a cardinal rule for getting on top of a case—listen to telephone conversations and survey the mail. He believed that what he obtained this way would give him enough information to penetrate any gang. When he had gathered all the pertinent facts of the Blonger group's activities, he got into the gang as a stock salesman, working on a commission basis. At the time Blonger was knee-deep in peddling phoney oil stock.

Koehn found himself with a twofold job: he had to report the movements of the group to Van Cise *and* also report on the crooked detectives who worked out of the police department; Van Cise had a one-man counterintelligence corps in agent Koehn.

After months of hard work, during which Blonger took many a hayseed and Koehn discovered a string of whorehouses and a little clique of dope peddlers, Van Cise, advised by Koehn, called the governor in order to arrange for raids. The DA was taking no chances of having the case against Blonger blown up in his face by corrupt local officials. The raids went off like clockwork. One of the largest churches in Denver was used to hold the hoods, whores, pushers and con men incommunicado. Blonger himself was picked up in the last raid. He had been surprised in his office, with all his equipment—phoney stocks, bank rolls, badges, and so on. The cooperation of the Denver press was excellent; none of the papers printed a word about the raids until every member of the gang was in. Van Cise and Koehn brought in thirty-four people; some had engaged in some half-hearted gunplay, but no one had been injured.

With Andy Koehn as the star witness, the trial got under way. The clever defense attorneys could not shake his testimony. Van Cise relaxed; this time Blonger and his gang had had it. The trial lasted two months. After all the work and danger, after all the efforts on the part of many, there came the convictions. Twenty of the gang, including Blonger, were expected to receive stiff sentences.

They didn't.

Blonger got seven years, which he could do in less than four; three others got three years and could serve them in twenty-five months. Blonger and his men, forbidding their attorneys to file appeals, walked briskly out of the courtroom, smiling. They said they could do the time standing on their heads. They said: "Well, we won."

And they had. The bench gave them, in spite of the ruin they had brought to Denver, in spite of the harsh punishment their crimes deserved, the lightest possible sentences. Van Cise and Koehn were furious and sad by turns. They had a right to be. But Koehn had to move on. There was more work for him.

Returning East, Koehn teamed with Malachi Harney to put the stopper on Lepke Buchalter. With Yasha Katzenberg, Jake Lovsky and Sam Gross, Lepke ran a plant in the Bronx which derived heroin from opium. The business was going so well by the middle thirties that Lepke decided to expand. Although he was careful to avoid direct involvement with the operations, we learned that he was indeed an integral part of it. Information, however, is not enough. Successful criminal prosecutions require evidence and witnesses. The facts must be proved and the witnesses have to be competent. And good prosecutors are needed. With Harney directing and Koehn in an undercover role, the Bureau set out to remove Lepke from the picture once and for all.

Even while plans were being set for the infiltration of Lepke's gang, Lepke was expanding his smuggling operation. He organized a group of "world travelers." (I mentioned this group in *The Murderers* along with other details of the Lepke case.) Harney and Koehn received word that a large amount of narcotics, delivered by one of the "world travelers," was due to arrive in New York. The shipment was from China and slated to be put through customs by a couple of dishonest inspectors. Following the route of the shipment to the wholesaler could have clinched the case against the Lepke combine. Agents waited, but nothing happened; the shipment hadn't come through. The Japanese-Chinese War with its resulting complications had upset the delicate balance of Lepke's international machinery.

There was no choice, however, but to wait for the break. Harney's men gathered bits and pieces of evidence in the meantime, and worked at fitting them into the larger pattern; Koehn continued in the dangerous job of working undercover. Fantastic as it seemed, Lepke's group was importing enough narcotics from Tientsin, China, to supply the needs of 10,000 addicts each year. Finally we had enough evidence to implicate more than thirty people in the Lepke combine. They would be picked up as soon as the next shipment came in, but in the meantime we had to keep a small army of agents poised and ready although other cases needed immediate attention. Further, could we jeopardize Koehn's position? Was the shipment even en route? Would the war in China hold up our plans indefinitely? And most important, could we nail Lepke for keeps if we moved at once?

We could put the inquiry and investigation on ice and hope to make the case later. On the other hand, we could move at once and hope for the best. It developed that we didn't wait and it was a good thing, too, for the Chinese-Japanese War became an almost total involvement for both nations.

Harney insisted, and rightly as it turned out, that with the help of the U.S. Attorney General and a grand jury, the risk in trying Lepke and his mob, without being able to use all of the evidence we wanted to, was worth taking.

To our great satisfaction the indictments were returned. Lepke became a fugitive.

A year or so later Andy Koehn returned to the underworld and spread so many fires and instituted such a campaign of harassment that the underworld sent word to Lepke that if he didn't give himself up, they would dump his body on the courthouse steps. A huge reward was offered for Lepke's capture, dead or alive. Lepke was caught in the middle and turned himself over to Walter Winchell and J. Edgar Hoover.

The Bureau of Narcotics and the Bureau of Customs had the honor and the risk of bringing about the first important convictions against the man thought to head Murder, Inc. While he was serving a part of his twelve-year sentence, other law enforcement agencies had time to perfect the cases which would lead to Lepke's execution for murder. Emanuel (Mendy) Weiss, called the chief executioner, and Jake Migden, a known torpedo, would be executed also. Both had jumped bond but were recaptured, Weiss in Kansas City and Migden in St. Louis where he had undergone plastic surgery in an attempt to escape detection.

James Attie was one agent who, unlike many other agents, never made a claim upon the arrest and conviction of Al Capone. Attie's family had come from the Middle East. A former boxer, he had fought several times in Madison Square Garden. He wasn't big, but he was fast on his feet. He was good-looking, with jet-black hair and dark, flashing eyes. He dressed like a prosperous racketeer. But Attie wasn't a party boy. He was our ace in the hole many times when the going got rough. He is the holder of more awards gained in the line of duty than any other agent in the Bureau.

Since he spoke several Arabian dialects, we used him to good advantage in undercover work in the Middle East.

One of Attie's biggest cases was made not for the Narcotics Bureau, but for the Secret Service. Involved in investigating the Mafia operations, he was able, through an informer, to secure $750,000 in counterfeit money. We handed the case over to the Secret Service. They weren't very grateful. They argued that the special employee, the informer, was also one of the big counterfeiters they'd been wanting to prosecute. But we needed the man to help Attie into the inner circle of the Mafia's dope traffic in Chicago.

The Chief of the Secret Service went to my Treasury Department superior and complained that we were obstructing justice by not turning the counterfeiter over to the Service at once. I explained to my chief that the Service people were looking a gift horse in the mouth; that when our aspect of the case was over the Service could do whatever they wanted to with the informer. The Chief agreed with me, but the Service people went on up to the Attorney General. The decision was once again made in favor of the Narcotics Bureau, and we were allowed to keep the informer on the job until he had introduced Attie to one of the most important Mafia criminals in the Windy City. The case Attie made against this man was so good that we didn't need the informer to testify. But before the Service could get to him he was found shot to death in a Chicago suburb. The murder has never been solved.

In Mexico City, Attie, after hard work, finally met a large-scale peddler known to police there as the Al Capone of Mexico—a man who, like Attie, was of Arabic background. Neither the Mexican federal or local police was able to catch and prosecute this man. After many negotiations in different hotels in Mexico City, after using many intricate covers and making transactions and deals, a buy was scheduled.

On the appointed night Attie showed up and asked to see the heroin. The Al Capone of Mexico, however, wanted to see the color of Attie's money. One of his aides stood by, but Attie was also covered by federal police who were stationed in rooms down the hall. After staring each other down for a few moments, the buy was made, at which point Attie, without notifying the police down the hall, said, "You're under arrest."

The gangster pulled out a forty-five and leveled it at Attie, who drew his own pistol. "Okay," he said, "we'll shoot it out. No one'll get out of here alive." The conversation was in Arabic. The hood's partner didn't understand what was being said, but he had sense enough to faint when he saw the drawn guns. Finally the Al Capone of Mexico lowered his gun. Attie took it and called in the police.

In another Mexican case Jim was supposed to step out of the picture when a delivery of heroin was about to be made. The idea here was that in order to achieve successful prosecution, no agent *provocateur* could be involved. Entrapment is an ugly word in Mexico, where the memory of dictatorship and suppression is strong. Shooting broke out before Attie could leave the scene, and a Mexican officer threw himself in the line of fire to prevent Attie from being hit. The Mexican press, believing Attie to be a bigtime narcotics peddler, took the police to task for not having arrested him. Although the government was grateful to Attie, they had to hustle him out of the country in the interests of law enforcement and because of prevailing public opinion. The Mexican police officer, who had been wounded, recovered and was awarded a gold medal for bravery by the American treasury department, but was not allowed to receive it until his retirement.

Like Jim Attie, Benedict Pocoroba also worked on many cases within and outside the States. Within the country, however, he was most often concerned with the Mafia.

Benny was just like having a loaded gun in the house; maybe you wouldn't need it, but if there was a crisis, it would come in handy. A Sicilian, Benny spoke with a thick accent and he looked like a small-time hood. Benny had worked with Bill Harmon in the Southwest on the Kok-Si case. Kok-Si, who seemed to be a pious, dedicated man, solicited money for the support of a "missionary school" in China. In truth, he was hustling opium. When Pocoroba and Harmon finally caught up with him he had caches of opium in a dozen different places in town and between $30,000 and $40,000 in his safe. Judge Ling of Phoenix sentenced Kok-Si to eight years, but the term was suspended on the condition that he leave at once for China.

Now Pocoroba had infiltrated the Charlie (Big Nose) La Gaipa mob. A former partner of Luciano in the narcotics racket, La Gaipa had broken with him and planned to take over the traffic in California. Benny got into the mob through a man we have never permitted in court; the Mafia doesn't suspect him, but he has opened many underworld doors for us.

Pocoroba was on the case for six months. There were times when we were out of touch with him for as long as a month, and we would wonder if there was anyone left to get in touch with. But it always turned out that Benny was doing one hell of a job. He was helping the La Gaipa crew hide hermetically sealed copper tins of opium smuggled from China. Later it would be passed through the Chinatowns as in the old days, or else processed into heroin. In addition, Pocoroba became the favorite cook of the gang; his Italian dinners were like none the hoods had ever eaten.

By now Benny had turned over to us all the information needed to proceed with the arrests. We made our raids and got the entire group except for Charlie La Gaipa. We left it up to Pocoroba to find him.

Nosing around Oakland one day, Pocoroba spotted La Gaipa's empty car. After examining the lay of the land and deciding that he was not walking into an ambush, Pocoroba inspected the car. There was a sticky substance on the dashboard that might be blood and flesh. Pocoroba called in the local authorities, who determined that the substance was brain tissue. We presumed that this was all that was left of Mr. La Gaipa, and that he had been dispatched by the local California boys, either on their own or at Luciano's request, because La Gaipa's incursion was much resented. Benny had no one left to cook for.

There was something so sincerely "old country" about Benny that whenever he came out with the inevitable line: "You're under arrest, I'm a federal agent," the crooks thought he was making an unpleasant joke. In one such case in Kansas City, a man with great political influence first refused to believe Pocoroba was sincere; then in a burst of anger he accused Benny of framing him. They exchanged heated words in Italian, until Benny said in English, "Why in the hell should I frame you? I get a government check each and every month."

Pocoroba's integrity was shared by all our agents with the exception of the few who "went Hollywood" or who tried to convert crime into profit for themselves. During the thirties the Bureau of Narcotics, while comprising only two per cent of the federal enforcement personnel, accounted for 12 per cent of the federal prison population. The average narcotic agent, therefore, was making 300 per cent more criminal cases than any other law enforcement agent in the country. Men like Benny Pocoroba were responsible for this record.

We thought this was a good record. It prepared us for the future. Our personnel of less than five hundred in the field and in the offices had come through the first years of the Bureau with distinction. But we had no time to rest on our laurels.

Few projects in which Harney and I were involved gave us more sleepless nights, headaches and fits of downright disgust than our long-time campaign to bring Frank Costello to the bar with a solid conviction.

We first came across Costello in the twenties when, under a plan set up by the Treasury Department, men from Customs, the old Prohibition Unit, and Internal Revenue were called upon to provide men to break up the combines of Canadian distillers who were conspiring to distribute liquor in the U.S. That task was arduous. Hundreds of individual acts revealing a picture of criminal-distiller collaboration had to be pieced together; "corporate veils" established by steamship companies, shipping companies, fiscal depositories and the like had to be torn away to discover what persons lurked behind them. It was discovered that many of the distillers had agreed to apportion among themselves the illegal American whisky market. But they fell out among themselves and took the case to court, where the judges threw it out but ordered the records sealed. Later, the Canadians settled out of court with a compromise offer of three and a half million dollars.

As a result of the investigation, the agents of the Bureaus involved in the undercover work, and who had wormed their ways into various gangs, got themselves listed in the "Who's Who of American Gangdom."

It was also in the course of this investigation that Harney picked up the information that later was to help the Immigration and Naturalization Service put a crimp in Costello's activities and challenge the validity of his citizenship. By the early thirties Frank Castiglia, or Costello, had a small piece of the slot-machine racket in New York City. It was difficult to determine how big he was then. His connections with Murder, Inc., Lepke Buchalter, Lucky Luciano and many others brought him under scrutiny.

Mayor Fiorello La Guardia, the "Little Flower," closed down Costello's slot machines and Don Francesco, as he is called by his intimates, lived quietly, working always out of sight and up the ladder to the peak of Mafia power. In 1943 a storm broke around him; he was being accused of having pressured for the nomination of Thomas A. Aurelio for State Supreme Court Justice. Aurelio was elected.

But let me make this quite clear: Judge Aurelio has an immaculate record.

Either the Mafia made a mistake, or the strong sense of nationalism its Italian and Sicilian members possess, could have been the major factor in advancing the Justice. There are cases where known Mafiosi have encouraged their relatives in law-abiding professions and worked hard to get them there. This, to many Mafiosi, is a superb and honorable achievement.

Murder, Inc., at one time seemed to be without attachment to any other group of criminals. It later became clear, however, that the organization was from the beginning controlled by the Mafia. Non-Sicilians and non-Italians were at the lowest organizational rung, and the most expendable. Sicilians are the hard core and Big Ones of the Mafia.

Abe "Kid Twist" Reles was a major exception; a number of ricottari gunmen of Sicilian or Italian extraction worked under him. When finally picked up, Reles named Albert Anastasia—a close associate of Joe Adonis and Frank Costello—as the boss of Murder, Inc. Before he could get to the stand, Kid Twist fell or was pushed to his death from the window of a Coney Island hotel while under the guard of six hand-picked New York City cops. Half-hearted investigations turned up nothing, as usual.

And again, after a great many stops and starts along the circuitous route to Frank Costello, we were at a dead end. Many law enforcement agencies turned to a close connection, Lucky Luciano.

In the scheme of things, Charlie Lucky was Costello's boss. The government would do better by him; he would be deported aboard the S.S. *Laura Keene* to Italy in February, 1946.

Don Salvatore came up rapidly. By 1920, at twenty-three, he was the right hand of Giuseppe Masseria. He had come from the infamous Five Points gang which had spawned Al Capone. Luciano's organizational genius was comparable to Capone's. Whereas Capone in Chicago usually eliminated rival gangs, Luciano set out to seek their cooperation as he dominated them. Thus, across the pages of criminal history, we find Jewish gangs, Irish gangs and Italian gangs interweaving with one another in New York and elsewhere. In 1935, Luciano, as the dapper Mr. Charles Ross, moved into the Waldorf Astoria, the citadel of prosperity and acceptance.

One of the most powerful capi Mafiosi to come upon the American scene, Luciano's connections extended to Tammany Hall, City Hall, the state government at Albany and into the nation's capital itself. No single racket was conducted without his approval. His payroll covered those enforcing the law and those avoiding its clutches. History may never know how many important legislators were on it as well.

Name it; Lucky controlled it.

But as Eve proved to be the downfall of Adam, so women toppled Luciano from direct control of the rackets. In the U.S. over 1,200 women worked in Lucky's parlors. That is a little over two women for every two of the 3,000 miles from coast to coast. They brought him $10,000,000 a year. But the high protection tariff and the strong-arm ricottari tactics bred a rebellion among the prostitutes in New York City. Lucky forgot that pride is almost always most strong among the deprived. Thus, when racket-busting Thomas E. Dewey was seeking witnesses against Luciano, three "gutless whores," as Lucky used to call them—Mildred Harris, Florence Brown and Nancy Presser—blew the whistle loud and clear.

Luciano was made on sixty-two counts under the charge of compulsory prostitution. In the meantime, the Bureau had gathered enough evidence for Dewey to prosecute for narcotics trading and extortion. But it was agreed to press for as many counts as possible along the white slavery angle. This violation of the puritan codes regarding sex in America could stir the greatest public outrage. It did. Bringing also the heaviest penalty, Luciano was sentenced to thirty to fifty years in prison.

How did Frank Costello figure in all this? It was still hard to tell, for Luciano would reach outside prison walls to continue to run his rackets; he would even, when the war came, gather the forces along the New York waterfront to combat sabotage by German agents. So important would he become to the U.S. Navy that it would successfully request Luciano's transfer from Dannemora to the Great Meadows Penitentiary closer to New York City. Joseph (Socks) Lanza would carry out his orders on the docks.

Long after the war German intelligence would report that saboteurs were quickly discouraged by the tight vigilance exercised along the piers.

Luciano would be placed aboard the battered old Liberty ship after the war and countless law enforcement officers would watch helplessly as the highest echelons of the Mafia, including Frank Costello, came to pay obeisance. Seven months after his deportation, Don Salvatore would be reported in Cuba, gathering his chiefs about him; Don Francesco would be there. Large amounts of narcotics would be prepared for direct shipment to the U.S. We would inform the Batista government of Luciano's presence in Havana and continued pressure would result in his being redeported to Italy.

With Luciano gone, we would turn our full attention to Costello, concluding that he might best be made through an investigation of his income tax returns; a dozen other high-level Mafiosi would be included with the blessing and towering support of Attorney General Tom Clark, now a Supreme Court Justice, and ace racket-buster Max Goldschein and a host of assistants and a grand jury.

The investigations would fall flat; there would be interference inside the government.

The coming war took us away from many immediate concerns, one of which was Frank Costello, although he was never completely out of our sight or mind.

Having foreseen the possibility of war, we had, in 1939, arranged with drug manufacturers to stockpile a sufficient quantity of opium to carry the U.S. and her Allies through a conflict. This was accomplished without Congressional appropriation by having the funds made directly available to opium manufacturers.

The Germans were nibbling at Central Europe; Poland went next. Next would almost certainly be France, the Germans wheeling once again through the Lowlands to outflank the Maginot Line.

The Japanese were poised in the Pacific, ready to begin construction of the empire of the Rising Sun. In Washington it was obvious that war was inevitable. But people in America hoped with a certain indulgence that it wouldn't come; they watched newsreels of the boys training with broomsticks, positive that it would all stop somewhere short of American intervention. On the other hand, as in World War I, certain elements strained toward the war, eager to get into the fight to save democracy, to link up once again with the old Allies.

Late in 1940, Garland H. Williams was called to Washington for an interview with Major General Sherman Miles, Chief of Intelligence for the Army. Williams had come fresh from the narcotics beat as a supervisor, with an enviable record in surveillance, interrogation, audits, seizures, arrests and prosecutions. He had even succeeded, so great were his powers of persuasion, in getting the indomitable and much loved Fiorello La Guardia to raze the block of houses on New York City's West 62nd Street that was known as San Juan Hill. The area had been an important haunt of dope peddlers and addicts since 1898, and no police officer was safe while he walked that beat.

General Miles, a rather old-fashioned regular army man said, "I've been told that you know something about secret operations and that you'd be a good man to organize some sort of plainclothes unit for the Army. We've already spoken to Commissioner Anslinger. You report for six months' duty to set up a secret police for us. You might as well know, we'll be at war before long and General Marshall says that we'll need a lot of trained people to fight spies and that type of thing."

General Miles' statement, of course, raises an old question: if military Washington expected war, how did the sneak attack on Pearl Harbor occur? Why were civilian conscripts training with mop handles?

In any event, the force that Williams was to organize was to become the Counter Intelligence Corps. Many of our agents were to follow him. One fourth of our men would be engaged in keeping army and other military camps free of narcotic peddlers and drug addicts. The Army Medical Services would find that about one man out of every 10,000 was a drug addict while, for World War I, one of every 3,000 had to be rejected for this reason.

What about the criminals, Mafia and otherwise?

If we lost the war, we would not have to worry about Costello, Luciano and the lesser people. But to be honest, many Mafiosi professed and displayed an intense dislike of fascism, almost as intense as their dislike of law enforcement.

# 8 AGENTS AT WAR AND CORRUPTION AT HOME

After his tour of duty with the CIC, Williams became the director of Special Training for the Office of Strategic Services, upon my recommendation to General (Wild Bill) Donovan. Williams secured two grand sites from the Department of the Interior, one of 12,000 acres near Frederick, Md., and another of 10,000 near Quantico, Va. Before long, hundreds of applicants were undergoing selection tests and operational training for espionage, sabotage and guerrilla tactics. Many would find their way to lonely European beaches and forests; some would set up on Pacific Islands. All would learn to kill quickly and quietly, if they had to. When President Roosevelt inspected one of the training areas, he liked it so well that he took over some of the buildings as a weekend rest camp and named it "Shangri-La." President Eisenhower later changed the name to Camp David. The place now has a history of its own because of the important meetings between our Presidents and the heads of foreign governments. In addition to his tasks with OSS, Williams had assignments with Parachute Infantry and the committees of the Joint Chiefs of Staff and Combined Staff Planners.

Also on my recommendation, Charlie (The Sphinx) Dyar was assigned to the OSS. It was still true that Dyar knew more about the Germans than most people, certainly more than anyone in the OSS. Dispatched to Berne, Switzerland, with the cover of a financial attaché, Dyar again made his mark as an intuitive, calculating, poised agent. His immediate boss was Allen Dulles, former head of the CIA, but General Donovan relied heavily on his reports. The Swiss Ambassador considered Dyar a financial wizard and often remarked that Charlie would have made an excellent international banker.

Later during the course of the war, I had the feeling that George H. White, another of our agents on duty with the Armed Forces, was one of the first nonscientific people to know that we had discovered how to make the atomic bomb. He never disclosed whether he had that knowledge or not.

George had come into the Bureau when the Hip Sing Tong was operating in Seattle. I was at first inclined to fire White for not displaying enough get-up-and-go, but he was responsible for the deportations back to China of many top Hip Sing people. A former West Coast newsman, George was a loner. He didn't like to carry the other men around on his back. He took all the responsibility. His reports were terse and to the point, a result of his newspaper training. White could almost smell a crook, and he had an obsessive hatred especially for trusted officials who abused public responsibility. When White started riding the behinds of some of those people, they could forget about getting off or away. Sooner or later, and mostly sooner, Mr. White would have them behind bars.

As round as he was tall, White looked like Buddha. Made a lieutenant colonel in the OSS, he worked with me on a project to find a truth drug. When this was over, he was sent to many places, performing a considerable amount of work at the risk of his life. On a mission in India, for example, he was forced to kill a Japanese spy with his hands.

Today, on the walls of his apartment, are pictures of three men, including the spy he had to kill in self-defense. While gruesome, the photographs are nevertheless a constant reminder of White's courage.

The OSS also took Charles Siragusa, who had come into the Bureau in 1939, hired by Garland Williams as a stenographer and as an apprentice under George White. Working with White on the surveillance of traffickers Isadore Kayne and Robert Gordon, who were also fugitives from narcotics and prostitution charges, Siragusa's watchfulness brought in Kayne and was responsible for the apprehension of Gordon in Chicago.

Siragusa's cover in the OSS was that of a Naval officer; his station was Italy where his chief function was to apprehend fascist spies, their Nazi recruiters, and to break up espionage networks wherever he found them. Behind the widespread spy network was a woman, Baroness Annabella. She remained free until the war ended, when Siragusa, accompanied by a teen-age patriot, chased the aristocratic and beautiful baroness through northern Italy, finally catching her ten miles from the Brenner Pass. Although she was carrying a half million dollars in jewels, she herself was considered the prize catch. Siragusa's coup vexed American military police and intelligence agencies and their Allied counterparts.

On the home front in Erie, Pa., a young cop named Edward J. Allen had been reporting "drops"—locations of the local policy racket controlled by Duce Calafato. Calafato had come to our attention in 1928 when he was importing and selling illegal whisky. And now, in 1943, it was well known to most members of the Erie Police Department that a policy racket was flourishing, but all turned blind eyes and deaf ears to it. Except Patrolman Allen.

Allen could not understand why the reports made to his superiors did not result in raids on the locations and on Calafato himself. The numbers boss revealed the reason in a private conversation: the police warned Calafato whenever Allen reported a drop. The crook suggested that Allen was getting too nosy, but, since he liked to get along, he would offer the rookie $1,000 in cash and $50 to $100 weekly "if they could be friends." They were riding in Calafato's Cadillac. There would be raids, from time to time, for the sake of appearance, Calafato said, but these would net little money and people of little value to the racket; and they could get off right away with a $50 or $100 fine. When Calafato dropped Allen off at the police station, the rookie placed him under arrest. Inside, the police superiors quickly concluded that the gangster's offer was not in itself evidence for prosecution.

Later, pretending to have considered the proposition and accepted it, Allen arranged a meeting with Duce Calafato. Three witnesses were hidden in the room where they met to have Calafato offer $500 as an immediate binder to the agreement. Allen then consulted with District Attorney Burton Laub, who advised lodging a charge of corrupt solicitation and bribery. But the grapevine had advised Calafato what was afoot and he fled for a time, finally surrendering to the alderman who had issued the warrant for his arrest. He was booked, mugged and freed on bail.

Allen might have expected a startling turn of events, what with the police department being riddled with corruption and the presiding judge at the trial believed to be mentally unfit, but he doubted his own sanity when he heard the judge fine Calafato only $750 and six to twelve months in the workhouse.

"Parole, your honor!" cried Calafato's attorney. "What about parole?"

The judge rambled on and on and finally directed that the sentence be suspended and the defendant placed on two years' probation.

The next month, Allen, disturbed and incensed over this gross miscarriage of justice, made a public statement attacking the judge for his inability to carry out the functions of his court meaningfully. Newspaper headlines followed. The judge sent word to Allen demanding that he come before him to "answer for certain remarks." But an attorney friend and U.S. Commissioner advised Allen that he did not have to appear unless and until charges were made against him. In the meantime, the local branch of the Fraternal Order of Police unanimously and quickly adopted a resolution censuring Allen and disassociating itself from him. Allen had been a member.

Whatever charge was to be placed before Allen became lost when the judge fell ill. He recovered long enough to sentence Calafato to six months when the gangster broke his probation. Calafato continued to prosper until he was blown to pieces while starting his car one day in the early sixties.

Edward Allen went on to become police chief of "Little Chicago"—Youngstown, Ohio, where, with the help of Mayor Charles P. Henderson and Governor Frank J. Lausche, he wiped out the racket rule of that city.

Chief Allen is one of the few top echelon enforcement officials who dare mention Mafia in public. Most people don't believe the Mafia exists or, if they do believe there is such an organization, they go to bed and pull the covers over their heads, fearful mostly of the political pressure these riccottari can exert. The bed jumpers include, I am sad to relate, the head of a state crime commission. He once resigned from a committee of federal, state and local police experts who were getting set to wage all-out war on organized crime. The crime commission man got up and insisted that the Mafia did not exist. But then, this man, entrusted with so many vital jobs, was always afraid of his own shadow. When Allen got up to address the group, I could see officials exchanging tolerant smirks and grins. It is for this reason that the Narcotics Bureau has withheld its confidential book on the Mafia from many, many public officials. Edward Allen and Jim Hamilton, head of the Intelligence Division of the Los Angeles Police Department, are the only two local officials in America to whom we have entrusted this carefully compiled document. When they leave office, the books will be returned. J. Edgar Hoover holds a copy.

The author of a book, *Merchants of Menace*, which dealt with Mafia connections in Erie and Youngstown, Chief Allen after long, active and unappreciated fight against crime in the East, moved West to head the police department at Santa Ana, California. With so much attention focused on the war, crime could have had a field day if men like Chief Allen had not been around. He did more than his share to keep the home front in order.

Another important battle was about to be decided, a battle that had commenced only a short time after the Bureau was established. Now, we had come to the moment of truth.

Allied forces invaded Sicily on July 10, 1943. Four days later the U.S. Supreme Court affirmed the judgment of a lower court in favor of the United States against the Direct Sales Company, Inc., the petitioner.

Direct Sales Company sold morphine tablets to doctors by mail order through government purchase forms. Many doctors throughout the country avoided purchasing the drug from local wholesale houses because, if they were addicted themselves or were selling morphine to addicts, there was less chance of getting caught. Because of this, we had kept surveillance on the company for some time.

In affirming the decision, the Supreme Court brought out the fact that, at the end of 1941, there were more than 1,350 wholesale drug dealers from whom physicians could order narcotics. Of 204 doctors convicted on narcotics charges, the court went on, 27 per cent were customers of Direct Sales.

When we had discovered unusually large sales of morphine being made to members of the medical profession in one section of the country, we made investigations of the surrounding community and picked up a number of peddlers to whom doctors had sold the drug. We knew the morphine was coming from Direct Sales, and even though Joe Bransky, who was on the case, issued warnings to them again and again, the company felt that it was within the law. Bransky told the officers of the company that if they sold any unusually large quantities of morphine to a doctor, they could be found guilty of conspiracy to violate the law.

In one fantastic case we ascertained that the company had filled an order for a doctor in the Midwest calling for 40,000 half-grain tablets of morphine. Testimony during the court arguments proved that the average doctor in the United States did not require more than *400 quarter-grain tablets annually for legitimate use*. We had been advised of the order before it was filled and urged Direct Sales not to comply.

We were able to bring Direct Sales before the bench mainly through its transactions with Dr. John V. Tate, whose dealings with other doctors was also subject to close scrutiny. Tate practiced in Calhoun Falls, South Carolina, a community of about 2,000 persons. Dr. Tate, together with three other doctors and the Direct Sales Company, were charged with conspiring to violate Sections 1 and 2 of the Harrison Act over a period of seven years, from 1933 to 1940.

It was through U.S. Attorney O. H. Doyle, a crusading prosecutor, that we had begun to gather the evidence necessary to stop this unconcealed diversion of morphine. In one instance, we found that from November, 1937, to January, 1940, Tate's purchases, which he was diverting illegally to his cohorts, amounted to the stupendous sum of 79,000 half-grain tablets. The shipments to Dr. Tate alone during the final six months of 1939 exceeded 6,000 half-grain tablets per month—enough, the government pointed out, to administer 400 average doses every day of the year.

The company itself grossed $300,000 to $350,000 annually, from 1936 to 1940, with about 15 per cent of its revenue and 2½ per cent of its volume in narcotic sales. Unlike its competitors, Direct Sales listed narcotics, like morphine sulphate, in quantities exceeding 100 tablets; its listings *began* at 500 tablets and proceeded upward to 5,000 tablet units. The company also offered 50 per cent discounts on narcotics and "pushed" quantity sales. Advertising of this kind attracted many customers, among whom were a dis-

proportionately large number of doctors who had previously violated the Harrison Act, some as addicts and others as suppliers.

Dr. Tate bought his morphine at less than two dollars per 100
half-grain tablets, and sold the same amount at from four to eight
dollars. When the drug was sold for the third time to addicts, it
cost as much as $25 per hundred tablets.

Doyle went into circuit court with this conspiracy case with the
evidence gathered by Bransky. Circuit Court of Appeals upheld the
earlier decision, and when Direct Sales appealed to the Supreme
Court on a writ of certiorari, the decision was resoundingly
affirmed. The conspiracy statute from the Harrison Act reads:

> If two or more persons conspire to either commit any offense
> against the United States, or to defraud the United States in any
> manner or for any purpose, and one of such parties do any act
> to effect the object of conspiracy, each of the parties to such con-
> spiracy shall be fined not more than $10,000 or imprisoned not
> more than two years, or both.

Joseph Bransky made Bureau of Narcotics history by being the
instrument through which the Supreme Court hammered home
the responsibility of the drug trade and medical profession alike
for alert narcotics supervision and control. The far-reaching judgment, that the United States hereafter was at war with those who
sought through those professions to aid the spread of addiction,
would for many reasons outlast the victories of the U.S. Seventh
Army in Sicily.

As the war approached its end, Benny Pocoroba was sent to the
Free Territory of Trieste, an area that was electric with illegal
narcotic activity. Working undercover and using his Sicilian dialect
to fine advantage, he made a great many cases for the Allied Forces
there and severely disrupted narcotics traffic.

The war reunited Ralph Oyler and General Donovan for a time.
In the early days when Donovan was an assistant to the U.S.
Attorney General with offices in Buffalo, New York, he prosecuted

all the cases Agent Oyler made through undercover work in the city.

Oyler was raised on an Ohio farm and it was said in the department that when he drove his father's manure spreader, he held the reins in one hand and a detective story in the other. Oyler was not at all averse to closing with criminals; he was a brawler and had his jaw broken many times. Some of our agents understandably dislike gunplay, but Oyler didn't seem to mind. He reported time after time with a puffed lip and after a while he had so many scars that he looked like a boxer. He was an excellent shot. On one occasion we went hunting together and he shot a pair of boar dead through the heart as they ran. When the butcher cut them up he said, "Christ, I'd hate to be in the sights of the man who shot these."

Oyler earned his reputation as a tough agent on a September night in 1921 when he was operating out of the Prohibition Unit. It was one of those warm autumn New York nights. A big, orange moon hung over the waterfront where the Greek liner, the S.S. *King Alexander*, was tied up.

Oyler had set up the ship's fourth officer, Sabbas Mendenis, for a purchase of opium, heroin and cocaine. On the night of September 8th Oyler went aboard with a group of agents who posed as a part of his shipping gang. He met Mendenis and a doublecross on the part of the Greek officer then followed. Oyler called to his agents to board the ship, which they did, sweeping through the passageways and over the decks. Gunfire attracted the harbor police, who joined the fight. The battle lasted only a half hour. From that time on, Oyler became master of the swoop raid and, when he was sent to Japan at the end of the war to break up the narcotic gangs that had quickly burgeoned in the confusion, he employed a series of mass swoop raids. The Military Government under General Douglas MacArthur could also thank Oyler for setting up the machinery to combat illicit traffic in the future.

# 9 A "CRIPPLE" TRIPS A GANG

Franklin Delano Roosevelt died at Warm Springs, Ga., April 12, 1945. Few people thought the former haberdasher and artillery officer, spry, crusty Harry S Truman, could follow in Roosevelt's footsteps. I've worked under eight Presidents and I must say for the record that I had more admiration for Truman than for any other President. He was crisp, a man of decision.

Some of his decisions disappointed me, but if I'd been in Mr. Truman's shoes, I probably would have made them myself. Two decisions involved Frank Wilson, the cigar-smoking agent who worked under Malachi Harney and whose labors were a key factor in bringing in Al Capone. But James J. Maloney, Chief of the Secret Service under Truman, enters the picture before Wilson.

A former New York State Trooper, Maloney was the epitome of efficiency. He performed his duties with snap and dash right up until just before the election results which would decide whether Truman remained in office or Dewey replaced him. This was in 1948. The press at large had convinced the public (and itself) that the former New York District Attorney was to be the next President. Maloney rushed to New York and threw a cordon of Service police around the Roosevelt Hotel, Dewey's headquarters. The figures were running top-heavy in favor of Dewey.

Then came morning. President Truman awoke in a suite in the Muehlebach Hotel in Kansas City and read (as he'd predicted) "Truman Re-elected." One of the President's first questions was, "Where's Jimmy Maloney?"

There was a lot of hemming and hawing before someone spoke up and said, "He's with Dewey." Truman instructed one of his aides to see that Maloney got fired the next day.

This was done with supreme alacrity. Maloney came to talk it over with me; he believed he'd got a dirty deal. "Look at the regulations," he insisted. "Here it says that the President-elect must be protected immediately upon his election."

"That's right." I agreed. "And your place is with the President until a new one is elected."

He disagreed violently.

"I'm not going to cry with you, Jimmy," I said. "After all, *you* wrote those regulations."

Maloney's dismissal resulted in the appointment of Frank Wilson. During the course of his government career he had worked with about ten men who now held positions in the Service; Wilson held some great reservations about these men, especially the one in charge of the White House detail. Wilson promptly replaced the man with one named Fred, for whom Wilson had great respect. As far as Wilson knew, Fred didn't drink or chase women and he and Wilson had been on the best of terms for years; Wilson was sure he could now relax about the White House.

Then President Truman scheduled a visit to his home in Independence, Missouri. It was Fred's job to furnish protection. He went out ahead of the President with a group of his men to set things up. The morning after Truman arrived some of his friends said, "What kind of a Secret Service do you have here? This guy Fred painted the town red from end to end last night."

President Truman was angered that Wilson had sent a man like Fred to protect him, and it was quite possible that he didn't take kindly to the ribbing his friends at Independence gave him. In any event both Wilson and Fred got the crisp Truman ax in the neck. Wilson later became coordinator of Treasury Law Enforcement Agencies and, after his retirement, president of the National Association of Retired Civil Employees.

Outside of Washington the narcotics traffic was gathering a full head of steam. During the war drugs coming from abroad fell off to zero. Cooperation between the United States and Mexico had tightened border controls in the Southwest. Measures had been taken to bring under federal control twelve new synthetic drugs developed during the war. At the height of the conflict, in 1944, the 107th Street gang had been crippled with a number of important arrests. But now, 1946, with the sea routes open again, it was back in business.

Late in the year the New York District Supervisor brought in Agent Oliver Dent from San Francisco to penetrate the gang and particularly to apprehend Joseph (Pip the Blind) Gagliano, listed as number 121 on the International List of Suspected Narcotic Violators. An associate, Charlie (Bullets) Albero, was also wanted.

For over ten years Gagliano had bossed one of the largest illicit narcotic rings in the nation. He had been convicted in 1942 and had drawn only nine months. This was the sole conviction of a man whose arrest record dated back to 1928. Although Gagliano and Albero headquartered on the upper East Side of Manhattan, their influences ranged from coast to coast and deep into Mexico, in spite of border patrols. Business was brisk; as the European market opened up, the two arch-traffickers were able to provide more drugs to more people. More than $2,000,000 worth of drugs were sold in or from this area every year.

Many of our agents were still cleaning up in the O.S.S. after the war, and the few men active in the Bureau ran a greater risk of being recognized by the peddlers. Garland Williams, recently discharged, was taking no chances; he wanted a new face.

With Oliver Dent in town, Williams laid elaborate plans to ensnare the Gagliano-Albero group and knock out the 107th Street gang. Gagliano was the first target; he was convinced that he had become so big that we could not touch him. Williams welcomed this challenge, his first big one since the war.

Dent was given a government car, one of the three hundred we pick up in the course of our work every year. Most of them are Cadillacs. (We prefer to use Chevrolets; they give the most and can take a lot when the going gets rough.) Dent's was no ordinary car, however; agents had made certain alterations in it, making it possible for a second, covering agent, hidden in the trunk, to see persons in the front of the car, see a short distance in front of the vehicle or persons standing at either side of it. The car was also modified so that conversations could be overheard.

Still another car was altered to appear as a commercial vehicle. Agents concealed behind the driver could observe in any direction and remain invisible to persons outside.

The second vehicle was not employed until Dent had painstakingly made contacts among the drug addicts and small-time peddlers. Dent let it be known that if a buy went well, if the junk was good, he would be interested in larger amounts. Planting information like this takes time; after the planting someone checks out the buyer, for there is always the risk that the Narcotics Bureau has planted the man; descriptions are flashed from addict to addict, peddler to peddler, and finally up to the top.

A buy was finally arranged. At four o'clock on December 11, agents gathered in the office to go over plans and insure against a slip-up. The purchase of heroin would be made later in the day.

Except for a few favored customers, Gagliano conducted his talks indoors, either at his home or in the rear of his bar on East 107th Street. A scheme had to be devised to bring him outdoors and into the presence of the covering agents.

Agent Oliver Dent became temporarily crippled.

His right foot and ankle were heavily bandaged and a crutch placed upright near the driver's seat. Agent Ross was assigned to the trunk. Meanwhile two other agents went in another car to 107th Street and happened to see Gagliano parking his car on 107th Street between Second and Third Avenues. The agents returned to the meeting place and advised the other four, who would be concealed in the commercial vehicle, of the whereabouts of Gagliano's Cadillac. Quickly the agents drove to the street and parked in front of Gagliano's car.

Dent did not arrive until five. He pulled up in front of the restaurant, lowered his window and began honking the car horn. "Puggy!" he yelled. "Hey, Puggy!"

Angelo Loicano appeared in the doorway in answer to his nickname. He was wearing a dark blue overcoat, a gray suit and hat. Puggy was partial to somber clothing. He was stocky, dark-complexioned. Under the hat which sat precisely centered upon his head, his hair was curly and dark. With a quick, sweeping glance around, Puggy crossed in front of the car and got in beside Dent. Taking in the crutch he said, "What happened?"

"I fell down the damned stairs a couple of days ago and got a bad sprain. Today they took pictures. I got a chipped bone. Hey, is Pip around? I want to see him."

"What do you want with him?"

"Tell you, Puggy, I got a customer for five ounces. I want to make him a good price, but I can't do it paying three and a quarter to you guys."

"Pip's at his mother's fixing up the dining room," Puggy said. "Why don't you go in?"

"Can't; have to keep weight off my ankle. And it's gettin' late and I'm in a hurry to get downtown. Go and call him for me, will you, Puggy?"

Loicano mulled over the request and then said, "Okay. Pull up a little bit. I'll show you where to stop." Dent set his car in motion. "Whoa," Puggy said. "Right here."

At a glance Dent saw that he had parked directly across the street from Gagliano's car, ahead of which, in the dull, commonplace commercial vehicle, were four covering agents. Dent shut off the motor. Puggy left the car. Gagliano emerged from a nearby building a moment later wearing a tan hat, suit and topcoat. He wore his usual loud tie. Gagliano climbed in beside Dent; Puggy had returned and he lingered nearby on the sidewalk.

"Hello, Pip. Puggy tell you what I wanted?"

"No. Just said you wanted to see me. What's up?"

"Pip, I can sell five ounces tonight, but the guy that's picking up the goods is paying three fifty. I want to get his business away from the guy he's buying from in Harlem. I can't do it paying you three and a quarter."

"Why not?"

"I don't think it's fair for me to be working on $25 a piece," Dent said.

"I'm charging everybody else three fifty or three and a quarter. You're getting the lowest price now."

"I don't want to lose this customer, Pip, and I don't want to work on $25 a piece."

Gagliano sighed. "The only thing I can do, then, is let you have these five pieces at three fifteen; anything else, you'll have to pay the regular price. This way you make an extra fifty."

"All right, Pip, but don't forget to okay it to Puggy."

"You know there's not much brown goods left," Gagliano said. He lowered his window and called to Loicano. "How much brown we got left?"

"One five-ounce package."

Gagliano turned to Dent. "Okay, this five is yours, but if you want more brown you'll have to wait a few days." To Puggy he said, "Dent can pay you $50 less on these five pieces tonight." Climbing out of the car, he said, "You two can get together and make a meet. I count on you guys to make sure these meets are changed."

"Don't worry, Pip," Dent said. "I'll see that they're changed."

Puggy got back into the car as Gagliano went back to his mother's house. "What time shall we make it—eleven?"

Dent said, "Whatever's best for you. The later the better, but I need it tonight."

"One o'clock?"

"Okay. Where?"

"Make it 85th and Broadway," Puggy said. "No, let's keep the hell off Broadway. Amsterdam and 85th, southwest corner. Are you going to have the money?"

"Yeah, I'll have it," Dent promised. "Will it be okay to give it to the kid when he delivers?"

"Yeah, me or the kid." Puggy left the car. Dent and the covering agents left the scene at separate times and returned to the Bureau of Narcotics offices where all made notes of the afternoon's events.

They met again at midnight and Dent's foot and ankle were wrapped again. The men checked their snub-nosed 38-caliber revolvers and set them in their holsters. The Bureau doesn't use automatics because they tend to jam—often when an agent needs them most—and then the agent is in a mess. The holsters contain spring clips so that the guns, once the draw is started, come flying out. Those extra seconds the spring provides can mean the difference between life and death.

Dent was given $1,700 in fives, tens and twenties with which to buy the brown heroin. All the serial numbers on the bills had been listed. Ross once again took his place in the trunk of Dent's car and was locked in. Should anything go wrong, Ross would have to fire through the peepholes and partitions of the car. The vehicle with the four concealed agents drove to the rendezvous area and parked.

At five minutes to one, Dent arrived at the predesignated spot and Puggy jumped in. "Let's start driving," he said. When the car had got underway, he said, "I can't give you any tonight."

"You mean you haven't got anything? What in the hell am I supposed to do?" Dent said indignantly.

"Listen," Puggy said placatingly. "After we spoke to you this afternoon, there was a coupla bad cars around."

"What do you mean?"

"I can't understand it," Puggy said, shaking his head. "There ain't been any agents around for a long time."

"You sure they were cops?" Dent asked, allowing concern to spread over his features.

"Yeah. Look—are you sure of this guy you're giving the goods to?"

"C'mon, don't be foolish. What're we, kids?"

"Anyway, Pip says nothin' doin' tonight; not with all this heat. Tomorrow. We'll make it tomorrow at five-thirty. Same place. I'll bring it myself."

Dent said, "What am I going to tell my customer?"

"Christ," Puggy countered. "It's not so bad. We're doing this to protect you as well as us. There's a cab; I'll grab it and go back. See you tomorrow."

Dent stopped and Puggy dashed for the cab. Now it was necessary to plan for the meeting of the next day. It was decided that since Gagliano and Puggy were suspicious of strange vehicles, the covering car with the four agents should not be used; it fell to Ross to provide maximum cover. For the third time Dent's foot and ankle were bandaged, and Ross, who hadn't so far complained of claustrophobia, was locked in the trunk of the car.

Puggy was waiting.

He got into the car and told Dent to drive south on Amsterdam, then east on 82nd Street to a spot midway between Columbus and Amsterdam. They parked.

Belligerently Dent said, "You caused me a lot of trouble last night."

"I'm sorry," Puggy said. "It couldn't be helped. We have to be careful. What time you got?"

"It's five thirty-three."

"I'm meeting the kid at twenty minutes to six," said Puggy. "You know," he said, breaking a short silence, "Charlie Bullets is burning up."

"What's the trouble?"

"Their working man was making a five-ounce delivery and as soon as the customer left, he was pinched. Now they got a thousand agents around here."

"When did that happen?"

"Last week." Another silence followed. Then both men checked the time again. "Dent, you can let me have the money now."

"How much?" Dent asked.

"Lemme see," Puggy said, starting to figure aloud, "three times five makes fifteen hundred; five times fifteen is—seventy-five. Fifteen hundred and seventy-five beans."

"I've got seventeen hundred. I'll take off one hundred and twenty-five, that leaves fifteen hundred and seventy-five. Want to count it?"

Puggy took the money and counted it. "It's all here." He placed the money in his pocket.

"Gonna lose it there," Dent said.

"Nah. I got a deep pocket there. Listen, pull up close to the corner, by Columbus." Dent drove to the place. "When will you be up to see me again?" Puggy asked.

"Saturday or Monday. Most likely Monday. Will you have brown goods?"

"Not Saturday or Monday, but maybe a few days later," Puggy said. "I'll have to make it up. Be very careful. Pip says you got to be extra careful when you come to see us again." Puggy left the car and walked to the southwest corner of Columbus Avenue and 82nd Street. He stood waiting. Dent watched him, glanced up and down the street. A minute later, a young man who would be identified as Anthony Lucente, appeared suddenly at Dent's window and handed a package to him. "Come around and sit down," Dent said. When Lucente was in the car, Dent asked, "What's your name?"

"Andy."

Dent fished out a bill. "Here, Andy, take this five and buy yourself a drink."

"Thanks," said Andy, pocketing the marked money, "I'll do just that."

"How much goods have you got in this package?"

"I think it's the five ounces." Andy left the car and joined

Puggy on the corner. Taking an evasive route, Dent drove back to headquarters. The trunk was unlocked and Ross was helped out. He stretched expansively. Dent gave the package to the other agents, who promptly began an examination of the contents. They found two large glassine envelopes containing brown heroin. Here, at last, was the evidence against Joseph Gagliano, alias Pip the Blind.

Accordingly, one week before Christmas Eve, three agents walked into the bar where Gagliano, Puggy and Andy Lucente were sitting. "You're under arrest," one of the agents said. Protests flew thick and fast, but the three were brought to the New York County District Attorney's office.

As indicated in the conversation Dent had had with Puggy, other agents had been closing in on Charlie (Bullets) Albero. Bullets and his two top aides, Armando Piragnoli and Nicholas Gnazzo, were taken into custody. District Attorney Frank S. Hogan asked Judge Francis L. Valente to hold Gagliano and Albero without bail and place the others under $25,000 bond. Hogan went on to say that none of the men before the bench were small fry. He accused Gagliano and Albero of having operated competing wholesale combines with points of distribution throughout the country; he further charged that they brought raw opium from Mexico into California and thence to Harlem where they processed it into heroin.

Gagliano and Albero were accused of representing "two of the biggest illegal drug syndicates in the United States." Their traffic, Hogan continued, was "worse than murder. The potential murder victim has a chance for life, but the poor addict has none."

Hogan then listed their associates: Albero consorted with Joseph Rao and Michael Coppola, both notorious East Harlem gangsters who once had been held as material witnesses in the slaying of Joseph Scottoriggio, a Republican district captain.

Garland Williams then linked Gagliano and Albero to the Mafia and declared that they held high positions in that organization. The defense counsel protested the high bail, but the judge set it at $150,000 for Gagliano, which he could not furnish, and $15,000 for the others, which was furnished. Albero's bail was to be set later. The two gangs, which may have been a part of one giant organization, were brought to trial within six weeks of each other; all persons were sentenced the same day, April 8, 1947.

During the trial the Gagliano defense, enraged because narcotics agents had provided the material for an airtight case, demanded that the identity of the agent who had made the case against them be disclosed. A petition had been made by the prosecution to clear the courtroom. Defense turned it down. Trial judge Mullen was forced to reveal the identity of our "Oliver Dent."

Mullen bristled when he spoke to Gagliano and his group before sentencing:

"Gagliano, Loicano and Lucente, you were each convicted before me by a jury of the crime of feloniously selling a narcotic drug. You have contested the prosecution at every step. My report indicates that you three constitute one of the three outstanding syndicates controlling the illicit drug business in this country; that you, Gagliano, at the head of it, and you, Loicano, as lieutenant, and you, Lucente, as the delivery man. The extent of your operations is difficult to tell, but there is every reason to believe that they have been most extensive and lucrative to you fellows.

"You went so far, even at the trial, to refuse an opportunity to keep secret the identity of a certain narcotics agent who testified here, and I am sure that you did it in order that other people in the drug business might know those narcotic agents and would be able to identify them if they saw them on the street. There was an application made on the trial when testimony was given by one of the narcotics agents—who was certainly one of the most courageous and most efficient law enforcement officers I have ever known—and this application was to clear the courtroom so that he would not be disclosed to persons who might thereafter be able to point him out in his law enforcement work. You fellows decided NO—you were going to have him shown up and put on the stand. That was your legal right."

Judge Mullen sentenced Gagliano, Albero, Lucente and Loicano to five to ten years in Sing Sing; Gnazzo drew from four to eight in Sing Sing, and Piragnoli two to five in Sing Sing.

Two days after sentencing, while he was still in the Bronx County jail awaiting transportation to Sing Sing, Joseph Gagliano, alias Pip the Blind, took the sheet from his bed and hanged himself from a high bar in his cell.

# IO MARIJUANA ON CAMPUS AND OFF

One could have almost predicted that, with the tension eased as a result of the end of the war, younger people would be attracted to drugs, or habits that would lead to drug addiction. College students surrounded by the wisdom of generations in their libraries were to be included among those young people seeking "kicks" to forget the war.

Near one large Eastern university, a young music student was discovered growing marijuana in a flowerbox in his mother's kitchen window. Near another, a small plot of marijuana grown by the students in the nearby men's dormitory was found and destroyed. In the West and Southwest, colleges near the Mexican border found their students driving back and forth across the line, transporting marijuana for their own use or to sell to other students.

This was 1948 and campuses across the country were crowded with returned vets studying under the G.I. Bill. One cannot lay the spread of marijuana smoking on them alone. In any event, most cases were confined to small groups of students out of student bodies of five to twelve thousand. What was most despicable about the marijuana smoking at one large Midwestern university particularly was that the members of this smoking group were ostensibly gathered to improve race relations. There seemed to be, at that time, a brief commitment on the part of many people to explore and better conditions; Hollywood produced a rash of movies dealing with the theme. New organizations made it their business to call attention to the inequities existing between black and white Americans. Moves like this should be applauded—but not when they become excuses for other activities, such as at this university.

The situation there had existed for a year before the local police advised us of it; they had been reluctant to move for fear of embarrassing university officials who believed that the situation would not last. Besides, the officials said, the people involved were young and had their futures before them, and the university did not want to appear unwilling to advance ideas of improvement between the races; an investigation would also discredit those other interracial groups which were sincerely concerned and actively doing something about the situation.

Along with the marijuana had come reports of "sex experimentations." Seven persons had been arrested the year before, some of them white girls and some of them Negro men from the town. A newspaper in a neighboring town threatened to break the story wide open unless something were done. University officials asked for and received permission to handle the case, but it had got worse instead of better and the Bureau was called in.

A girl—I shall call her "Greta Busch"—had attended many meetings where, it was said, "sex experimentation" and marijuana smoking took place. Her absences from home became so frequent that her father asked for an accounting. She told her father about the group and stated that she was determined to break it up. This is what she also reported to our local office when her father insisted that the police be notified; they in turn called us. We learned also that a cub reporter had been assigned to penetrate the group and write an exposé. The co-ed and the reporter, they said, were working together. The two young people were ordered to step out of the picture at once. There was some question of the credibility of their stories, especially the girl's. The reporter's story checked out, but at what point did he stop working and join in the fun? The girl and boy insisted that they remain on the case, pointing out that they would have a better opportunity to make contacts than the police or our agents, because they not only knew the smokers but the peddlers as well.

Their insistence did much to increase our faith in them and, once more employing the agent hidden in the car trunk, we set out to make contact with the men who sold the marijuana cigarettes. We were in search of the man considered to be the chief trafficker, but, after purchasing a total of thirteen cigarettes from three different people, the agents were unable to locate him. It was decided that, after the third trip, the girl would no longer be used. The cub reporter was familiar enough with the local criminal element. It was this group, rather than students on campus, who were selling. The arrest of the major trafficker and some minor ones would break up the ring and there would be no more cigarettes on the campus; the university, therefore, would suffer little embarrassment.

Local police and agents got a break.

They had not been able to find The Man, because he had been planning a robbery. No one knew this until twenty-four hours after the robbery occurred. Police answered a call from a pharmacy and found that a number of checks and narcotic drugs had been stolen, along with a safe containing $1,200.

When The Man appeared at the local bank next morning to cash the checks, he was picked up. Two of his accomplices were hauled in within the hour. The burglary created a problem. The local police could not withhold action on the burglary and that meant that the case we had been building on the marijuana angle could not be pursued. We had planned not to use the co-ed as a witness. Had the reporter made a buy from The Man, we would have used him alone, for we did not want to create the specter of wild sex and drugs with the girl and her Negro contacts. Mainly, I suppose, because there was more to her story than could ever have met the eye. In any case, we had no recourse but to help the local police press for burglary and theft of narcotics charges against The Man and his accomplices; we could not even bring in the three small-time peddlers without implicating the girl.

But another problem developed. One of our agents had failed to come along as rapidly as we'd hoped. He could not understand that working for the Narcotics Bureau was not a nine-to-five, but a full-time job. His supervisor, after repeated warnings, called the agent in and asked for his resignation. The agent submitted it without question. But within two hours he reported to the local newspaper editor that we had not liked the way the local police handled the situation. The police chief squelched the story the ex-agent had already called in to the paper, saying that he had never had better cooperation. The agent also said that the Bureau had changed its mind and now wanted to use Greta Busch as a witness. Her father called us in great agitation. He was afraid, he said, that if she were put on the stand she would be ruined because no one would understand that she had been of great assistance to us. Perhaps he too was beginning to feel uneasy about her story.

With The Man and his crew out of the way, we hoped the students would settle down to business. The university was too proud and famous an institution to have had its name besmirched by an unthinking selfish few whose activities clouded the genuine efforts of others to find a solution so that all races could live in harmony.

Joseph Orofsky lived not far from the campus, but he wasn't a student. He was a veteran and, like thousands of people, was caught in that first postwar depression of 1948. The twenty-eight-year-old metalworker was jobless and engaged to be married. If he could find work soon enough he would go through with it, if not, well—it would have to be postponed.

He lived with his brother in an old house, in the industrial part of town. Orofsky was a tough man, but he liked flowers. One day, after making the rounds of the factories and other establishments, he bought an envelope of bird seed for five cents; he would plant them in the yard and see what happened. Flowers would make him feel better—any kind. It looked as though any day now he would have to break his engagement.

With good weather the seeds germinated. A wild mixture of plants and flowers bloomed in the yard, many of which Orofsky didn't recognize, and he had to go to the public library to identify them. They proved to be hemp.

Orofsky knew that the plant was used widely in Asia and had certain effects when dried and smoked, but he didn't pay any attention to this; his mind was on his girl, Molly. If the job situation didn't break by the fall, they'd have to put off the wedding. His only income was the famous 52–20 club of that time—$20 per week for 52 weeks for veterans—and he could not afford to buy packaged cigarettes. He began looking around for a substitute.

By now the hemp plants had grown quite tall and Orofsky cut them down. In a day or so he found himself fingering the leaves which had dried rapidly in the sun. He gathered some of them and crushed them and rolled them into a cigarette. He smoked his first one that night while reading in bed. He smoked a second. Soon he began to feel anxious and he expected something terrible to happen, he could not imagine what. Then he experienced a sudden onset of throbbing and palpitation. His limbs became unbearably heavy and erotic images began to come to him. Small dark men sat in colorful furniture, their legs crossed. When Orofsky rose to get some air to clear his head, it was three in the morning. He returned to bed, and when he awoke he felt very drowsy. Later in the day he told his brother and Molly what had happened; his brother was unimpressed. He wanted Orofsky to find a job and move out and get married. But Molly was curious.

She decided that she would smoke one of the cigarettes and, at ten in the evening, alone with Orofsky, she smoked about two-thirds of one. Orofsky finished it and lit another. At the moment, nothing seemed so bad; he wasn't even envious of the college students. Nothing seemed the matter with Molly. She fell asleep. As she had often done this, Orofsky paid no attention until he decided to take her home. She awoke with a start and fought him off as though she were afraid of him. Her hands moved nervously and her eyes were brighter than he had ever seen them. Molly wanted to know where she was, but despite this fear of the moment, Orofsky noticed that in another couple of minutes she was quite contented and happy. A half hour later, as he was walking her for air, she became coquettish, more affectionate than he had ever known her to be. Gone was the girl who had brooded over his inability to find a job. Now she rubbed against him and kissed him in a way she had never kissed him before. She insisted on being close to him, touching him everywhere.

At first filled with desire, Orofsky became alarmed when, after some time had passed, Molly did not return to normal, and he rushed her to a doctor. The doctor noted that her lips were red, as though painted, although she was not wearing lipstick. He recorded that she complained of dizziness when she stood and walked. Although she was talkative and excited, her speech was slurred. The pupils of her eyes were dilated, but contracted rapidly to light. Even in the doctor's office, she continued to embrace and kiss Orofsky, and when the doctor succeeded in getting her fiancé out of her grasp, she seized him instead.

Since her condition did not improve, the doctor called a police ambulance and Orofsky and his girl were taken to a hospital for further examination. He was only slightly affected, but Molly's condition was so severe that she was kept at the hospital overnight. By morning she had recovered and, perhaps to Orofsky's dismay, had become rather shy again. The plants in Orofsky's yard were destroyed except for some leaves which were taken to a laboratory, where they were found to be *Cannabis sativa*, a plant used in the East to create erotic effects, as in Molly's case, or, as Orofsky experienced fleetingly, a sense of well-being mixed with anxiety.

# 11 AGENTS IN THE MEDITERRANEAN

In 1948, even with Gagliano dead and Albero in prison, illegal combines flourished with international help. It was my opinion that a few good agents overseas might help dry up the traffic at the source. The cooperation of a number of European countries had enabled us to put agents overseas as early as 1935 on special assignments. Now we were going to establish an office. Although deported, Lucky Luciano was still active and considered to be the head of a multimillion-dollar narcotics ring. Frank Costello was free. Garland Williams and George White were our two choices for overseas assignments.

Once there, they found Luciano's old and inimitable knack for setting up cooperative deals still at work, especially with the Corsican criminals of France. The method and outlook of these criminals is similar to that of the Mafia. Generally speaking, they control illicit traffic through the port cities of France, importing opium from Turkey and Iran, converting it to heroin and transporting it via courier to America.

George White was due for a "vacation" anyway. Shortly before he went to Europe, he learned that a district attorney was associating with a Mafia leader. White made certain unmistakable charges, and the district attorney called him up before a grand jury. White refused to give the jury the name of the informant who had supplied him with material on the DA after White had seen him with the Mafioso. White was promptly jailed but was later released, purging himself from a contempt charge by divulging the name of the special employee; two months later the man was found dead.

George went to Turkey, tracking the source of opium which was passed through Luciano's Italy and on into the eastern and southern seaports of the United States. On one assignment in Istanbul, White, an accomplished actor, masqueraded as a hotshot pilot and arranged for the purchase of $6,000 worth of opium which otherwise would have gone to Italy.

The Turkish police, who have always been most cooperative with us, were as anxious as we to dry up the illicit narcotic source. They surrounded the building where the transaction was taking place, disguised as laborers. The signal to bring them at the gallop was the lowering of a window shade in the room occupied by White and the traffickers. But somehow the police became engrossed in their work and did not see the shade going up and down in panicky jumps.

Inside the room, the opium dealers, suspecting that something was amiss, advanced on White. He backed up, pulled out his gun and sent a chair crashing through the window. Forgetting their picks and shovels, the Turkish police were up the stairs in a rush and the arrests were made.

A similar incident of crossed signals occurred in Naples. White had set up another buy. The Italian police were to step in when he walked into a courtyard and tipped his hat, signifying that a purchase had been made. But hat tipping is customary in Europe and for a few seconds White and the police stood there raising and lowering their hats. Then the cops remembered the signal and seized the criminals.

Those were a couple of the light episodes in the campaign by White and Williams and various European and Middle Eastern police to disrupt illicit narcotics trafficking. They were amusing because White lived to tell about them.

What happened to Williams? Our feeling was that European police, although they never said so, resented his diplomatic manner. They felt that our cops should fit the image of James Cagney, for example; Williams did not. Further, foreign police could not understand our problems with illicit drugs any more than we could understand theirs on a day-to-day basis. We agreed, certainly, that the effect of uncontrolled drugs upon various populations could be horrible, but we did not always agree on the method of eliminating the traffic. Williams smacked of official Washington and the police over there, like their governments, took a dim view of Washington venturing into places where it was not only unwelcome but not overly tolerated either.

No matter, for when the Korean War broke out, Williams was called to duty again. He formed a completely new type of intelligence organization and became the first commander of the 525th Military Intelligence Service Group, training specialists in all fields of intelligence work. When training was completed, Williams' people formed into combat-ready units and were shipped to Korea in large numbers. Others were sent to many places in the world. Some are still deployed and heavily engaged in the war against communism.

Thus, in the absence of Williams, George White became our second man overseas and Charles Siragusa the third.

On the day of his discharge in 1946, Siragusa hunted down an old informer in New York's Chinatown. The man was glad to see that Siragusa had returned safely from the war, but insisted that he could not give him a tip on such short notice as to who was currently smuggling opium. Siragusa insisted; he wanted to prove to himself and to us that he had lost nothing during his hitch in the Navy and the OSS. The informer gave him the information and Siragusa went out singlehandedly and arrested Sing Hop, a seaman who only a few days before had brought in 10 pounds of crude opium. Squad leader George White and Supervisor Garland Williams were impressed that Siragusa had made a pinch within twenty-four hours of his discharge, but they gave him hell for doing it alone.

Before I could get Siragusa packed and off to Turkey where he was very much needed, United States Attorney Philip Herrick requested assistance to fight a growing narcotics problem in San Juan, Puerto Rico. Reluctantly, I dispatched Siragusa. During his two months there, employing his high school Spanish with a mixture of Italian, he conducted classes for a force of forty Puerto Rican Treasury police. He took his pupils out and gave them practical training including lessons in how to recruit informers. A week before the classes graduated, Siragusa and his students had booked a total of thirty prosecutions in federal court, and had arrested more than forty-five persons including those responsible for smuggling heroin and marijuana to the United States, fugitives from stateside prosecutions, and medical doctors and dentists guilty of diverting legal narcotics to addicts and local pushers.

From Puerto Rico Siragusa went to Athens where he gained the confidence of George Bouyakas, a man with a long history of narcotic offenses in Europe and the Middle East. Upon the delivery to Siragusa of one kilogram of pure heroin which the agent was supposed to deliver to a New York customer, Bouyakas, considered the heir to the toppled Eliopoulos criminal empire, was arrested.

In Trieste, where Benny Pocoroba once roamed, Siragusa easily assumed the character of a deported Italian mobster looking for a connection to supply his boys back in New York. He pitched into this task with his customary verve and, knowing Italian and its dialects, played the role with ease, securing 10 kilos of heroin and bringing in more than twenty persons, many of them Yugo-slavs and major dealers in crude opium.

This case, as we knew almost any of them might have, in-volved Lucky Luciano. We were not surprised to learn that the 107th Street gang was also implicated. It was a little hard to dis-cover that pure heroin had been diverted especially from the Schiapparelli Company of Turin, Italy, and other licensed manu-facturers and wholesalers in Trieste, Modena, Milan and Rome.

Professor Carlo Migliardi, a chemist executive of Schiapparelli, alone had diverted almost half of the 1,500 pounds of heroin to professional gangsters; this amount would represent on the New York market from four to forty million dollars.

Working with the Italian Guardia di Finanza, Siragusa had made this case through piecing together the movements and connections of Joe (Peachy) Pici of Pittsburgh (Pici had been deported on the *Laura Keene* with Luciano), Francesco Coppola, the Frank Callaces, uncle and nephew from the 107th Street gang, Eugenio Giannini (who had been charged with murdering a policeman but had got off), and a host of others. Now operating out of an office in Rome, Siragusa had been clearly able to see the endless ramifications of the Mafia. He had even got one of the rare, trickling tips from Luciano on the activities of Coppola who had annoyed Luciano with his attempts to break in on the traffic.

Giannini's tracks had been easy to follow; he had lived in opulence and liked to travel that way. Apprehended in Italy and faced with a long term in an uncomfortable jail, he blew the whistle on Mafia operations and was deported back to Idlewild and released in $15,000 bail. He immediately set out to have transported to America via courier unknown to the Mafia, a half-dozen kilos of heroin; he planned to sell it himself. The new courier he contacted was agent Anthony Zirilli, who, with Siragusa and the Guardia Finanza, arrested Giannini's brother, the safekeeper of the missing heroin, in Salerno.

The arrest of so many top suppliers and aides, the seizure of quantities of heroin, made the Mafia murderously angry. Under no circumstance does it tolerate a doublecross, not even for a small amount of heroin. Certainly Giannini must have known that, at the moment he decided to steal six kilos of the drug, he was as good as dead.

He was found one month after his release under bond, shot to pieces beside a garbage can at Second Avenue and 107th Street. The gang had claimed its own.

Professor Migliardi was more fortunate; he received a sentence of fourteen years. Joe Pici was given a long sentence. One of Migliardi's distributors, also hauled into court, was dismissed. We appealed to Ambassador Clare Booth Luce to have the case reopened, but her efforts were useless. The Italian police named Luciano as defendant in the same case, but the judge, who came from Lucky's home town, said the evidence against him was insufficient. But Italian authorities conducted successful civil actions against him for income tax evasion and the illegal importation of an automobile. He was declared a social menace and placed under restrictions which were to have kept him out of Rome, off the streets after dark, away from race tracks and other public places, and prevent his consorting with other known criminals. He was scheduled for exile for violating these police regulations, but they were found to be unconstitutional.

Although Siragusa was doing herculean work, illegal heroin continued to flow into America, and the 107th Street gang and its satellites continued their operations as Bill Davis' case proved.

# 12 THE SCENE IN NEW YORK

It was almost eleven P.M. A thin, spring drizzle of rain was falling upon the streets of New York's Hell's Kitchen, on the West Side of Manhattan. Sixty-year-old James Edwards McReynolds was walking north on Ninth Avenue near 56th Street when he noticed two men standing near a car. One, a Negro, was ordering the other to raise his hands and stand against a wall. McReynolds, with the inbred caution of a New Yorker, promptly crossed the street to the far corner.

Suddenly the white man turned and dashed west on 56th Street. McReynolds then saw that the Negro had a gun which he raised high in the air. "Halt!" he cried, firing a shot in the air. The other man kept running, his feet slapping hard against the pavement, even above the sounds of the busy Friday-night traffic. The armed man called out once more, then lowered his arm and fired. His target kept moving. Another shot barked out and the man staggered and fell.

Agent Bill Davis, who hadn't been able to make the Bureau's

pistol team, had brought down Angelo Paccione with two bullets, one in the heel and one in the back near the lower spine.

Davis was one of the thirty-five Negro agents in the Bureau—more than in any other federal law enforcement agency. The thirty-five agents represent a far cry from the thirties when, in some parts of the country, individuals balked at working with Negro agents and even withheld commendations from them when they did work with them.

For example, a dangerous situation existed in New Orleans because of the narcotics traffic. But we could not get a white agent to work undercover in the Negro section which was booming with illicit drugs. Through Bill Harmon, three Negroes were hired and, working full time undercover, made sixty-two cases, most of them marijuana. A. Miles Pratt was the Collector of Customs then and he blocked the commendations which the three men—two guards and an inspector—had coming from the Secretary of the Treasury. Harmon discovered what was going on and immediately wrote the Secretary himself. The Secretary then personally instructed Pratt to call in the three agents at once and present them with their citations. The Collector was also ordered to place copies of the citations in the files of each man and on the office bulletin board so that the entire staff could be apprised of their bravery. Pratt wasn't happy, but he followed the orders from Washington and never had any use for Bill Harmon after that.

Bill Davis had been on the case three months before he was forced to shoot Paccione, and had worked through a special employee, an informer. The first contacts were established deep within the boundaries of the 107th Street gang. Davis, posing as a Newark peddler, finally met the wholesale gang in a bar at First Avenue and 100th Street. He was alone; the informer had done his work and returned to the shadows. Now Bill spoke with a man he'd met the night before, known only as John Doe. Davis stressed the urgency of his need for heroin for his customers and John Doe asked, "How many pieces do you want?"

"One'll do," Davis answered.

"Right," said John Doe. "Sit there. I'll send a kid in. Name's Tony." John Doe left and a few minutes later a young man entered and identified himself as Tony. "I can let you have a quarter of an ounce. You can make five times that when you cut it because it's straight stuff."

"That's not what's worrying me," Davis said. "It's the price. You want one-six-oh beans."

"Got to get $160 for it," Tony said.

"I wouldn't go for it if I didn't have to," Bill complained, but he paid in advance. Tony counted the money carefully, put it away and said he would return in a few minutes. Then John Doe number 2 came in and approached the agent. "You Bill?"

"Yes."

John Doe number 2 studied him carefully. "Walk up to 101st Street and turn left. Tony'll meet you."

Davis went out and met Tony. "Look under the steps in the hallway of 338 East 101st Street." Tony said. "I'll wait to make sure you get the stuff." In the drop, Davis found a double glassine bag filled with white powder.

Other agents had had Davis under surveillance. Now they returned to the office, tagged the drug as Exhibit 1, and put it through an examination. The heroin content was 65.7—not "pure," but pure enough to suggest that Tony and both John Does had a worthwhile source of supply. It is almost standard procedure among drug traffickers that the first buy contain "good stuff" in order to hook a steady customer who, by cutting carefully, could increase his profit five to ten times. The heroin content of the next buy would drop to 47.2, and the third to 15.2 per cent.

After the second "connection," New York City detectives were notified. Two of the three men Davis had dealt with were picked up but were released in $10,000 bond. The men were now identified as Anthony Musarra, Nicholas Constantino and Paccione, who had not been picked up. Being under bond did not slow these fellows up. Exhibit 3 was sold to Davis by Paccione and Musarra.

It was decided to make an arrest as a fourth delivery was being made and take this crew out of circulation altogether. Davis then arranged for a meet on the evening of May 7th. Agents Katz, Marshall, Dick, Slotnick, Young, Doyle and Mercado were stationed in the area. But Musarra and Paccione called off the buy until the following evening. Ten ounces of heroin were to be delivered at the price of $100 an ounce; they didn't want to take any chances.

The next night Davis fretted alone in his car. Delivery was an hour late. The other agents in nearby cars shifted restlessly. What had gone wrong? The plan called for Davis to turn on his car lights as soon as the meet was made and he picked up the connection. The other agents could then follow and precede him and keep him covered.

Davis himself, thinking the meet had gone up in smoke once more, climbed out of his car and was pacing back and forth beside it when he saw Paccione hurrying toward him. "They're still bagging the stuff," he said. "You'll have to wait." Paccione got into the car. "Drive out of this block, quick. I want to see if anybody's following us."

Davis remained outside the car. If Paccione was on the alert, he could not drive away with the lights on; the buy would be fluffed. Davis tried another tack.

"Damn it, Angelo, let's do business right here. I don't want you to take me around the corner and run into some of your boys who'll stick me up."

Paccione's expression was one of hurt. "Bill, Bill, look at me. Would I do a thing like that? Besides, the stuff's up at 50th Street."

"So bring it here."

"Bill, it's got to be done my way."

Seeing that Paccione was firm, Davis shrugged; he would make the move and let the other agents cover as best they could. Now he got into the car and let Paccione direct him to the drop. When they arrived Paccione said, "Hold it right here and keep the

motor running. As soon as I get back make a quick left turn and
go north on Tenth Avenue."

As Davis sat waiting, he saw Agent Doyle drive past and turn
left on Tenth Avenue. Would he park and wait? And the others,
where were they? At least they had caught on about the lights.
Paccione came running back. "I've got it. Let's get the hell out
of here," he said, scrambling into the car and urging Davis to
move quickly. He laid a brown paper package on the seat between
them. "You want to check this out, Bill?"

"Damn right I do," Davis said as he drove. "I don't want to
lay out a thousand bucks until I see what I'm getting."

"You're going the wrong way!" Paccione yelled.

"Oh, yeah." Davis had bungled directions on purpose to give
his fellow agents a chance to find him. He finally pulled up at
56th Street and Ninth Avenue and started to count the glassine
envelopes.

"Hurry up, will you?" Paccione was anxious to collect and get
away.

Under the pretext of surveying for police, Davis stepped out of
the car; now he could reach for his gun and badge. When he spun
around, he had the badge in his left hand, the gun in the right.
"I'm a Narcotic Agent, Angelo. You're under arrest."

Panicked, Paccione cried, "Bill, Bill! Don't do this to me. I've
got a wife and five kids; I don't want to go to jail."

"Slide out on this side."

However, Paccione slid out on the opposite side, but Davis ran
around and ordered him to a nearby wall. It was at this point
that McReynolds passed and crossed the street.

When Davis stood over the man he had just shot, he asked
McReynolds to call the police. The other agents arrived and then
the city cops. Statements from witnesses, including McReynolds,
were obtained. Paccione was hospitalized under guard and then
jailed. While behind bars he threatened to "mess" Davis up. The
threat wasn't carried out; few of them ever are, against our agents.

But five years later we were to receive anonymously the following information:

Rose & Tony Candy Store, 243 E. 105th Street, should be looked after night & day. Sell dope to kids, boys and girls; every kid should be inspected that goes in there. Owner very wise also her daughter Ann, she got some line. Go there nights and days and see also back room. Investigate her son-in-law king of drugs with his wife Anna near E. 105th Street. Send the kids home so they could go to school and be with their families. Act soon and save the lives of kids.

Our files indicated that Nicholas Constantino who had recently completed a federal narcotic sentence as a result of Bill Davis' work in the Paccione case, was alleged to be a part owner in the candy store. During the same investigation, Davis had had contact with the woman named Anna, but failed to find clear-cut proof of her involvement. All the skills and risks that went into Davis' work would have to be repeated.

About two years later, Frank Costello, to whom Paccione perhaps owed a great deal of allegiance, escaped by millimeters his moment of truth on New York's Central Park West, a near victim of the organization that had made him its prime minister.

The mind reels in its effort to fathom the reasons why Costello had been ordered assassinated. Were we at last closing the gap and making it too uncomfortable for the Mafia to continue business? Were the young *riccottari*, the gunmen, getting restless with wanting to break the rigid restrictions placed upon their blood membership in the Mafia? Had a new prime minister been chosen to guide the fortunes of the rackets in America? If so, who? Most important, had Lucky Luciano himself ordered the deed? None of these questions have ever been answered. This was no effort on the part of the Mafia to frighten a man into more strict adherence to its codes; Costello's death was intended.

The New York City Police Department, convulsed with the ramifications of the attempt, pulled out all stops and Vincent (The Chin) Gigante was arrested and brought before the bench.

This time Costello was on the side of the People—unwillingly, as it turned out, but such a twist of fate would have made the gods howl.

It was submitted by the state that Gigante had slipped out of his car and called to Costello as he entered the building where he lived. Costello had turned and Gigante had fired, the bullet creasing Don Francesco's skull and tumbling him to the floor. The *riccottari* always aim for the head, lessening the chances that the victim will live long enough to identify the killer or killers.

Costello had had a date at the hour the would-be assassin's bullet hurled him to the floor of his lobby. The date was an extremely lovely model, one of those who doubles in clothes and out of them. She had been secured for Costello by a former New York City official.

Since Costello had to undergo immediate medical attention, his date was automatically canceled. The girl was one of his favorites and he assigned a bodyguard for her, through his attorney—one of the top criminal lawyers in the country. As it happened, the man assigned to the task was one of our former agents. Costello's girl fell in love with him. Every night while Costello was under care or incommunicado, the lovely girl and her guardian were proving their love for one another in bed.

But even if he had known, Costello's mind would have centered on the coming trial.

Law enforcement officials from every level of government—city, state and federal—jammed into the courtroom, hoping against hope that something would come out of the trial to crack the Mafia wide open. Surely a rift existed. Would Costello, a legendary figure in and out of the underworld, his pride frayed by the burn of an assassin's bullet and the fear that death, once decreed, would ultimately be carried out, blow the lid off with his whistling?

District Attorney Alexander Herman carried the attack to Costello; Judge Mullen, who had passed sentence on the Gagliano-Albero combine, presided. Herman hammered at Costello;

Costello barked back, his throaty voice quivering with threats. No, he hadn't seen his assassin. Herman pointed out, however, that the bullet had entered the *front* of Costello's hat and that the would-be victim must have been facing the street when the shot was fired. Had it been the accused, Gigante? Defense cast doubt on the credibility of the doorman's identification of the fat gunman. Who, Herman asked Costello, would want him dead? No one that Costello could think of.

Did he know Anthony Strollo, alias Tony Bender?*
Only vaguely. . . .

The result of Costello's refusal to identify Vincent Gigante as the man who had tried to kill him, resulted in Gigante's acquittal. The police were to a man convinced that, despite the jury's verdict, Gigante was the man and Costello the victim—almost. As bruised as his ego must have been, Costello had kept the Mafia code of *omerta*, the code of silence on pain of death.

The Mafia scene in Italy appeared unruffled by the attempt on Costello's life. Luciano, although he had narrowly avoided police action in the case involving Dr. Migliardi, continued his world-wide operations. The perpetual machinery of crime did not stop just because Costello had been grazed, nor did our activities.

Luciano had arranged papers and passage for three important criminals against whom we had made cases. They jumped bond and with Luciano's help, seemed to have vanished into thin air. They were Frankie (The Bug) Caruso, Vincent Mauro and Salvatore Maneri. A tip came in advising us that the trio had visited the Bahamas. Our agents, working with the police in Nassau, located the record of their arrival and departure aided

---

* Tony Bender vanished one night in 1962. On April 7, 1963, The New York *Post* reported the following item: "Four skin divers, under the direction of Hudson County Prosecutor Tumulty, were searching an abandoned quarry in North Bergen, New Jersey, this weekend, but the prosecutor wouldn't say what they were looking for. It was believed they were seeking the bodies of two missing mobsters, Anthony (Tony Bender) Strollo, 62, and Anthony Castellitto, 51. Tumulty wouldn't even tell New York Police why he was looking in the quarry near Tonnele Av. at 74th Street."

by false Canadian passports furnished, we later discovered, by John Papalia.

From Nassau their trail led to Kingston, Jamaica; Caracas, Venezuela; Nice, France, and London. For two of the fugitives the chase ended in Barcelona; the third was found on the resort isle of Majorca. Working with the Spanish police, we were able to have them extradited back to America to stand trial before Federal Judge Croake. The four, Caruso, Mauro, Maneri and Papalia all pleaded guilty to a conspiracy to smuggle more than $150,000,000 worth of heroin into the States. Eleven other members of this group were convicted in absentia.

One of these was Silvestro Carollo, a deported hood who had terrorized New Orleans, killing a narcotics agent in the process. Carollo was trapped by Siragusa and the Italian police in the Italian foothills of Terracina. With Mafia money, Carollo too had tried to escape the punishment of the law. His apprehension was made concurrently with Siragusa's investigation of the death of Lieutenant Petrosino, an American and chief of New York City's famous "Black Hand" squad, a group of brave policemen who fought the Mafia hand to hand before it was ever recognized as a world threat. Siragusa was able to identify the two killers of Lt. Petrosino even though the murder had been committed in 1904. One of the killers had died; the other was seventy-six years old and had lived in Palermo for the past fifty years without visible means of support. Siragusa discovered that the man was being given a pension by the owner of a large Rome newspaper. This information was turned over to the Italian police, although Siragusa knew that the statute of limitations, the length of time during which a man may be legally prosecuted for a crime under existing treaties between the United States and Italy, prevented action. But the information enabled New York City police to close the case on the Petrosino murder.

It was for these and other exploits that I recommended Siragusa for the Treasury Department's highest decoration, the Exceptional Civilian Service Gold Medal for narcotics law enforcement accomplishments in foreign countries. Siragusa, working out of District 17 which is Rome, was too busy to come to Washington for the ceremony. At that time his force consisted of only four men. We mailed him the medal. He also won the "Columbo Award—Italian-American man of the year for 1960," the Knight of Merit of the Italian Republic award and the Gold Medal of the Italian Treasury Department. He was made Assistant Deputy Commissioner in June, 1960, and then Deputy Commissioner a short time later. He is now head of the Illinois State Crime Commission.

# 13 *DIALOGS OF DEATH*

It was late in August, 1950. St. Paul, Minnesota, fried under the blistering Midwestern sun. District Supervisor Anker M. Bangs received a call from the Federal Bureau of Investigation: a girl wanted to talk with the proper government law enforcement agency about narcotics and a Chinese man. The girl's name was Mickey Anderson.

Shortly afterward Bangs met with her in the lobby of the Lowry Hotel. Mickey Anderson was a commonplace woman whose single claim to doubtful fame was that Chinese men liked her and cared for her. She had been living with John Wong at the Glendale Hotel and had discovered smoking opium in his closet. She invited Bangs to come with her—Wong was away on a trip—and examine the apartment himself. Bangs found several large jars of smoking opium and a quantity of yen shee, the residue of the smoked drug. From a dresser he took a fully loaded 32-caliber pistol. Other Chinese men in the building were associated with Wong, and Bangs took their descriptions and apartment numbers from Mickey Anderson.

Why was she giving the Narcotics Bureau this information?

John Wong, she said, was in the process of getting rid of her for another girl.

Returning to his office, Bangs started an intensive investigation of Wong and his connections. He also discussed the case with the U.S. Attorney General's office and received search warrants for two apartments in the Glendale Hotel. It was suspected that Wong was away for the purpose of picking up opium or delivering it.

At 7 A.M. on the morning of September 24, Bangs, with agents Joseph Winberg and Magnuson, went to the Glendale Hotel to arrest John Wong. What happened then is best described in Winberg's own words, recorded at a St. Paul hospital some five hours later. County Attorney Richard Ryan put the questions to the agent.

RYAN:     Do you feel up to talking a little bit?

WINBERG:  Okay.

RYAN:     You and Bangs were on the third floor of the building and took Wong to the second floor, right?

WINBERG:  That's right.

RYAN:     Can you tell me very briefly what happened when the three of you went down to the second floor?

WINBERG:  Well, we went down because he [Wong] said he had the smoking opium in his room. That's all. We went in there. He went into the closet and he brought out this jar of opium and gave it to us. Bangs asked him if that's all he had, so he reached back in there and he whipped out this gun. I don't remember what he said, but when he whipped out the gun, we both jumped him and he shot me first and I fell and the three of us were in the closet and wrestling around, and he shot Bangs too, and I grabbed hold of his gun to keep him from shooting any more and Bangs finally pulled his gun out and shot Wong. I don't know how many times, and I didn't have my gun with me because I had given it to Magnuson to keep the other fellows covered upstairs. I think Bangs unloaded his gun in Wong and I am pretty sure Wong still had a couple of shots left in his, and we both tried to make it towards the door to get out of the apartment, because Bangs' gun was empty and we didn't know how many shots Wong had left.

RYAN: You and Bangs got to the door. You didn't know if Wong's gun was empty and Bangs' was.

WINBERG: We both crawled out in the hall and I heard a couple more shots and I didn't know who was shooting.

RYAN: Did Wong ever come out of the room?

WINBERG: I don't know.

RYAN: Now, Winberg, you've heard the above statement read to you. What is your understanding of your physical condition?

WINBERG: I am critical.

Meanwhile the reports were being made out on Bangs: "Federal agent shot and killed while attempting to make an arrest. This man was found face down in the hallway of the Glendale Apartments. He was DOA. The only visible wound was a bullet wound through lower spine."

An hour after Ryan questioned Winberg, he was taking testimony from Wong:

RYAN: Wong, where did you get the gun?

WONG: I haven't got any gun. I wish I had one now.

RYAN: You got that gun in the closet, didn't you?

WONG: I wish I had one now.

RYAN: How many shots did you fire down there?

WONG: I didn't fire any.

RYAN: Who did shoot, then?

WONG: They shot themselves.

RYAN: You expect us to believe that?

WONG: Yes.

RYAN:     Who shot you? Did you shoot yourself?

WONG:     [No answer.]

RYAN:     What were you being arrested for, Wong?

WONG:     Narcotics.

RYAN:     Had you been smuggling narcotics?

WONG:     No.

RYAN:     Did you have any in the room this morning?

WONG:     [No answer.]

RYAN:     Wong, did you have a gun in the room this morning?

WONG:     Not that I know.

RYAN:     Wong, the other narcotics agent that was there has made a statement that you had the gun in your hand and that you shot him. There is no way you can refute that in court. Why not put an end to it? It's bad enough. Tell what happened. How many times you shot and who shot you.

WONG:     [No answer.]

The questioning of John Wong ceased at 2:25 P.M. when he was taken to the operating room where, for four and a half hours, he underwent surgery for gunshot wounds in the finger, abdomen and right chest. His condition, like Winberg's, was critical.

Both Winberg and Wong recovered. Winberg was the key witness against Wong, who was charged with killing a federal officer and assaulting a federal officer. The jury found him guilty of second degree murder. He was given a life sentence. Wong filed a $75,000 suit against Bangs' widow, claiming that the warrant issued the Supervisor was for apartments on another floor of the hotel—not his. The claim was tossed out of court.

# 14 *THE BROTHERS*

A month after the Korean War broke out, agent Henry Giordano was put on a case in the Pacific Northwest. A massive narcotics ring seemed to be in the making, encompassing Seattle, Portland, Tacoma and Spokane. And there was every indication that San Francisco and also Vancouver and other cities in Canada would be included.

This was the case of the Mallock brothers, George and John, and four years were to pass before it was closed. Officials and agents of three nations—the United States, Canada and Mexico —would be involved.

The end was predictable. Hank Giordano, chunky, dark-haired, usually soft-spoken, would rise on the basis of his work in this case to District Supervisor and on up the ladder to the post I held for over thirty years, Federal Commissioner of Narcotics.

By August 23, 1950, officials of the Royal Canadian Mounted Police were certain that heroin was being smuggled from Vancouver into Seattle. There was no positive proof; the information had come in a steady trickle from informers and was so persistent that Giordano had already made a brief prior contact with George Mallock. It appeared that the informers were playing both sides of the fence because it took so long to make real headway in the investigation. The delay proved providential, for it brought the younger Mallock, John, into the picture.

Armed with the information that the Mallocks had not been avoiding Giordano, the RCMP called Supervisor A. B. Crisler in Seattle and requested that the agent be permitted to work in Vancouver to establish that heroin was crossing the border. Crisler cleared through channels and Giordano was allowed to re-establish contact with the Mallocks in Canada.

The Mallock brothers, only a year apart, were of Canadian-Ukranian background. George stood only five feet six, a stocky man with fair complexion and blue eyes. Sometimes he wore a wig over his thinning brown hair. His criminal record listed breaking and entering, theft, auto theft, shop-breaking, possession of dangerous weapons, and unlawfully wounding with intent to do grievous bodily harm.

John was a half inch taller than George. Running almost to fat, he hoisted a bulky 185 pounds, twenty more than his brother. His criminal record consisted of theft, assault, causing bodily harm, breaking and entering, burglary, and receiving stolen property. Both men were usually armed and considered dangerous.

The informers had repeatedly said that an undercover agent would not be able to make any purchases from the Mallocks; they were too shrewd, too tough to be taken in by anyone they didn't know. A final appraisal of the situation was made and Crisler and J. J. Atherton of the RCMP Narcotic Branch and the Bureau, decided once again to give it a try. Giordano was given $650 with which to purchase heroin from the suspected traffickers.

Driving a Lincoln convertible, Giordano drove to Vancouver on September 21, three days before Anker Bangs met his death in the Glendale Hotel in St. Paul. The Vancouver special employee was brought to the RCMP office and plans were laid to contact a man named Carter who was the pipeline to the Mallocks. Giordano had met Carter before, but found that he had moved. Giordano reported his early moves:

On September 21, 1950, at 11 P.M. [the informant] and I drove to Dode Jones' place, the Cozy Chicken Inn. I talked with Dode Jones and obtained the telephone number of Robert Simpson. [This was Carter's alias.] I checked and found that this number had been changed. Mrs. Simpson answered the telephone and told me that Bert Simpson was not in. She told me to call back about 2 P.M. I told her that Harry from Seattle was calling and gave her my room number 1016 at the Georgia Hotel. At 2:40 P.M. I again telephoned Mrs. Simpson's residence and again talked to Mrs. Simpson. Simpson was still not in. I told Mrs. Simpson that I wanted to see Bert and talk to him that evening. She gave me their address and told me that if we missed connections to come out to the house.

Some six hours later, Giordano drove to Simpson's where he chatted briefly with Simpson, his wife and a relative. The agent waited an hour for a call from Mallock, whom Simpson had called and who, Giordano was sure, was aware of his presence in town by now. When he did not get a call at Simpson's, Giordano drove back to his hotel to continue his wait. Arriving there, he found a message stating that a man named Murdock had called at 7:45 P.M. and would call later. There was no doubt in Giordano's mind that the caller had been George Mallock.

The agent made himself comfortable and settled down to await the call.

At 9:45 the phone rang. Giordano answered.

"Is Jack there?"

Giordano said, "There's no one here by that name."

"Do you have a friend at [Simpson's number]?" Mallock asked.

"Yes, I called that number. This is Harry from Seattle—don't you remember me?"

"I don't know any Harry," Mallock said, "but I'll meet you in the rotunda of the hotel in twenty or twenty-five minutes. I'm at the edge of town now."

The two men met in the lobby and went into the coffee shop. "How's business here?" Giordano asked.

"Very good."

Giordano said, "I understand that the prices have gone down and that stuff's cheaper here."

"A lot of stuff came in from Toronto, but it wasn't any good. We cut our stuff to meet the competition. We have two grades, the good stuff, six dollars a cap, and the bad stuff, four dollars a cap. We're cutting our stuff with milk sugar and putting in some theobromine—the hypes [addicts] like it, and if that's what they want, they'll get it. We're selling some of the poor stuff which is cut way over half of what's good and we're making more money. Now tell me: how're things in Seattle?"

"Not much happening down there. Prices're high, that's why I'm here."

Mallock said, "You didn't get a sample last time. I'll give you ten caps of the good and ten caps of the bum stuff. You take it back to Seattle and try it. See which you want."

"I don't think I want any of the bad stuff," the agent said.

"Do you know how to test it to see how good it is?"

"Well, there's the acid test," Giordano said.

"That's too difficult," Mallock said. "I'll tell you what to do. Get a spoon and put some in. Then put in water. If it all dissolves, it's good. What doesn't dissolve remains on the bottom, that's what it was cut with. Take the samples back and try it. Get hold of an addict you can trust and let him try it. After you test it, I'll call you and see you when you come back."

Mallock left the hotel promising to return later. Giordano called RCMP Corporal Price and reported the meeting.

The meeting had been conducted along business lines: "good stuff" and "bad stuff." "To meet the competition. . . ." The supreme callousness of the drug peddler was implicit in Mallock's statement, "Get hold of an addict you can trust and let him try it."

Corporal Price instructed Giordano to carry on with his plans.

Accordingly, the agent was in his room when George Mallock knocked at his door twenty-four hours later. "Let's not talk here," Mallock said quickly. "These rooms are bad places to talk. They have them wired."

"Okay," Giordano said. "Let's go."

"Somebody I want you to meet," George said as they passed down the halls to the lobby. It was Johnny Mallock. The three men got into a car and drove around the city talking.

After some time had passed, Johnny said suddenly, "He's okay. That was my first impression and I find that first impressions are usually right." He turned an approving look on Giordano.

"You're satisfied," George said. "Well, good. I want to give Harry some samples." Then he said to the agent, "You'll find our stuff is the best. We want to keep the market. This is a business with us; we're in it to make money. We can't afford to lose customers and have people dissatisfied."

"What's the beef?" Giordano asked.

"The last time a piece was $650, but I think we can let you have it for $600. Of course, if you want the cut stuff, we'll let you have that for $300."

Johnny said to his brother, "How about letting him have it for five bills American?"

"Okay with you?" George asked Giordano.

"Five hundred and fifty in foreign money," Johnny said.

"And make it big bills," George cut in.

Giordano said, "What size?"

"Hundred-dollar bills," George said. "How many pieces do you think you'll want the first time around?"

Giordano, the $650 we had given him resting snugly in his pocket, said, "I don't know. I'll have to see if I can contact my friend in Portland."

Magnanimously George said, "Whatever you want. I'll deal only with you and I expect some protection."

Johnny broke in excitedly. "We want that business down there.

We can handle a hundred pieces. You should be able to take care of the Seattle, Tacoma and Portland markets with stuff you have."

The conversations went on, sounding strangely like a Madison Avenue marketing conference.

The following day, at 12:10 P.M., Giordano received another call from George Mallock, who told him to pack his bags and check out and meet him at the gas station where the agent had parked his Lincoln. When they were alone George said, "Everything's set. We're giving you a sample in powder form instead of caps. It's easier to carry and makes a small package. It's in two or three folds of a rubber [condom]—that way it doesn't break. Carry it in your mouth, then, if you're stopped, you can swallow it. Later you can bring it back up or else it will pass out in a day or two."

George picked up his brother and once again the three men cruised around in the car. After a while George said, "Johnny, roll down beside that pole."

Johnny parked and got out of the car.

"Everything all set?" George asked him.

Giordano looked warily from one brother to the other. The street was deserted.

"Everything's set," Johnny answered. Now George got out of the car and the brothers walked to a nearby corner, leaving Giordano in the rear seat. The brothers returned to the car and, leaning in, George said, "Your sample is right over there by the telephone pole."

"Where?" Giordano asked looking around but seeing nothing.

Johnny said, "Over there." He pointed. "Five feet from the pole in a Winchester box."

"I don't see it," Giordano said.

"No?" George said.

"No."

"Aw, you can't miss it. It's by the pole. See it now?"

"No," Giordano said once more, straining to see the box.

"It's on top of the grass. Go over there. You'll see it," Johnny said.

The agent got out of the car then, shook hands with the brothers and told them he'd see them in a couple of days. He walked to the telephone pole and picked up a crumpled cigar box.

"That's it," George called, and the brothers drove off.

The purpose of this action was to insure the brothers time to get away if "Harry" did turn out to be an agent.

As soon as the brothers' car was out of sight, Giordano hurried to a phone and called the RCMP, then waited for officers Price and Robson to arrive. He turned the sample over to them. Dominion analyst H. I. Edwards later ascertained that the sample contained diacetylmorphine (heroin) of high quality. The weight was fixed at 15.4 grains.

Just in case the Mallocks should check him out, Giordano drove to Seattle, conferred with Supervisor Crisler and returned to Vancouver. Little cover had been given the agent during his rendezvous with the Mallocks for fear of upsetting the delicate balance of the operations. Now the Mallocks had accepted Giordano as a bona fide trafficker. A conspiracy case could be made against them on the evidence already gathered, but it was considered better for the agent to continue in his present role long enough to make an actual purchase of an ounce of drugs.

George called Giordano soon after he arrived back at the Georgia Hotel and a meet had been arranged so the agent could buy. Now the RCMP swung into action.

Fluorescent powders and ultra violet ray lamps to treat the money to be exchanged were readied.

Two adjoining rooms were rented at the hotel where the meeting was to take place.

The RCMP arranged for one of its officers to act as the hotel clerk.

There would be an open line from the hotel to the sheriff's office during the evening.

Additional police cars, three equipped with radio, were ordered to stand by.

At 8:00 P.M. on September 26, all law enforcement officers concerned took up their posts.

Forty-five minutes later Giordano entered the lobby of the hotel and bought a paper; this he would read under the observation of Constable W. Kowtun of the RCMP Narcotic Branch. If Giordano had to leave the hotel with Mallock to secure the narcotics, advanced planning called for him to leave the paper behind.

Another fifteen minutes passed. George Mallock was seen on Georgia Street parking his Studebaker sedan. He walked into the lobby of the hotel and signaled Giordano, who, still carrying the paper, left with him after a brief discussion. The departure was observed both from inside the hotel and from the street.

The movements of the two men were relayed by police radio and they were tailed by Corporals Price and Robson in separate cars. Traveling at speeds up to 70 mph, Mallock and Giordano were last seen by Sergeant Mathers' observation party on the east side of Vancouver. Since all members of the stand-by team had been advised by radio or telephone that Giordano had *not* left the paper behind, they returned to their original posts.

Three and a half hours passed. Nothing was seen or heard of Giordano. Five radio cars were dispatched from time to time to areas where Mallock might have taken him.

The stand-by force at the hotel breathed a sigh of relief when Giordano finally returned to the hotel and turned over to Corporal Price an oilskin-wrapped package containing an ounce of white powder. Giordano also reported that both brothers had been involved in the transaction that had taken place in their home on McHardy Street. One or both of the brothers was scheduled to meet him in a half hour at a nearby gas station, Giordano said, but the covering force should use caution since George had been drinking heavily and had been firing a revolver as they drove along the highway.

The members on stand-by deployed to apprehend the Mallocks. Three radio cars were poised to block off the street as soon as the suspects entered it. Johnny Mallock, driving alone, was seen circling the block twice. As he approached the gas station, Corporal Robson and Constable Jensen forced his car to the curb; the other cars closed in. Johnny, spluttering his surprise, was found unarmed and taken to the nearest RCMP office. No incriminating evidence was found on his person save traces of fluorescent powder seen on his hands with the infrared lamp.

Meanwhile, Sergeant Mathers and Constable Wallis and officers Gostling and White drove to the Robert Simpson (Carter) home and found him with his wife and four children. Under the powers of the writs of assistance, the home was searched, but no incriminating evidence was found.

While this action was taking place, Giordano was relating what had happened when George Mallock picked him up.

George had driven him to his home, asking him en route, if the sample had been all right. Giordano had answered that it was and that he had tried it on an addict as George suggested.

At his home George said, "In the future, don't go to a hotel. Come here and stay at our place." He showed Giordano the house key hidden at the base of the fence post by the gate. Inside, Johnny Mallock tried to get Giordano to take more narcotics, and said that they would soon be buying in kilos. "The price'll be better then," he said.

"I'll just take an ounce for now," Giordano said.

"When do you want it?" Johnny asked.

"Right now. I'm ready."

George told Johnny to get the piece from the "plant," but Johnny protested and a brief argument followed. Johnny wanted to know why George could not get the ounce. "The stuff is put up in half-ounce lots in glass jars with sealed tops," Johnny said, sulking. "This keeps it dry when it's buried." He rambled on, saying that he had some friends in Seattle who were in town and who wanted to buy.

"If you're going to do business with someone else from Seattle," Giordano snapped, "we might as well forget our deal. I don't want competition."

Giordano was gambling, for if the brothers had insisted on selling to other parties from Seattle, he would have had to back out of the deal, as would any peddler seeking a wide open market. Then the investigation of the Mallocks, now two months old, would have to begin all over again with another undercover agent.

Johnny hesitated, but George said, "Okay, that's the way you want it, we'll deal with only you." He looked at Johnny, "Go give your friends the brush and bring back that stuff for Harry."

As it happened, the other buyers were the Talbots, people Giordano had originally come to Vancouver to investigate. When Johnny left it was 10:20.

"Do you know Jack Sieman?" George asked the agent as they waited.

Giordano was cautious: "I think so, why?"

"I saw him at the race track the other day and he said he knew you."

Giordano watched George pick up the heavy forty-five revolver he had been carrying all night; he watched him and thought of Jack Sieman.

Before the Bureau had been established, Jack Sieman had been considered one of the most important illicit dealers in narcotics on the Pacific Coast. With two associates he had been arrested in 1929 for the sale of 20 ounces of morphine hydrochloride and the possession of 20 additional ounces of the drug plus 20 ounces of cocaine hydrochloride. Held in $30,000 bond, the three men jumped it and were then classified as fugitives. Almost a year later Sieman was caught in Vancouver and vigorously fought his extradition, but in vain. He was returned to the States and after trial and conviction, was sentenced to ten years and a fine of $5,000. Sieman had been around a long time. Did he know Giordano was an agent? Had he told the Mallocks? Was this the cat-and-mouse game before George told him the play-acting was over? George opened the magazine of the gun and took out some bullets. He placed them back again. He said nothing. Giordano waited.

Johnny returned about midnight, bringing two small glass jars with screw tops. "This okay, or too bulky?"

Giordano was relieved; he had thought that when Johnny came back he too would be armed. "Too bulky," he said. "I'd rather have it in one package."

They went into the kitchen and Johnny held each bottle under hot water and removed the wax sealing. "This is pure, pure stuff," he said. "Right off the boat. New York would like to have some of *this* stuff."

As they were unsealing the jars, the three men talked. Giordano said when he got started good he would move down to San Francisco. The Mallocks said nothing. The agent had been hoping to get some names of operators there. Instead, they said that they often made trips to Buffalo, New York, "a great city for business." When the drug was finally prepared and the treated money passed, they got into the car to return Giordano part way to his hotel. George had been drinking all evening. Now, on the way to the hotel, he made Johnny stop and he got out and fired his gun. Johnny was unable to get him back in the car, and he left him. It had been 12:20 when Giordano arrived at the hotel and plans were carried out to pick up Johnny and Carter, alias Robert Simpson.

Now, new plans were drawn up to apprehend George. Three cars containing fourteen men proceeded to the McHardy Street address. The house lights were out, but George's car was parked outside. A search of it produced eight condoms. With two men remaining outside the police entered the house simultaneously from the front and rear entrances. George Mallock wasn't inside.

The investigation of the premises revealed the two glass jars which Johnny had brought. They had been rinsed in vinegar. Also found were milk sugar, an envelope containing eleven empty # 5 capsules, paraffin and Kodak scales. In the radio was found the treated money, five $100 bills, and in the bedroom, ninety-eight condoms.

The officers stationed themselves in various rooms to wait for George. At 6:20 A.M., he was seen through the front window placing something under the front seat of his car. When he entered the house he was placed under arrest. No narcotics were found on him.

On the morning of September 28 the charges were lodged against the Mallocks and William Carter.

Between the first day of July, 1950, and the 28th day of September, 1950, George Mallock, John Mallock and William Carter did unlawfully conspire, combine and confederate together to commit an indictable offense, namely, to sell a drug, to wit, a salt of diacetylmorphine; to wit, diacetylmorphine hydrochloride, to a person, to wit, Henry Giordano, save and except under the authority of a license from the Minister presiding over the Department of National Health and Welfare first had and obtained, or other lawful authority and contrary to the provisions of the Opium and Narcotics Drug Act, 1929, and Amendments thereto.

Bail was set at $20,000 for each defendant and the case was slated to be heard January 15, but was delayed a week. At that time Giordano, who had returned to the States, left Minnesota, his new post, to return to Vancouver for the trial. But on January 22, only one of the three defendants was present in court—William Carter. The attorney for the Mallocks stated that because of illness, the brothers would be quite unable to appear until that evening. Justice Klein thereupon ordered a further delay of twenty-four hours and, when the Mallocks were again absent, he issued a bench warrant for their arrest. Carter was found guilty, but the Mallocks had jumped bail.

Before the trial of Carter and the Mallocks had come up, the RCMP liaison officer, C. M. Bayfield had advised Deputy Commissioner Harney as follows:

"I am in receipt of information that the principals in this case [George and John Mallock] will most likely make efforts to locate the Agent responsible for their apprehension, who, as you know, is your Agent Harry [sic] Giordano; and they have said that when they find him they will arrange to have him 'knocked off.' Since it is felt that the Mallocks, with their Canadian and United States underworld contacts might use any means of preventing Mr. Giordano from appearing at their trial to give evidence, we feel some concern for his safety.

"Although we realize that Mr. Giordano has now been transferred to Minnesota, it is not known whether his family preceded him or are still in Seattle, and while our fears might be unduly aroused, it is deemed advisable that you should be informed of these facts which have already been brought to the attention of Mr. A. B. Crisler, your District Supervisor in Seattle, Washington, by the officer in charge of 'E' division. . . ."

Neither Giordano nor his family were molested in any way. The agent went on the witness stand and the Vancouver courtroom found it hard to believe that here was a genuine undercover agent. The press praised his bravery. After the trial, Giordano passed out of direct and active participation in the case. The Mallocks were now officially listed as fugitives, and the hunt for them continued.

On April 11, 1951, liaison officer Bayfield notified Harney that he had received word that George Mallock was in New York and that he was most likely to be spotted at sporting events such as prize fights, hockey matches, and so forth at Madison Square Garden and St. Nicholas Arena.

While agents probed New York, other trails seemed to open up in Hollywood, Chicago and Carrol, Iowa. All persons interviewed or placed on telephone or mail check were, or had in some way been connected with one or both Mallocks. In November Bayfield again wrote Harney advising that his latest information definitely placed John and George in New York in the company of Rheo Gauthier and Lucien Rivard. We had a dossier on Rivard for violations under the Opium and Narcotic Drug Act. The Mallocks were not found in New York.

During the first week of 1952, information was received that the brothers were hiding in a hunting lodge near St. Paul and Minneapolis. Agents from the St. Paul district office located and raided the lodge, finding only a man named Carl E. Boyd. Boyd was a major narcotics violator himself and he was taken into custody and held in $50,000 bail. A search of the cabin turned up a letter from Winnipeg in which the writer, a man named Twaddle, said that he had seen George Mallock during a recent trip in the Northwest and in British Columbia. The RCMP in Winnipeg questioned Twaddle without results and the trail was picked up in Hollywood again, from where, in August, it turned briefly to blaring, garish Las Vegas where George had been seen in a casino.

And then contact with George was made.

Agent Anthony Zirilli, back from Rome where he had worked with Siragusa, learned of George's presence in New York through an informer. George was reported to be holding down seven kilos of heroin and looking for a buyer. Zirilli set out to be that buyer and on December 9, after a previous contact to set up the buy, Zirilli met Mallock at 57th Street and Second Avenue. Two days later George was arrested. He agreed to return to Vancouver without extradition proceedings, and on March 1, his trial was completed before Justice A. M. Manson. He was found guilty of selling, giving away, and possession of narcotics. Henry Giordano, now a District Supervisor at Kansas City, Missouri, went to Canada to testify. George drew seven years on each of the three counts, and another seven years in default of the fines also imposed.

Now efforts were turned to the apprehension of Johnny Mallock, reported to be in Mexico.

Mexican authorities, acting on information from the U.S. Bureau of Narcotics, almost arrested him once, but he made good his escape in a car. Assuming the name Hatchett Horta, Johnny was forced to go on the run; the tips were coming in with disconcerting regularity. Mexican police, chagrined over his escape, pressed the search with new vigor.

On April 9, 1954, Johnny, with Carlos Ortega Cano and Efren Iniguez, left Mexico City, heading northward to Guadalajara. Ten miles outside the city of Querétaro, their 1947 Cadillac collided with a truck. When the dust settled Johnny Mallock was unconscious from a cerebral concussion. Ortega, whose left arm was so shattered that it would have to be amputated, was also unconscious. Iniguez had been killed instantly.

Johnny Mallock remained unconscious until the 16th of April, then he seemed on the road to recovery although his condition remained critical. On April 22, just fifty-three days after his brother had been convicted, he died. The case of the Mallock brothers was closed.

# 15 HYPOCRITES OF THE HIPPOCRATIC OATH

Fifteen years after World War II the Bureau found it necessary to readjust its operations. The goal of an agent on an investigation was not to develop an addict-possession case, but to ferret out evidence against the big wholesale boys, the interstate and international peddlers. If, however, a possession case can be made against one of these people, we will do it, but it must help us get the men at the top. The routine possession and addiction charges are the task of the local police. Our staff, in order to avoid accusations of being like the Gestapo, has remained the same size as it was when the Bureau was established.

The success of Siragusa and White and others abroad proved that we could most effectively halt illicit narcotic traffic by maintaining offices overseas and thus block shipments of drugs before they could be loaded aboard ship or plane for the United States. Agents now work in Europe, the Near East, Middle East and Far East and in Central and South America.

While around 80 per cent of the Bureau's activities are concerned with the illicit traffic, the other 20 per cent has been admirably used in establishing cordial and cooperative relationships with the professions and industries interested in legitimate narcotic drug activities, including the medical professions and the pharmaceutical industry.

Sometimes doctors violate the oath of their profession and break the narcotic laws; sometimes, in spite of the fine relations we have with the medical profession, a few doctors can create some of our biggest headaches—doctors like John Tate and Carlo Migliardi. Because of the nobility of the profession, the aura of respectability, the doctor who violates the narcotic laws will find himself the object of more publicity than others charged with the same offense.

Dr. Leopold Brandenburg could have been a brilliant physician. He had been superbly trained and he had that instinct for the right move when training ran out. It was conceded by doctors who knew him that he could have scaled any heights he chose to.

For twenty years Brandenburg engaged in a variety of illicit enterprises; he was the real-life version of the underworld doctor of the George Raft and James Cagney films. For all his illegal activities, he roamed free from 1925 to 1945 when he was sentenced to three years in prison for a narcotic violation in New Jersey, where he had been an important figure in that state's political picture. This was his first prison term, and he didn't stay long.

A number of convictions had been made against him, but they were always reversed by one court or another until we nailed him with the narcotics charge. Dr. Brandenburg's first conviction was in 1933. The Terrible Touhy gang of Chicago had staged a robbery, netting more than $100,000 from a U.S. mail truck in North Carolina. When $10,000 of the stolen money turned up in the doctor's bank account, he was indicted and tried for conspiracy. He was alleged to have accepted the money for treating a wounded member of the Touhy gang. The decision of the federal jury in Newark, however, was reversed by the U.S. Circuit Court of Appeals, which pointed out that no evidence had been presented to show that the doctor knew the money had been stolen, and Dr. Brandenburg went free.

Some time later, police in Waco, Texas, arrested a motorist who was taken in for fingerprinting. To their amazement, they saw that the man had had skin grafts on the tip of each finger; these had almost obliterated the identifying whorls. "Just try to prove who I am," the motorist gloated. "It can't be done."

The Waco police were sure they had a big one and hastily summoned the FBI experts, who found enough old ridges around the edges to prove that the mysterious motorist was Roscoe James (Cocoa) Pitts, a graduate of Alcatraz wanted in North Carolina for blowing a safe and helping himself to its contents. Angered that the operation designed to remove his fingerprints and thus his identity had failed, Pitts disclosed how Dr. Brandenburg had sliced the skin from his fingers, then inserted the raw ends into pockets cut into his chest. It took six uncomfortable weeks before the flesh of the fingers and chest healed so that the hand could be cut away. Brandenburg was convicted, once more in Newark, this time for concealing a fugitive from justice. He was given a three-year sentence, but again the Court of Appeals came to his rescue, deciding that altering finger tips wasn't a federal offense; concealment was not considered.

After that incident, Dr. Brandenburg remained in relative obscurity until January, 1944, when he was arrested as a material witness in an unsolved Montclair, New Jersey, killing four years earlier. The details of the case were bizarre.

John Longstreet Ely, a retired farmer, lived with his son-in-law, J. Raymond Tiffany, a former district court judge and attorney general. According to the newspaper reports, Ely sat up late one evening playing solitaire in his sunroom. The next morning the maid found him dead with a bullet in his brain. It was determined that the shot came from a high-powered rifle aimed from a nearby clump of bushes. Detectives suspected that Ely had been mistaken for Tiffany. As the case unwound, it was revealed that Tiffany had represented two of Brandenburg's former wives in distasteful lawsuits against him. In addition, the doctor had a collection of high-powered rifles and was an efficient marksman. Brandenburg was cleared when it was proved that none of his rifles could have fired the shot.

Our conviction against the doctor in 1945 was on the evidence that he prescribed narcotics solely to satisfy an addict's craving and for monetary gain, and that he did so without any attempt to ascertain whether these people had a medical need for narcotics.

It was not that Dr. Brandenburg was careless; rather, he did not care at all. This was our opinion when one of our agents, posing as an addict, went to the doctor for drugs.

"How about getting a prescription today, doc?" The agent had already been introduced to Brandenburg and had described a few symptoms.

"Sure," the doctor said, "how much do you want?"

"Two prescriptions for twenty-five quarter-grain morphine tablets each."

Brandenburg wrote out the ticket with a flourish. "That'll be ten dollars. What date shall we use? I'm supposed to keep a record of each prescription, but . . ." His voice trailed off and his mind seemed to wander. "Oh . . . I'm too busy."

The agent made another visit sometime later and requested another prescription.

"How much this time?"

"A hundred half-grains."

After a third visit, Brandenburg was arrested, and despite the overwhelming evidence we had against him, his conviction was reversed in the U.S. Court of Appeals and he was granted a retrial. Found guilty and sentenced to five years, two more than he was given on the original conviction, the doctor appealed to the Supreme Court, and went free on bond while awaiting the decision.

Then a New York newspaper announced still another angle of Brandenburg's practices:

Abortion Mill Raid Catches Physician to the Underworld

New York, Sept. 4—Dr. Leopold Brandenburg, once known as the "physician to the underworld" because of some of his clientele, was charged with criminal abortion today following his arrest in a raid on an alleged assembly line abortion mill in the Bronx.

Police said the fat, tall, 61-year-old doctor was the brains and chief surgeon of a syndicate that netted $500,000 in illegal operations annually.

Four others were taken into custody yesterday and questioned about the operations of the "Rose Ring."

The ring got its name by using a rose as a countersign. Tipsters would steer pregnant women to a member of the ring. Each woman would be instructed to wear a rose pinned to her dress as identification.

The rose badge would enable the women to get an operation for which fees of $200 to $400 were collected, police said.

He had just completed an operation on a woman in the Bronx apartment when he was arrested.

The raiders allegedly found Brandenburg counting money on a kitchen table on which he had performed three operations.

Dr. Brandenburg was convicted in New Jersey in 1946 for criminal abortion and was sentenced to from four to five years imprisonment, to run concurrently with the sentence imposed as a result of the narcotic charges, and fined $1,500. In addition, Brandenburg's license to practice medicine was revoked by the New Jersey State Board of Medical Examiners.

Dr. Oedipus, unlike Dr. Brandenburg, was not a jack of all trades. His one specialty was narcotics, and he dispensed them not for money but for merchandise. In one month alone he issued sixty-five prescriptions for more than 1,000 grains of morphine. In less than nine months he issued three hundred scripts for over 9,000 half-grain morphine tablets.

One of our agents posing as an addict agreed to give the doctor merchandise in exchange for a prescription. Marked merchandise was used and Oedipus was quickly arrested. During the trial it was revealed that Dr. Oedipus' morbid acquisitiveness was directly related to the strange attachment he had to his mother, long since dead. Her body was kept in the local mortuary because he could not bear to think of her being underground. It was because of her, he told the court, that he had gone into medicine. He had wanted to help alleviate suffering in the world. Instead, forgery and the illegal dispensing of drugs had been his lot.

His state medical board revoked his license, but less than two years later it reversed itself and put him back in business again, chiefly because Dr. Oedipus had been quickly paroled after his conviction. But an investigation conducted soon after showed that he was no longer dispensing narcotics. Perhaps he learned his lesson. However, one wonders, if his mother's body remains in the mortuary.

One of the most fantastic "doctor" cases in our files is that of Howard L. Groves of Royal Oak, Michigan. Groves, a blond, personable, twenty-five-year-old faker, never went to medical school, yet he served on the staffs of four hospitals, delivered numerous babies, diagnosed scores of cases, assisted in countless major operations, performed autopsies and prescribed medicine without ever being questioned by hospital heads of colleagues.

"Doctor" Groves, who was actually a radio repairman, held a 4–F Selective Service classification which explained why, during the early years of World War II, he was not in uniform. But it was a time for uniforms; nearly one American out of every fifteen had on some kind of service suit. It was only natural that Groves, the "Great Pretender," should have posed in his spare time as an ex-army colonel and one time flight surgeon of the famous Flying Tigers.

1943 found Groves in a private hospital in Detroit as a laboratory technician, a task which required no great skill. He read medical books for a month and a half then, because he wanted to be a doctor right away, was fired. He took himself to another Detroit hospital and posed as a third-year medical student from Washington University in St. Louis, specializing in X-ray. This time he managed to learn something about the job. Perhaps his conscience got the better of him, because he quit and returned to the job he knew best—repairing radios. Two years later, again posing as a third-year student, Groves turned up at a Flint, Michigan, hospital where he made blood counts, urinalyses, tested blood smears and throat cultures. This was the place where Groves started down that long road to addiction.

Unable to sleep one night because of a pain in his leg, he took some Dilaudid, one of the most powerful narcotics available. "I liked the effect of it," he said later, "and I began to take it regularly." Before long Groves switched to morphine, but he had to write fake prescriptions for the patients who had no way of knowing that he was using the drug for himself. Sometimes he stole quantities from the hospitals where he worked.

At still another Flint hospital, Groves assisted in surgery. Perhaps considering himself well trained now, the affable young man drifted over to Windsor, Canada, and somehow became the house doctor of the hospital there. He diagnosed cases, prescribed medicines, attended childbirths and performed autopsies. He also perfomed appendectomies, hysterectomies, leg amputations, gall-bladder removals and skin grafting.

By July, 1945, Groves, now a hard-shell addict, returned to Flint and took over the offices and patients of a physician too ill to practice. Groves took the doctor's diplomas from the walls, pasted his own name over his predecessor's, took them to a photo offset shop and had copies made. The original names, he explained to the printer, had been inscribed in Latin, but he preferred English. He displayed the copies prominently in his new office.

The practice was surprisingly profitable, aided no doubt by Groves' charm, of which he had a great deal. Before long Groves owned not only a fine car but an airplane too. It was said that after only three hours of dual-control flying he was able to pilot the plane alone. During his unbelievable career Groves bought no less than three planes, and although he never held a pilot's license he was considered by flyers who flew with him to be an expert pilot.

Without a doubt Groves was some kind of untutored genius.

Meanwhile an unusually large number of prescriptions were flooding the drug store of William Benton of Flint. Suspicious, he reported Groves to the Bureau of Narcotics. Upon investigation, it was learned that Groves was not registered with the Bureau as required by law, and that the registry number he was using was in fact assigned to a Detroit druggist. Groves somehow learned of our inquiries and hurriedly left home, leaving his baggage in storage. Four days later, when the storage company received a request to send his baggage to the Billingshurst Hotel in Detroit, agents waiting for just such information wired Detroit and Groves was taken into custody.

By this time Groves was taking 12 to 14 grains of morphine a day.

There is no record of the number of patients who may have died or were crippled as a result of his fraud. When federal judge Frank A. Picard of Bay City, Michigan, sentenced Groves to two years in prison, he warned him not to pose as a doctor while there. Unable to resist the urge to practice surgery, Groves attempted to cut his way out with a hacksaw, but was caught and given an additional year to serve.

Groves was a phoney who might have been an asset had he been reached in time. Obviously he was in some way mentally unbalanced. But the doctor who practiced in an Oklahoma town, a trained, genuine, practicing physician, over a two-year period bought and shipped to people he didn't even know, 122,000 morphine tablets and other opium derivatives. He was not unbalanced, but crooked. This gross violation was repeated by doctors in St. Petersburg, Florida, and in Medford, Oregon. The doctor in Medford sold hypodermic injections of morphine in his office. These doctors had their licenses lifted and were given heavy fines and sent to jail for long terms.

Doctors are not immune to the tricks resorted to by clever and desperate addicts. In Russell, Kentucky, a woman named Laura Light brought a seventy-year-old man to a doctor's office and introduced him as her father, a victim of cancer. Actually the man suffered from hemorrhoids and was not related to Miss Light at all. The doctor prescribed pain-killing morphine at each of several visits. It was Miss Light who was taking the drug, the old man turning over the prescription to her upon her usual payment to him of five dollars per visit. When the old man died, Laura found another old-timer who looked something like him. Apparently the doctor did not notice the deception and continued to write the prescriptions. So many of them were coming through—362 scripts covering nearly 19,000 morphine tablets—that we ordered an immediate check, and upon completion of the investigation, arrested Miss Light. She was given probation on the condition that she enter the U.S. Public Health Service Hospital at Lexington and remain there until her addiction was cured.

Of course, all doctors have not been traffickers or dupes, not by a long shot. Dr. Lawrence Kolb, former medical director at Lexington, was one who for a number of years devoted a great deal of time to the study of the addict. He explained that the treatment fell into three main groups—abrupt, rapid, and slow withdrawal of drugs. "About 20 per cent of any large group of relapsing addicts will truthfully tell you that they have had many treatments and that at some time during their addiction they have, without assistance from physicians, kicked the habit at home, showing, of course, that the process is rather simple. Addicts with strong habits and even those who are mildly addicted react very differently to withdrawal treatment.

"Some will suffer uncomplainingly. Others, especially certain temperamental individuals or those whose desire for treatment is not strong, will whine and complain bitterly as soon as they begin to feel restless or uncomfortable. Some vomit, are very restless, and have mild twitchings or other symptoms showing that they are going through severe withdrawal, but will tell you that they are doing very well.

"Others who have scarcely any objective symptoms of discomfort will complain bitterly, especially if they feel there is a chance that the physician in attendence will give them morphine or give them more than he has been prescribing."

Dr. Kolb's opinion was that "any treatment that has as a part of it the withdrawal of the opiate, will effect physical cure of the addiction. A large proportion of the treatments that have been advanced cause more suffering and more danger to the life of the patient than abrupt withdrawal. The treatment of choice, based on present knowledge, is rapid withdrawal in fourteen days or less, supplemented by certain supportive measures."

The person, once addicted, can find no easy way out; he comes off or stays on, increasing his dosage more and more, for his tolerance becomes greater, his habit more expensive. Unethical practices by doctors only worsen the condition. Today, the cases we are forced to make against doctors are few and far between; this was not so a quarter of a century ago. Proof of the constantly improving relationship between the medical and allied professions is the number of citations they have issued the Bureau.

# 16 JAZZ AND JUNK DON'T MIX

Billie Holiday, the lady of the white gardenias and boxer pups, of *Travelin' Light* and half a hundred other heart-breaking songs, was arrested by agents of the Bureau of Narcotics and charged with violation of the federal narcotics laws in Philadelphia. She was then twenty-nine and had been addicted for four years. The Associated Press reported her sentencing May 28, 1947:

### SINGER CONVICTED AS DRUG ADDICT
#### Negro Blues Soloist Victim of Parasite Gang

Sober-faced Billie Holiday, Negro blues singer, was on her way to a federal institution today as the aftermath of a sordid tale of narcotics addiction unfolded in U.S. District Court.

The attractive singer, who sobbingly testified she "guessed" her earnings last year were between $40,000 and $50,000, was sentenced to the federal Reformatory for Women at Alderson, W. Virginia on a criminal information filed by Assistant U.S. Attorney Joseph Hildenberger.

Hildenberger declared, however, that Miss Holiday was the victim of the worst type of parasite imaginable.

"They followed her around," Hildenberger told Judge J. Cullen Ganey, "and charged her $100 for dosages of narcotics that cost ordinary buyers only $5 or $10. She made a quarter of a million dollars in the last three years and all of it is gone," he added.

The tall, slender singer, visibly moved, confirmed Hildenberger's statement. She declined counsel, stating that she wanted to plead guilty and be sent to a hospital.

Judge Ganey told Miss Holiday, in imposing sentence of a year and a day yesterday, that the government was going to give her "benevolent" treatment at the reformatory. In return, the jurist said, Miss Holiday must cooperate to the fullest extent with federal agents in their efforts to track down the source of the heroin supply she was receiving.

"Don't hold out on those who are trying to help you," Judge Ganey told the tearful Miss Holiday.

Joseph Bransky, head of the Federal Narcotics Bureau in this area, made a plea for Miss Holiday, telling Judge Ganey that unless she is isolated from those who got her into addiction, "she doesn't have a chance to break herself of it."

Federal narcotic agents told the judge Miss Holiday was arrested in New York last Tuesday on a tip from the Chicago office. She recently completed a two-week engagement at a local theatre.

A million words have been written about Lady Day. She told her own story as well, with certain embellishments, but the true sorrow of her life is in the lines of her testimony to the court in that fateful month of May before sentencing by Judge Ganey.

Q. You are advised of your constitutional rights. If you do not care to make a statement, you do not have to. Is that clear?

A. (Miss Holiday) Yes, that is clear. What do you want to know?

Q. What is your name and how old are you?

A. My name is Billie Holiday, and I'm twenty-nine years old.

Q. When were you born?

A. On April 7, 1918.

Q. Did you attend school?

A. Yes, in Baltimore.

Q. Are you married?

A. Yes. To James Monroe, in California. We are separated.

Q.    When did you begin to use narcotics?

A.    Three years ago.

Q.    Under what circumstances?

A.    You know how show business is. Always looking for a thrill.

Q.    What kind of narcotics did you use?

A.    Heroin caps. In Washington.

Q.    How much did it cost you?

A.    $50, $100 or $75.

Q.    Did you take it by the dose?

A.    Yes, three or four times a day when I needed it.

Q.    After every performance?

A.    Whenever I felt like I needed it.

Q.    When you left Washington, where did you go with Joe Guy? [She had been arrested with Guy, a trumpeter, and James Asendio, her manager.]

A.    All over the country.

Q.    Five months ago you went to California. What did you do there?

A.    I made a picture—*New Orleans*.

Q.    During the making of the picture, were you using narcotics?

A.    Yes, Joe Guy gave me it three or four times a day, whenever I needed it.

Q.    How much did he sell you and how did he sell it?

A.    Always in packages. He had to get the stuff for me by the doses. About fifteen caps during the day.

Q.    Do you know from whom he purchases the narcotics?

A.    No.

Q.    Was he driving around the country as your husband?

A.    Yes. He said he was my husband. I said no.

Q.    What is Jimmy Asendio to you?

A.    He wanted to be my road manager.

Q.    Do you know James Jordan? Did you at any time purchase narcotics from Jordan?

A.    No.

Q. During your stay in Chicago, was Joe Guy there? At your hotel?

A. Joe Guy was in Chicago, but I don't know what hotel.

Q. Did Joe Guy give you any narcotics?

A. Yes, about $300 worth.

Q. In whose possession were the narcotics and equipment kept?

A. Mine.

Q. Where did you keep them?

A. On my person or I hid them someplace.

Q. Did Guy hold the stuff sometime?

A. Yes. He would administer heroin into my arm.

Q. Did you take the cure before you went to Chicago?

A. Yes. At the Park West Hospital in New York. Doctor Gilbert was attending me for four weeks.

Q. What did it cost you?

A. $1,850, and in about three or four weeks I was cured.

Q. After you left the hospital, how long were you off the stuff?

A. About a week. Later Joe Guy came to see me and he wanted money. I gave him $150 and he bought the stuff.

Q. What did he buy?

A. Cocaine or heroin.

Q. Did he tell you from whom he made the purchase? Where were you living?

A. No. I was living at the Braddock Hotel in New York at 126th Street and 8th Avenue.

Q. Did he administer the heroin?

A. Yes.

Q. When did you take the engagement at the Earle Theatre in Philadelphia?

A. On May 9, 1947.

Q. When you left New York, who accompanied you?

A. Joe Guy and Asendio and the driver of the car.

Q. Did you stop at Morristown?

A. Yes, to pick up Bobby Tucker. [Tucker, a pianist, was a witness.]

Q. Did you have heroin in your possession?

A. No. Joe Guy had it; quite a bit. Fifty caps I guess.

Q. How much did you pay him?

A. $200.

Q. Did he administer the narcotics to you?

A. Yes, at 17 Cleveland Avenue, Morristown, in the home of Bobby Tucker's mother. I went with Joe Guy into the bedroom. In the bedroom I took the package which was wrapped in a nylon stocking and he administered a dose to me. Then we went to Philadelphia.

Q. Where did you stay in Philadelphia?

A. We stopped at the Attuck Hotel at 6 A.M.

Q. Under what name did you register?

A. I did not register. Asendio did that.

Q. What room did you have?

A. Number two, with Joe Guy.

Q. Where did Tucker and Asendio stay?

A. Room number seven.

Q. You had room number four also. Is that right?

A. Yes. Jimmy Asendio had a girl friend.

Q. After you registered, when did you have your first performance?

A. Rehearsal at 8 A.M.

Q. Did you have a dose before rehearsal?

A. Yes, I had a dose before rehearsal from Joe Guy.

Q. Did you keep any heroin in your dressing room?

A. No.

Q. From May 9th to the 15th, was Joe Guy with you all the time?

A. Well, Joe left on Wednesday and I left on Thursday when the show closed.

Q. When Joe left, who carried the heroin for you?

A. Asendio. He knows I was a narcotics user. He saw Joe give me an injection. And I also know that he uses cocaine.

Q. How do you know that?

A.     He sniffs it in his nose.

Q.     Do you know where he keeps it?

A.     I saw him use cocaine and he always kept it in his room.

Q.     Do you know what was said when Joe turned the heroin over to Asendio?

A.     He told Jimmy to keep the stuff away from me and only give it to me when I felt sick.

Q.     Did Jimmy administer it to you?

A.     No.

Q.     After your first performance at the Earle, what did you do?

A.     I took a dose and then wrapped the stuff in a stocking along with two needles and a black spoon. I then gave it to Asendio to hold for me. There were ten empty caps and sixteen full ones of heroin.

Q.     What did you do then?

A.     I told Asendio and Tucker to pack my clothes. I then went to the restaurant to get my food. I then parked. I sent the driver out and he said there were detectives in the apartment. I drove to New York with the driver and the dog. He drove me to the Hotel Crampton. I paid him $35.

Q.     Did you try to communicate with Asendio and Tucker in Philadelphia after you came to New York?

A.     Yes, my manager, Joe Glaser, called Philadelphia.

Q.     Did you meet anyone?

A.     Yes. I met Joe Guy.

Q.     How many doses did he give you?

A.     Four doses of heroin for $90.

Q.     When did you open at the Club 18?

A.     On Friday, May 16, 1947.

Q.     How many times did Joe Guy visit you in your dressing room?

A.     Three times a day.

Q.     When you were placed under arrest in front of the hotel as you were going to your room, number 32, you were told

by the manager that the key was gone and that Joe Guy
was in there. Is he occupying the room with you?

A. No.

Q. Are you afraid of Joe Guy?

A. No, but he's always sick and needs money.

Q. During your acquaintance with Joe Guy, how much did
you spend for narcotics?

A. About $10,000 to keep me under the influence of heroin.

Q. Is there anything else you'd like to say?

A. No.

Q. You can correct any part of this statement you wish. Is that
clear?

A. Yes.

Q. You have given this statement of your own free will and no
promises have been given to you. Is that correct?

A. Yes.

Billie's cure at Alderson didn't take. Soon after her release
while fulfilling an engagement in California, she was arrested for
attempting to dispose of a quantity of opium, but was found innocent. Her attorney was the famous criminal lawyer, Jake Ehrlich.
Once George White called me from the Coast to advise me of
Billie's presence.

"Is she clean?" I asked.

"No."

"Then you'll have to bring her in."

When White appeared in the clubs where she worked and requested a number, she would sing it for him. We thought that
by 1950 we had her again when her driver was found to have 317
grains of heroin in his possession. He claimed that Miss Holiday
had no knowledge of his activities and he was sentenced in a
state court. We were sure that Billie had a firm and loyal friend
in the driver, loyal enough to do the time for her.

Our information was that she was a constant user of heroin and
as a result was moving into the shadows. She had slipped from
the peak of her fame; her voice was cracking. Trying to regain

the pinnacle of her success, she went to Europe in 1958 and had some minor trouble with us because she had failed to register upon her departure and return according to the provisions of the Narcotic Control Act of 1956. The Act aided us in keeping a check on users going abroad for the possible purpose of obtaining drugs and smuggling them back into the States.

In Europe, along the French Riviera she had, it was reliably reported, some of the most pleasant moments of her shattered life.

Then it was 1959. Behind her now was her last major concert appearance at Town Hall in New York. The host of agents who at one time or another had had contact with Lady Day—George White, Nick Surrell, Joe Bransky and others—had no inkling when she collapsed in her apartment on May 31st and was carried to Metropolitan Hospital, that she would never leave it alive. She staged an amazing comeback and the music world and well wishers generally were delighted. While she was on the comeback trail, someone smuggled cocaine to her and an alert nurse saw the powder on her nose. This resulted for a time in the stationing of a police guard. Billie died on July 17; for her there would be no more "Good Morning Heartache."

Jazz entertainers are neither fish nor fowl. They do not get the million-dollar protection Hollywood and Broadway can afford for their stars who have become addicted—and there are many more than will ever be revealed. Perhaps this is because jazz, once considered a decadent kind of music, has only token respectability. Jazz grew up next door to crime, so to speak. Clubs of dubious reputation were, for a long time, the only places where it could be heard. But time brings changes; and as Billie Holiday was a victim of time and change, so too was Charlie Parker, a man whose music, like Billie's, is still widely imitated. Most musicians credit Parker among others as spearheading what is called modern jazz.

Primary investigations were completed on Parker, on June 15, 1948. At noon, agents John Cusack and John Boxhill went to room

342, Dewey Square Hotel, in New York, the residence of Parker and his wife, Doris. Only one week earlier, agent Daniel Belmont had received word that Parker and four other musicians engaged at the Royal Roost, on Broadway, were all addicted. It was felt that since leads on Parker had been followed for two months, he would be the likely man to implicate his four colleagues, if they were dealing with the same peddler.

As they were questioning Parker, the agents found, on top of a small table, sixty-seven empty capsules, two syringes, three hypodermic needles, one spoon and one empty glassine envelope which contained traces of heroin. Parker admitted ownership of the equipment and said that he had been using narcotics for the past several years, but that he had never been addicted. He got his supply, he said, from the many peddlers in the neighborhood of 112th Street and Fifth Avenue.

Agents Cusack and Boxhill arrested Parker and took him downtown. When the facts of the arrest were presented to the United States attorney for the Southern District of New York, he declared the evidence insufficient. Parker was released.

Nevertheless, it was evident that Parker was an addict. There was no indication that he was being supplied by a large combine. His addiction began not in 1944 as he claimed, but when he was a teen-ager in Kansas City, at that time a place where criminals almost openly carried on a brisk trade in illegal narcotics and booze. It is said that one of Parker's most famous records was made while he was under the influence of heroin. After the recording he collapsed and was sent to Camarillo State Hospital in California.

Only thirty-five years old, Parker died on Saturday, March 12, in the Stanhope Hotel on Fifth Avenue. Billie Holiday had been forty-one. Because of persistent rumors about his death having been caused by an overdose of heroin, and because a congressman requested an investigation, we went out again.

We questioned the doctor who had twice been summoned to the apartment where the musician died. Then we talked to a newspaper editor and the New York City assistant medical examiner who listed the cause of death as lobar pneumonia. An examination of the intestines revealed no traces of narcotics. Baroness Pannonica de Koeningswarter, in whose apartment Parker had died, was questioned at length, but again there was nothing to substantiate the rumors that the musician had died from an overdose of drugs. The story of Parker's death was reported three days later in *The New York Times*:

CHARLIE PARKER, JAZZ MASTER, DIES
A Be-Bop Founder and Top Saxophonist
Is Stricken in Suite of Baroness

Charlie Parker, one of the founders of progressive jazz, or be-bop, died here last Saturday night.

The news of the death of the noted musician, known as "Yardbird," spread quickly last night through Tin Pan Alley where he was affectionately referred to as "The Bird." A virtuoso of the alto saxophone, Mr. Parker was ranked with Duke Ellington, Count Basie and other outstanding Negro musicians.

Mr. Parker had appeared several times in Carnegie Hall and had played in Europe. More than five years ago the Broadway jazz hall at 1678 Broadway was named Birdland in his honor.

Mr. Parker died while watching a television program in the apartment of the Baroness de Koeningswarter in the Hotel Stanhope, 995 Fifth Avenue. He had called on the Baroness last Wednesday on his way to Boston to fill an engagement. The Baroness, who is 40 years old, is the former Kathleen Annie Pannonica Rothschild of the London branch of the international banking family of Rothschild. She and Mr. Parker had been friends for many years.

Disturbed by Mr. Parker's appearance, the Baroness called Dr. Robert Freymann with offices in the hotel. He urged the musician not to drive to Boston and advised him to enter a hospital immediately. Mr. Parker refused, but the Baroness persuaded him to stay in her suite until he recovered.

At 7:30 Saturday evening Dr. Freymann found Mr. Parker in satisfactory condition. Forty-five minutes later he collapsed and when the physician returned Mr. Parker was pronounced dead.

Dr. Freymann, who notified the Medical Examiner, attributed death to a heart attack and cirrhosis of the liver. The body reached the Morgue at Bellevue Hospital about 2 A.M. Sunday. Last night

Chief Medical Examiner Milton Halpern said an autopsy had disclosed death was due to lobar pneumonia. . . .

Trumpeter Chet Baker, at twenty-three and twenty-four, topped the jazz polls as the world's best jazz trumpeter, and then he stuck a needle in his arm and started downhill. "From being the fastest-rising jazzman in the business, I became the world's best-known junkie. Police, medical authorities, the customs men of a dozen countries, Interpol, the FBI [I think he means the Narcotics Bureau] and the British Home Office all keep watch on me."

Baker was little more than a boy when Billie Holiday was tried and convicted in 1947. Growing up, he listened not only to Lady Day, but to the greatest phenomenon in jazz at that time, Charlie Parker. Baker's first success came with his singing "My Funny Valentine," a song whose poignancy matched his vibratoless, retreating voice. His trumpet playing was also distinctive, breathy and slurred.

Like Parker, Baker began smoking marijuana at an early age. He observed other musicians taking the hard stuff—cocaine, morphine, heroin. He listened to their skills fade and disappear. He saw them crumple from human beings to whining wrecks whose minds were plagued with but one thought: *get some junk!* He kept away from the hard stuff until 1956.

That was the year when his drummer, Dick Twardzik, died in Paris from an overdose of heroin. Completely shaken by the experience, Baker, instead of retreating from it, ran head-on into it; he "went on."

Since then, he said in an interview with the British publication, *Today,* "I have pumped enough dope in me to kill a quarter of a million normal people. . . . My arms have been punctured more than thirty thousand times to get morphine and heroin into my veins. Why? Hadn't Charlie Parker, one of the greatest jazz talents America has ever produced, been an addict? Couldn't I, too, be a genius with the intravenous aid of narcotics?"

Baker had never been around when Parker said that drugs never helped anyone to play better. Eventually Baker realized that himself. "If there is a short cut to complete musical fulfillment, drugs don't provide it. They're a short cut to the nut house and the grave."

Wise words indeed, but—as always—too late. Like many musicians who feel they will have easier access to drugs, Baker at this writing is in Europe. Billie Holiday and Charlie Parker paid the supreme price for their addiction; there is no doubt that being addicts made them too weak to fight off the sudden illnesses that carried them off. What about Baker? Will he collapse some day on the Via Veneto, in St. Germaine, and go the same way? Time will tell.

What can time tell about the woman I shall call "Princess Livia"?

She had been in our files for three years when, aboard the S.S. *Constitution*, Charlie Siragusa came to know more about her. It was July, 1958, and the ship steamed over calm waters to sweltering New York City. Siragusa was coming home from Rome with his family, and he was spending the last of the ten days' trip relaxing in a deck chair.

"Mr. Siragusa?"

Siragusa looked up. "Yes, how do you do?"

"I'm Mrs. Caldi. I learned who you were through your son."

Siragusa invited Mrs. Caldi to sit down and she began her story. She was the wife of a doctor and lived in an expensive suburb of New York. She was concerned with a new neighbor of hers, a woman called Princess Livia, who was reputed to be a member of an old and prominent European family.

What was there about the Princess that disturbed Mrs. Caldi?

First of all, she didn't believe the Princess was genuine; none of the other neighbors believed it either. Second, a lot of strange people visited the Princess' home at odd hours; many of them played jazz music until early in the morning. The Princess held frequent, loud parties in her $60,000 house. What was so strange about the visitors? Siragusa wanted to know.

Some of them looked like seamen, she said, and many of them were Negroes. She said this last hopefully, as if she wanted Siragusa to agree with her immediately that something strange indeed was going on.

Instead, he asked if Mrs. Caldi had reported the disturbances to her local authorities. She had, she said, and a detective had called at her home. She had given him the license number of a Cadillac sedan she had observed at the Princess' home. A few days later the detective returned and said that the Cadillac was registered in the name of John White, a known narcotics trafficker with one conviction against him.

Now Siragusa sat up.

Mrs. Caldi continued, saying that at first she thought the Princess' home was being used as a bordello but, since it contained only two bedrooms, could not possibly have handled all the traffic. She had since reached the conclusion that as John White was often on the premises, the home was being used as a center for narcotics distribution.

Even though there was something of just plain feminine curiosity here, and even jealousy, Siragusa was intrigued by the news of John White. Perhaps there was, after all, the specter of a large narcotic ring in the making or one still unknown. It was this that led him to ask Mrs. Caldi if she could make available to the Bureau a room of her home for use as an observation post.

We knew that the Princess was here on a permanent visa. Considered a patroness of jazz, she had indeed come from a distinguished family and lived in considerable affluence here, supported by her divorced husband.

She stood five feet six inches tall, somewhat on the plump side, with dark hair and eyes, and pale skin. Some people thought her attractive in a strange way; others considered her ugly. During one previous contact and investigation of her, many allegations were made as to her connections with the illegal narcotics traffic in

New York. None could be proved. It was established, however, that many of her friends were or had been addicts. She admitted that, years before, she tried to smoke opium, but felt no reaction and from that time on had no interest in narcotics.

The stake-out of the Princess' house revealed nothing, but in October, three months after Siragusa's first meeting with Mrs. Caldi, we learned that Princess Livia and two musicians had been arrested by the Delaware State Police.

En route to Baltimore where they had an engagment to fill, and accompanied by the Princess who drove her car, a Rolls-Royce, the group had stopped at a Delaware motel. The owner asked them to leave the premises. One of the Negro musicians refused and, becoming belligerent, insisted on staying. From the distance of time and place, I would hazard a guess that the motel keeper had refused the trio accommodations; two Negro men and a white woman constitute grave problems in Delaware, one of the first states to throw up opposition to the Supreme Court decision of 1954, outlawing segregation in the schools. The innkeeper summoned a state trooper.

When he arrived, the trooper asked the Negro, who was raging back and forth across the motel grounds, for identification. The musician, a pianist, refused, then went to the car and got in, joining the Princess and the other musician, a saxophone player. The trooper warned that he was going to call for assistance. The trio sat in silence. When the trooper went to his car to put in the call, the Princess drove off. The trooper quickly hung up and sped after them, finally forcing them to the side of the highway. This time he removed the keys from the Princess' $19,000 automobile. Highly incensed, the pianist cursed him roundly, and was told he was under arrest. At that moment four other troopers arrived and the pianist was told to leave the Princess' car. He refused, and the five state police officers advanced upon him and pulled him bodily from the vehicle and shoved him into one of theirs.

At the magistrate's office he was charged with breach of the

peace, assault, and resisting arrest. The Princess and the saxophonist had followed the troopers to the office. Needle marks were
found on the pianist's arm. They were asked to submit to
a search of the car. The Princess agreed. Now, the pianist had
come to our attention before, during an investigation involving
the late Charlie Parker. The evidence against Parker was not considered complete and he was dismissed. That evidence had mentioned the piano player and implied that he was an addict.

The troopers pulled the luggage out of the car. In one suitcase,
within a box, they found a quantity of marijuana. Asked where
she got it, the Princess said she had found it in her yard and, not
knowing what it was, had pulled it up so that her doctor could
examine it. The troopers nodded sympathetically and then charged
all three with violating Delaware state narcotic laws. A hearing
was set for the following day.

The trio secured the services of a Philadelphia attorney and
were freed on $5,000 bail each. They continued on their way to
Baltimore. Meanwhile the District Supervisor of the area where
the Princess lived was advised of the arrests and of the Princess'
statement about the marijuana. An agent was quickly dispatched
to her home and a thorough search proved that no marijuana
grew there.

After a six-day continuance, the hearing was set for October
21, at Newcastle, Delaware. The pianist was not present. En
route to Penn Station from his home in Manhattan, he collapsed
and was taken to a sanatorium. The Delaware police verified his
presence in the hospital by teletype and charges against the
pianist were held in abeyance. Princess Livia and the saxophonist
pleaded not guilty to the narcotics violation and were continued
in $5,000 bail.

There the case hung fire. The musicians—the pianist had recovered—continued to work, and the Princess carried on as the
Patroness of jazz, but no one was quite sure what her patronage
consisted of.

# 17 *THE WOMEN*

In contrast to women like the Princess, there are some like the
Nurse, whose name can't be disclosed because she could be called
up before the Nursing Board for disclosing confidential information. And there is Rita, who must also be nameless.

The Nurse came to us out of indignation and jealousy. Nevertheless, her help was of great value to us.

For a number of years she cared for a former United States
Senator in his Washington home. He had become addicted to
morphine through careless medical practice. The attending doctor
became frightened when it was apparent that the Senator's need
for the drug was not strictly medical. The doctor realized that
he would have more trouble than he needed if he continued to
supply the morphine. He discharged himself.

But soon after, the Senator himself made contact with the
underworld, and was able to obtain a regular supply of heroin
from a connection in New York. The Senator had become
dangerously addicted; it often required two shots just to settle

him down. His condition proved highly profitable to the connection, the wife of a New York City bondsman. She charged the highest prices, cashing in on the ever-present threat of blackmail. When the bondsman and his wife went on short vacations, they called the Nurse to tell her where they could be reached in case of emergency. Emergencies were frequent, and the wife made the journey to Washington dressed in mink, expensive dresses and jewelry.

Now, the Nurse worked long hours, mostly on her feet; she was entrusted with the most valuable property under the sun—life. Sometimes no pay seemed enough for the tasks she had to perform. I think I can understand why she eventually became envious of and infuriated by the tony, dope-peddling woman from New York. More than that, the Nurse was genuinely shocked at the woman's greed, the cold-blooded way she took advantage of the Senator's condition and position.

Owing perhaps to his addiction and plagued by the worry that his awful secret would eventually become known, the Senator died. That was when the Nurse first made her appearance in the Bureau offices and told of the connection. She was mad. Why should she work long hard hours at respectable work and have nothing to show for it, while the crooked doll from New York reaped the harvest from a life of crime? "If it's the last thing I do in this world," she told me, "I'm going to put that dirty, rotten, blackmailing bitch in prison."

"Will you set up this woman for us?" I asked.

"With pleasure!" the Nurse said vindictively.

We had a rather distinguished-looking agent whom we fixed up to look like a Southern gentleman. We booked him into an Alexandria, Virginia, hotel as a patient of the Nurse. As instructed, the Nurse called the "blackmailing bitch" and told her that the Senator had died, probably from an overdose of heroin. She now had another patient, she went on, a Southern colonel who needed heroin just as much as the Senator had. Immediate delivery was necessary as the colonel was suffering withdrawal pains.

The connection refused to make any deliveries in Virginia, saying that the courts were too tough there and if anything happened she wouldn't know her way around. She wanted the Nurse to move the patient to Washington where she could make the delivery without too much trouble. If anything happened in the District of Columbia, she wouldn't have to worry, she said; either she or her husband could take care of things.

When the conversation was reported to me, I wasn't surprised at all; that's the way Washington was. We moved our colonel to a hotel on Pennsylvania Avenue. The Nurse called the connection again and told her the move had been made and to bring about $7,000 worth of heroin. The amount the colonel seemed ready to pay for heroin startled the woman; her greed knew no bounds and she was in Washington in about three hours. I had taken a personal interest in the case and was outside with one or two agents when the woman entered the room. As she came out, I grabbed her handbag. "Our dough's in there, and it's as hot as a sheriff's pistol," I told her.

She fussed and fumed and stamped her foot and shook her mink until we identified ourselves; then she shut up. She asked only to be booked and refused to give her name. She wasn't worried, she said, during the booking; she could take care of everything. Damned if she wasn't right. She went to trial after being out on bond, and got a six-month suspended sentence. That stuck in my throat for a long time. The Nurse was fit to be tied. She came storming into the office screaming, "If that's the way the feds want it, good-bye and to hell with all of you!"

It was my opinion and the Nurse's that the woman should have got a far stiffer penalty. At that time the District of Columbia didn't have a mandatory minimum penalty for trafficking. Peddling was an easy business, and suspended sentences were the rule of the day. With the passing of the Boggs-Daniel Narcotics Control Act in 1956, however, pushers in the capital get the highest average sentences in the United States, which is usually about seven years.

A second-generation Sicilian, Rita saw her father, a greengrocer who had resisted extortion by the Mafia, gunned down in the street. Without fanfare or being asked, Rita dedicated her life to rooting out crime. Small, with piercing dark eyes and an unusually good figure, Rita refused many offers of marriage and secured a position in a big law enforcement office where she quickly learned a great deal about the underworld. Detectives, assistant U.S. attorneys, deputy sheriffs and other law enforcement officials passed in and out of that office and Rita filed away in her mind everything she heard or saw. Her specialty was the fugitive from the law. She turned up many of them for us. She was trusted by people on both sides of the law, but she herself worked only for justice. All her information came to me directly and sometimes, but not very often, indirectly.

When Tom Dewey was searching for the fugitives of Murder, Inc., Rita fingered the number two man of the combine, who was posing as the president of a phoney goldmining outfit in Denver —a man with so much influence that he played poker regularly with judges of that city. Another tip she gave us on the same gang resulted in the arrest of a hood who thought that operating a hardware store in northern California was disguise and distance enough.

Rita also bailed us out of another of those nasty border hassels with the Canadians. The RCMP were after a man named Pinkus, charged with narcotics conspiracy. They accused us of heel-dragging, since the man was loose somewhere on the Eastern seaboard. The fugitive's attorney had been in contact with an assistant state's attorney; we reported this to the Canadians and assured them that we were doing everything possible to help them get their man, but we were obliged to move according to the processes of the law. Then Rita delivered a bombshell. There was an unusual tie-up between the fugitive's lawyer and the assistant state's attorney; that's why they seemed always in conference. She had overheard a conversation in the office of the state's attorney concerning the validity of Canada's claim on the fugitive and surmised that Pinkus was not far from the attorney. She warned me that the attorney would call to check the extent of our interest. When he did, I told him that Canada certainly did not have any further interest in the fugitive, so neither did we—which was a lie. As soon as I hung up, I dispatched some of our agents to call on the young state's attorney that very evening. They found Pinkus in the attorney's apartment, reading the paper. He was extradited to Canada at once, convicted and given a sixteen-year sentence. The next time I saw the young state's attorney, he avoided looking me in the eye; needless to say, we always had our eye on him.

Rita's knowledge was sometimes uncanny. She once led us to a fugitive we had crossed off our list. When she called, he had taken another name, owned a string of horses and was a big-time gambler. Rita advised us that if we visited a certain track at a certain time, not only could we pick up the man but some of his associates who were wanted also. Her information was accurate, as usual.

We had also been searching for a man who had been peddling great amounts of morphine throughout the Southeast, bragging that he could supply the drug to anyone in any amount desired. He vanished. Rita told us he could be found in Panama. All we found, however, was a body that had been washed up along the banks of the Panama Canal with cards indentifying it as Dr. Albert C. Timbs. This was not our man; we wanted Dr. Riley C. Hammers, who had jumped a $10,000 bond while awaiting trial for violation of the Federal Narcotics Laws, and who remained a fugitive for over a dozen years. His violations extended over almost twenty-five years and at one time he supplied seventy-two addicts on a weekly basis.

As a matter of routine the fingerprints of Dr. Timbs were sent to the FBI. Then we discovered that Timbs and Hammer were the same person. Rita had been right again.

The underworld would like to get its hands on Rita. They'd like to know where she lives, where she works, how she spends her spare time, if she has any relatives against whom they can take reprisals. But the identity and whereabouts of this fearless woman will never be disclosed.

Molly Wendt worked the other side of the fence.

Young, beautiful, crafty, she was the daughter of the Minister of Justice of the Communist party regime in Manchuria. She was bored with life, considered it utterly wasted until an international gang which had bilked the Riviera casino tables of hundreds of thousands of dollars settled in Shanghai.

The gang was made up of various European nationals, men and women. They had operated in the Continental casinos, dressed in black ties and tails, the women in the latest fashion, all of them exceedingly well-groomed and poised. One man would station himself near the roulette wheel, the others at the opposite end of the table. At some point during the evening, the group would commence to argue loudly. The argument would reach fever pitch; even blows might be exchanged. During the ensuing disorder, the lone member near the roulette wheel would substitute a ball containing a magnet for the original ball. The substitute could easily be broken in half. When order was restored, the loner would ask to see the ball and, upon getting it, promptly break it open, "discovering" the magnet. With great indignation and anger, the member would shout that the casino was crooked. In order to preserve the reputation of the establishment, the management would pay off handsomely. When the French police caught on and began to make arrests, the gang moved to Shanghai.

This kind of sophisticated group was precisely what Molly required; it was she who organized these experienced con men and women into a world-wide narcotic smuggling syndicate.

No rear-rank general, Molly herself accompanied several trunks filled with heroin from Shanghai to California. She made several trips before she was arrested by customs agents. Her booty represented the largest catch on the Pacific Coast in ten years. Working frantically against time, agents held her incommunicado for several days in order to check on communications to her. They would give us her contacts, points of delivery or pickup. Any court in the land would castigate us for holding an arrested person without speedy referral to a magistrate. We had to take the chance —and it paid off. A Polish count, a member of Molly's group, living in Havana, sent her a telegram. We notified Cuban police, who had him bound for New York under guard the next day. Our agents were waiting for him with a warrant, but it was never served. The count had hanged himself, suicide being preferable to Molly's wrath.

In the meantime we kept close watch on the "Dragon Lady" in her hotel room. Molly claimed she had bladder trouble, and for that reason was always going to the bathroom. One morning she went and stayed a long time. Her guard became suspicious; there had been no answer to his knocks. He broke in the door, to find that Molly had gone. An open window told the story. The mob had rescued the boss.

All points of departure were carefully screened. The Secretary of the Treasury, who followed the case with extreme diligence, ordered her arrest within forty-eight hours, or else. Outgoing ships were carefully searched. A day slipped by, and half of another. Agents were ready to give up when a customs guard remembered that a young Chinese girl wearing sun glasses had boarded a ship at seven in the evening. After the vessel left, it occurred to the guard that sun glasses and twilight didn't mix. (Today we'd have trouble; people wear dark glasses even at midnight.) A Coast Guard cutter was dispatched to overtake the liner. Molly only smiled when the agents came aboard. In some ways she was a stoic, or maybe she was just a patient young woman.

When she was sentenced to five years in Alderson, West Virginia, she disclosed nothing about her operations or the people in it. Even though we had the handsome Molly Wendt behind bars, we had to start from scratch, piecing together what information we had and hoping for the best.

We could tell when we were on the right trail because someone invariably committed suicide. A German member of Molly's ring had mixed bamboo slivers in his food. The slivers caused a horrible, agonizing death by puncturing holes in the digestive tract. The man was found stretched across a grave in a Shanghai cemetery; he had learned that the Chinese police, at our request, were going to take him in for questioning. Other members of the group killed themselves by equally bizarre methods.

In Mexico City, the son of a former Paris police commissioner who had handled the Paris end of Molly's business, cut his throat. Pinkus, one of the fugitives Rita led us to, leaped to his death from the third tier of the Montreal prison, rather than be questioned about Molly Wendt.

We kept reaching dead ends filled with dead bodies, and so, after a year of that, I went to visit Molly at Alderson. I hoped she would be cooperative so we could break up the ring. And I was personally curious to know what power she held over her associates who preferred suicide to being apprehended. I did most of the talking. I worked my way through her operations from Shanghai to Japan and California. Every time I came to a crucial part—"Who else was involved in that city?" she would say, "Excuse me, please. My bladder," and would be away ten minutes. I talked about Cuba and Europe, but every time I got to the important questions, she excused herself. She went to the bathroom three times that afternoon, twice for ten minutes and the third time for twenty. When I left I told the superintendent that Molly was not entitled to any consideration when parole time came around. She served her full time and was deported. She must be pretty big in Red Chinese circles by now.

As indicated earlier, the South used to have a great narcotics problem; it was also a hotbed of bootlegging and continues to be so today. But I want to set down the statement of an addict from the South. Her name is Jane and her statement is all the more grim for being so listless and apathetic. It was not that Jane didn't care; the last lines of her statement told us that she did. She just couldn't help herself.

My name is Jane ———. I am married and live with my husband in a little house on ——— Avenue, just back of the landlord's house. We have been living in this house about two weeks. Prior to that we had a room at ——— Street.

At one time I was a waitress at the Kentucky Home Boarding House up on ——— Avenue. When working there I used to spend some time at the Golden Sun bar.

While my husband and I were living at ——— Street, I met a man whom I later knew as Slim and who Mr. Raithel [a narcotics agent] just told me is Donald Mathieu. I had previously seen him hanging around the ——— and he asked me if I didn't use junk (he had seen the scars on my arm) and I said yes. He asked me how would I like to have a shot and I told him I could use one. He asked me if I had any money and I told him yes. He then told me to come on with him and we walked over to a house with a porch in front, and a green rocker on the porch. When we got to this house Slim told me to wait on the porch and watch for the landlady while he went into the house and fixed me up a shot. I sat in the green rocker and waited while he went inside. He wasn't inside very long. He came to the front door and said "Come on," and I went into the house with him. We went to the second door left (I'm not sure of this, but I think it was the second door) and we both went into the room. On the dresser was a dropper and a hypo needle, there was a liquid in the dropper and a beer top or Coca Cola top that he had used to cook the shot in. After we got into the room Slim said, "There it is, give me a dollar and a quarter." I handed him $1.25 and he then picked up the outfit and shot the contents of the dropper into my left arm, just above the wrist.

I used morphine for about four years prior to Christmas, 1936, at which time I kicked the habit myself. This was the first dose I had had since I got cured, and I know from the action and the way I felt that he had morphine in the dropper that he shot me with.

After I took this shot we got into a conversation and Slim told me that if I would buy morphine from him every day, he would let me have the shots for a dollar. I told him I'd see if I could get the money. The first shot I got from Slim was about three weeks ago. After I got this shot we went to the front door and Slim told me to go out first and if I wanted to see him at anytime, he was always at the Golden Sun bar. I left and then I got worried for fear that I would get the morphine habit again. In fact, I told my husband that I thought it would be best if we moved entirely away from that neighborhood because I had met a dope peddler and I was afraid I'd get on the habit again if we stayed down there. That was when we moved out to the house in which we are now living.

The first shot Slim gave me made my face turn red and Slim got scared because he thought he'd given me too much. But I told him it'd be all right. That's why I got scared and wanted to get away from that neighborhood. After we moved to our present home, I stayed around the house and didn't go downtown for about a week. About a week ago, I went back to the Golden Sun bar for a beer, and after that I dropped in almost every day. Several times I saw Slim in the Tommie restaurant across the street.

On Friday afternoon, I met Slim just across the street. He came up, asked if I wanted to see him, and I asked him where we would go and he said he didn't know. I told him that I knew a girl who lived on —— Street. Her name was Dorothy. While we were walking over there we met a policeman and I asked Slim if anybody knew he fooled with it and he said, "No." We went over to Dorothy's place; she was home. I introduced him to Dorothy. I didn't know his name, so I called him Jimmy, Sammie or something. Slim said something about wanting to fix some dice and went into the bathroom. He closed the door and was in there just a short time when he called me. As I started into the bathroom he came out and told me to hook the door in case someone came in. The dropper and needle were lying on the washbasin and I took a shot. It was morphine. After I came out of the bathroom we both told Dorothy good-bye and left. As we were going down the hall I gave Slim $1.25. This was when he told me that if I would buy from him every day the price would be a dollar a shot, but he wouldn't let me carry any away. While we were walking down the street I told Slim that I would want a shot the next day and he told me to meet him at —— Street. He had a name pad in his pocket and he wrote it down.

On Saturday morning I went to the little place called ——. It was nine o'clock. I had a Coca Cola. Slim came in and drank beer. Then we walked away together and went over to my house. He came in with me. My husband wasn't there when we got there. On the way to the house I told him I wanted a shot and he told me he would fix it at the house. He went into the bedroom and cooked up a shot, using a beer bottle cap to cook it in. I saw him cooking up the shot and put it into the dropper. He shot it into me in my left arm and it raised a lump on my arm. I paid him a dollar for this shot and he left, but before he left, we made a date for another time. He would come to the house and fix me up, if my husband wasn't home.

On Sunday—today—shortly before ten o'clock, Slim came to our house. I was in the kitchen and my husband in the bedroom. I was standing at the door and motioned for Slim to come in. He came into the house and asked if my husband was home. I told him yes. Slim said he wouldn't do it with anybody there; he told me to meet him at the place where I met him yesterday in thirty minutes. He left the house. About ten minutes past ten, I left home and walked until I saw Slim and crossed the street to meet him. He told me to come into some brush there and he would fix me up. I stood out on the street while Slim cooked up a shot behind the bushes. After he cooked it up he called to me and I went in. About 15 feet from the street the brush is pretty heavy, so we couldn't be seen from the outside. Slim had the shot ready and he shot it into my left arm. It was morphine that he shot me with. While we were still there he told me that it was a "good big bang" and I told him I would give him $1.25 for it. I opened my purse in which I had five one-dollar bills which I had gotten from my husband. It was on the table in a box we keep our rent money in, and I took it out. I paid Slim for the shot. He told me he was short and didn't have any stuff and asked if I would lend him another $1.25 and I did. I gave him two quarters and two dollar bills. I left him and walked down the street to my home where I was later arrested by officers.

I am making this statement of my own free will without promise of reward or immunity, solely because I want the true facts to be known and, too, I don't want anything to happen to my husband who is a hard-working man and doesn't know anything about dope except what little I have told him. [Signed] Jane.

Sometimes addicts find themselves so far gone that, with the supreme, almost superhuman effort they turn themselves in, not waiting for the law to catch up with them and bring shame to their families. Mrs. C. was such a person.

She appeared in the Minneapolis office of the Bureau and expressed a desire to be committed to Alderson for treatment.

District Supervisor O. A. H. de la Gardie knew of the thirty-eight-year-old Mrs. C., and knew that she had had the advantages of a good education, wealth and refinement. As shabby as she was when she presented herself, there could be no mistaking her good breeding. She was now a common prostitute trying desperately to earn enough money to support her habit.

She had been addicted to morphine for fifteen years and, although she received treatment on about ten occasions, she had always suffered relapses. Some of the "cures" were taken in private institutions, but most were merely incidental to her incarcerations in local jails for various petty offenses which she had hoped would get her enough money to pay for her drugs. Prostitution seemed the surest way to make a buck and she had been engaged in that for some time.

Mrs. C. expressed the opinion that she did not think an addict could be rehabilitated unless restrained in an institution for at least one year. The matter was discussed with assistant United States Attorney George Heisey who was willing to extend his cooperation. However, the federal grand jury was not scheduled to convene for another two months and Mrs. C.'s condition was critical without drugs. It was decided to permit her to enter a plea of guilty to an information alleging the concealment of morphine in violation of the Narcotics Drugs Import and Export Act.

Accordingly, Mrs. C. appeared before a U.S. District judge, read and signed a waiver in open court to all rights under the Fifth Amendment to the Constitution, pleaded guilty to the concealment of morphine on the previous day, although there was no evidence of this other than her own testimony, and was sentenced to serve a year and a day at Alderson, and to pay a fine of one cent.

The legality of the law was most certainly involved here. But also involved was the life of a woman who through her own experiences knew that her salvation lay in what she asked from us. We could do nothing more than admire this courageous step and help her, although we wished the law could have provided a better answer.

Since this particular section has been devoted to women, the question might arise: Do we use woman agents?

The answer is no.

Why not?

We do not believe they can stand the tough going, no matter how rugged they think they are and no matter how much time they have spent in the WAC. However, we do hire female special employees or informers.

Malachi Harney's opinion, expressed in his book *The Informer in Law Enforcement,* is that a woman informer may prove extremely valuable simply because she is regarded by the hoods who surround her as a "part of the scenery." Important matters are discussed before her which the hoods would not think of talking about in front of their friends. Harney is also impressed by the ability of women to remember details.

Once won over to the law, the female special employee proves loyal. But Harney also warns of the dangers of a protracted relationship between an officer or an agent and the female informer, citing that once, many years ago, he asked the superior of one of his officer friends what had happened to him. The superior remarked that officer Smith had to be let go. Harney was surprised. The superior assured him that it was not for anything criminal. "We had him assigned on an undercover job in Pennsylvania with a female informer," the superior explained. "Some farmer complained to the state troopers about unusual goings on at night in his orchard. The troopers made a patrol down a lonely road—and there was Smith, with his female informer. He said he was obtaining information."

Sometimes our agents show remarkable initiative, finding

women informers who have not been authorized by the Bureau. They usually say that they *thought* the women had been authorized. We have to tell them, sadly, no. Even the authorized informers can be very difficult to handle in undercover work; why look for excess trouble?

# 18 A FALLEN IDOL AND AN IMPOSTOR

"Roger Crattle" was a well-loved man. Millions of Americans knew him; he was a tough, warmhearted guy—a professional boxer, a light-heavyweight. He had fought the best and was a champion. It was said that his right cross, traveling only six inches, could put a man down and out for fifteen minutes.

Crattle's story began long before we came to know him. When we entered the picture his days of glory in Madison Square Garden, the Cow Palace, Comiskey Park and other arenas were already behind him. But when he was introduced at fights and swung himself up through the ropes, bouncing lightly on his feet, the cheers lasted minutes on end.

For us, Crattle's story began the night he stepped from the glare and noise of Times Square into a drug store. He moved, still lightly, on the balls of his feet toward the prescription section and handed the pharmacist a piece of paper; it called for Dilaudid, five times more powerful than morphine. The druggist looked at the script; it seemed to be in order. One thing bothered him, though: it was *too* legible. Still musing, he went to prepare the drug. When Crattle had gone, the pharmacist called a friend who was a narcotics agent. "I've got a forged script here," he said.

"How can you tell?" the agent wanted to know.

"I can read the writing."

"Come off it. Have you looked up the doctor, or called him?"

"What's the point, the man's gone now. Why don't you call him?"

The agent came in for the prescription and called the doctor whose name appeared on it. The doctor existed, but he had never made out a prescription calling for Dilaudid for a man fitting the description of the forger. He would only recommend Dilaudid in rare cases anyway. The agent checked other drug stores in the Times Square area and found that a number of druggists had accepted scripts from Crattle. They were asked to notify the Bureau the next time the addict came in and to delay him as long as possible without arousing suspicion. It had been confirmed that every one of the scripts was a forgery.

Inevitably, Crattle did appear and a druggist called us. Agents were at the drug store within minutes. At that time we did not know Crattle's name, although he looked familiar.

He was brought downtown to our New York offices. He seemed relieved.

How long had he been addicted?

A long time, before he went into service in World War II.

How had he got on?

Nutsing around and before he knew it he was hooked.

It was sad listening to him. His way to the top of the boxing heap had been rough. Born on the lower East Side, he learned early how to take care of himself; he had to. He anglicized his European name. Kids idolized him. Play-fighting in the streets they told one another, "I'm Rogie Crattle."

How many prescriptions had he written and passed, where did he steal the pads from?

He had passed scripts all over the country and had swiped the pads from various doctors.

As much pity as we felt for him, Roger Crattle had violated the narcotic laws. We went into a huddle and the U.S. attorney agreed to hold the charges in abeyance if Crattle went voluntarily to Lexington. This decision was influenced by the presence of a few newspapermen outside the office who had recognized the boxer. It was felt that here was an excellent chance for the government to show its humane side. The decision made, the attorney stepped outside and announced to the reporters that Crattle had come of his own free will for help in fighting his addiction. This was the information that was so widely published. We received a great many letters commending us for our decision. As a rule, if we can find a reason to help an addict who has no criminal record and who is sincere in trying to kick his habit, we give him every break. The rest is up to him. But should an addict run afoul of the local police who now maintain under their jurisdiction more addict-possession cases, he finds another problem. This is not to say that local police cannot be as generous as the Bureau, but the Bureau can afford to be generous because its scope lies far beyond the single addict; it wants the big peddlers whose stuff has seeped down to him. Local police are concerned with local crime and they must call the shots as they see them.

Crattle went down to Lexington and became a problem right away. He was still considered a celebrity and was always surrounded by inmates, who secretly may have enjoyed his fall from grace. Addicts tend to be jealous of those who are able to kick the habit and very often urge them back on. And when a celebrity is picked up as a user, the ordinary addict then can think that he has done nothing very bad himself. Crattle basked in the adulation, but it upset the chief medical officer. "Can you get this guy out of here?" he asked me. "Discipline and morale are going to hell because of him."

However, the doctor had no choice but to enforce the discipline of the hospital, Roger Crattle or no. Discipline became so strict that Crattle decided that it was time for him to leave. He contacted me and told me he was going out; but I warned him that under the "Blue Grass Law" he could be picked up at any time and sent to jail instead of a hospital. Any Lexington patient who skips the hospital while under treatment is subject to this law. Pressure from us and his family made the ex-boxer reconsider. Any wise person would have chosen the few months' treatment Crattle had remaining to the year in jail.

After his cure and release, we learned that Crattle was hitting the bottle very heavily. This was the sure road back to addiction. The quickest way to get over a roaring drunk is to take a shot of hard stuff; it straightens you up pretty fast. We did not know to what extent he was becoming readdicted; we knew only that he had fallen again into old patterns. A lone wolf, he prowled about, taking in movies, walking the streets and sitting in bars. He seemed to be avoiding his wife and family. Crattle was odd. Even though he was often alone, he told me that if there was one thing he liked it was being with people, yet he felt uncomfortable with them.

He decided to write a book. When it was completed, his agent came to me and let me go through the manuscript. "What's this?" I said. I had come to a part of Crattle's autobiography in which he claimed to have become addicted as a result of being wounded in the Solomon Islands with the Marines during World War II.

Now, every Navy hospital corpsman attached to a Marine combat unit has a registered number of morphine syrettes. The corpsman has only to remove the protective plastic tip and insert the needle in the arm. The syringe is rather like a short, blunt toothpaste tube. The dosage is enough to kill pain for certain kinds of wounds; combatants with head wounds, for example, never get morphine. Afterward, the marine is given sulfa powders (that's what was available during a great part of World War II) and removed at once to the rear for surgery. I cite all this because Crattle implied that corpsmen handy with the morphine syrettes were responsible for his addiction. Navy corpsmen are among the best nonprofessional medics in the world. It was unlikely that Crattle could come by his addiction at their hands. Secondly, I reminded the agent, the boxer had told us that he had been addicted before the war.

The agent said, "Well, we put it that way in the book to make it a dramatic story. Does it matter how he got it? The fact is that he's over it."

"It's not fair to the Corps and it's not fair to his admirers who're not going to like him so much when this lie comes out. That's what it is—a lie, not drama."

But the book was published and Crattle became a greater hero than ever. Once more he was looked up to and invited into the ring before a major bout. He was asked to speak at banquets and such. We kept quiet, as we usually do. Crattle seemed to be coming along all right, although once I warned him about hitting that bottle.

We still count on this man. We put a lot of blue chips on him and so far he's paid off well. As for his big lie, it was obvious that, unlike many, he regretted very much that he had ever been an addict.

The "Reverend Father André" was a much bigger liar; he lived his lie night and day. He tried to pass himself off as a Roman Catholic priest when, in reality, he was a minister—and not a good one at all—of a splinter sect.

This is how we first came upon the man known originally as Reverend Father André:

Pasquale Moccio and four other defendants were on trial in New York for various violations of the narcotic laws. As the trial progressed, a priest identified only as Father André appeared in presiding Judge Bicks' chambers to plead for Moccio. Later it was made clear that Father André had made his move because only one witness had appeared against the defendants and Father André believed his testimony not strong enough to withstand a plea from him. The priest was a tall, handsome, soft-spoken man with sparkling black hair. He spoke eloquently of Moccio's character, his two children and his family background. After listening to him, Judge Bicks said that the presence of the clergy could not and would not in any way influence his decision; the merits of the case were his sole concern. After a three-week trial Moccio and his associates were found guilty and Moccio was sentenced to five years and fined $10,000.

Between the time of conviction and sentencing, Father André had telephoned Judge Bicks and insisted once more that Moccio was a devoted husband and father, and that a prolonged separation from his children would cause them undue psychological hardship. André told the judge that Moccio's children went to his parochial school. Judge Bicks replied that he chose to be merciful toward the other children in the school in preference to Moccio's, in view of the nature of the crime he had committed.

At the time Father André first appeared in court, agent John Cusak contacted the Chancery of the New York Archdiocese and spoke to Monsignor Nash. Cusak believed that Father André wanted to take the stand as a witness for Moccio, and he wanted to advise the priest of this fact. But Monsignor Nash told the agent that he did not know the priest and that it would be hard to trace him. The man could be of any Catholic order, stationed anywhere in the city. In any case, Father André had not cleared through Chancery, which all priests are required to do if they plan to testify as character witnesses.

Now it was believed that the young priest had been duped by Moccio and his hoods. When U.S. probation officer John Connelly began his investigation, Cusack asked that he also try to identify the priest and his parish. Later Connelly reported that when Moccio and his wife were questioned, they were evasive when asked about Father André. Mrs. Moccio, however, claimed that he was from the Holy Redeemer parish in New York.

But agents soon determined that there was no Father André at the Holy Redeemer parish, on Third Street in Manhattan. Father

André, that office reported, might be the one who was posing as a Roman Catholic priest and about whom some inquiries had been received. A few days later, agent Clifford Melikian spoke with Father O'Brien of the Chancery concerning Father André. It seemed that inquiries dating back to 1954 had been made about him. The most recent had come from St. Vincent's Hospital in New York, asking the name of the priest who had driven to the hospital in a flashy convertible and visited an unidentified patient. Double checking, the Bureau discovered that Moccio had suffered a heart attack about that time and had been confined to St. Vincent's.

Father O'Brien went on to state that a Father Nicholas Carlino of Little Ferry, New Jersey, knew an Andrew Penachio who was suspected of impersonating a Catholic priest.

Agent Melikian visited Father Carlino, who said he had had a casual acquaintance with Penachio in high school in the Bronx before World War II. For some reason Penachio looked him up at the time Father Carlino was about to be ordained. Some time later the New Jersey priest learned that Penachio had been expelled from a couple of Catholic seminaries because he was a homosexual.

Father Carlino further stated that he had heard that Penachio had been ordained as a priest or minister in a Protestant sect and that he had made two trips to Europe, but had no specific information about them. Describing Penachio as a very vain person, Father Carlino said that he had once worked as a model. Penachio always boasted about the celebrities and important politicians he knew, and how he used these relationships to further his personal interests.

Was it possible that Penachio could have served or was serving as a courier for an international gang of drug smugglers? It seemed within the realm of possibility, yes. Who would suspect a priest of carrying drugs on his person? Who would go through his luggage as though he expected to find something? We stepped up our investigation.

Penachio had lived at 205 East 82nd Street, but upon moving had left forwarding addresses for a post office box and the Liberal Catholic Church at Danbury, Connecticut. He also had listed the St. Thomas Apostle Liberal Catholic Church, 147 West 144th Street, New York, as a reference.

Judge Bicks and the United States attorney were both notified that Penachio was strongly suspected of impersonating a Roman Catholic priest. Judge Bicks told agent Cusack that he was very interested in the case and wanted to see Penachio immediately, if he could be found.

Almost a week later, agent Armando Muglia saw a priest who fitted Penachio's description. Muglia watched him enter the U.S. Court House and then notified agents Cusack and Melikian who, checking with the probation office, found Penachio conferring with Miss Evelyn Panella, a U.S. probation officer.

When Penachio came out of Miss Panella's office, Cusack told him that he and the other two men were narcotic agents and would like to talk to him. Penachio became nervous and wanted to know if the talk would take long. He was taken to the office of the special squad and served with a grand jury subpoena. After brief questioning, he was brought to see Judge Bicks.

The judge asked Penachio whether he had not represented himself as Moccio's parish priest and claimed that the defendant's children were students in his parochial school. Penachio admitted that he had asked the judge to consider Moccio's children before passing sentence, but he denied that he had ever said that Moccio's children were in his school. He denied even that he might have implied this. Judge Bicks insisted that Penachio had said those things. Penachio admitted knowing Frank Costello and of going to Judge McGohey's home on Costello's behalf just before the judge sentenced him for income tax evasion. Penachio also said he knew Vincent Mauro, number 291 on the national list of wanted persons. When he was allowed to leave, Penachio was warned that he was still under subpoena and would be directed to appear before the grand jury at a later date.

On the same day agents Cusack and Melikian questioned Ann Drakas in the presence of probation officer Panella. Miss Drakas was serving a term under probation for a check forgery. She said that Lola Polite of Bedford Street, New York, had introduced her to Penachio through one William Kersey, a homosexual. Kersey was described as an intimate friend of Penachio who had been trying to get Miss Drakas a job out of town. She could not take the job, however, being on probation. Penachio had told her that he had spoken to the judge and the judge had said it would be all right. Miss Drakas had not believed him. She also described him as vain and a homosexual who spent a great deal of time trying to impress people with his importance. He bragged about the famous people he knew and Miss Drakas gave the agents a number of photographs that had been taken of Penachio in the company of well-known people. One photo showed Penachio and Sharon Dumont. Miss Dumont was the paramour of Ralph Jiminez who had been convicted for smuggling large amounts of heroin into the United States from Cuba. She was working as a stripper in one of the clubs on West 52nd Street. Anthony Strollo (Tony Bender), Vincent Mauro and Pasquale Moccio managed numerous clubs in that area. It was believed that Jiminez worked with this group. It was also reported that Strollo was the actual owner of the San Remo bar in Greenwich Village, a place frequented by Penachio, and a notorious hangout for homosexuals and the Strollo mob.

One week later, agent Melikian interviewed Bishop James Roberts of the St. Thomas Apostle Liberal Catholic Church. Bishop Roberts said he had been consecrated a bishop in the church for the New York and West Indies territory several years before. He also said that Penachio, with whom he was familiar, was vain and boastful. He gave Melikian duplicates of the photos Ann Drakas had shown. The bishop said that Penachio had been ordained a priest in the Liberal Catholic Church in Hollywood in 1952, and that shortly afterward he came to New York to take up

an assignment at St. Thomas'. In the beginning he said mass a
few times and then disappeared.

Going through his records, the bishop found that André
Penachio was born in 1927 in Norton, Connecticut, and was married
to Josephine Polito of the Bronx. (Marriage of priests is allowed
in the Liberal Catholic Church.) The marriage ceremony was
performed by Bishop Matthews at St. Thomas'. Bishop Roberts
commented that he could not for the life of him understand why a
twenty-eight-year-old man would want to marry a forty-two-year-
old woman. Penachio left his wife after a year.

Agent Melikian asked Bishop Roberts the current status of
Penachio in the Liberal Catholic Church and was told that he
had resigned. Melikian took Penachio's letter of resignation.

It was now clear that Penachio's method was to avoid making
a direct statement that he was a Roman Catholic priest. His Italian
name, his dress, his attitude tended to make one believe that he
was a "Catholic" priest. He identified himself as a priest of the
Liberal Catholic Church only when pressed for indentification.
It was our opinion that he duped several people on behalf of the
underworld. In addition, before the investigations were completed,
information was received that a person described as a Roman
Catholic priest was allegedly delivering packages thought to be
narcotics to cities in the Midwest and West for the Moccio-
Mauro group. We also had reason to believe that Penachio was a
courier for transatlantic shipments of narcotics.

But when Vincent Mauro, Frank Caruso and the others were
caught, André Penachio was not among them.

Unlike Roger Crattle, Penachio seems to be living a lie. It will
catch up with him one of these days.

# 19 MOONSHINING AND COUNTERFEITING: STILL GOING STRONG

The Bureau of Narcotics is but one of twelve operating bureaus and offices under the jurisdiction of the Treasury Department. The others are: The Bureau of Accounts, Office of the Comptroller of the Currency, the Bureau of Customs, the Bureau of Printing and Engraving, the Bureau of the Mint, the Bureau of the Public Debt, Office of the Treasurer of the United States, the U.S. Coast Guard, the U.S. Savings Bonds Division, the U.S. Secret Service and the Internal Revenue Service.

The Alcohol Tax Unit of the Internal Revenue Service was established in 1933 to administer the production, warehousing and tax payments of distilled spirits, alcohol, wines, fermented liquors, cereal beverages and denatured alcohol. In 1952 the tobacco tax was added to the Unit's responsibilities and it was renamed the Alcohol and Tobacco Tax Division.

Earlier in this book, I discussed bootlegging, and now, toward the end, I find myself forced to say that bootlegging did not die with the repeal of Prohibition. Indeed, it flourishes today perhaps to a greater extent than it did even during Prohibition. At least fourteen states in the South have for many years had a record of vast amounts of illicit distilling, particularly in the mountainous sections. The distilling technique has been handed down from generation to generation.

These fourteen states comprise the area that makes campaigning presidential candidates shudder. It is known as the Bible Belt. Alcohol and Tobacco Tax agents have been the victims of more on-duty killings by lawbreakers than any other government agency, and they know first hand the inherent duplicity of the area.

Three Northern states—New York, New Jersey and Pennsylvania—while considered large-scale-operation areas, are easier targets for the Alcohol and Tobacco Tax agents because the illicit distilling plants are for the most part close to large urban centers.

Controlling the production of distilled spirits was first tackled by the Massachusetts Bay Colony in 1633, eight years after the first American saloon was opened in Boston. The first Internal Revenue statute assessed a distillery tax of 54 cents on every gallon of still capacity and seven cents for each gallon of whisky produced. That was in 1791. Three years later, a series of mass meetings of people from four western counties in Pennsylvania culminated in the Whisky Rebellion. Some 7,000 whisky makers or drinkers were involved, and President George Washington had to send out Governor Henry Lee of Virginia with militiamen to put down the protest. Liquor taxes are said to have paid one-third of the Revolutionary War debt.

Congress abolished internal revenue taxes in 1802, but quickly reinstituted them in 1813 to pay off the debt of the War of 1812. Five years later the taxes and even the offices were once more abolished. The Act of July 1, 1862, established the Bureau of Internal Revenue, and is the basis for the current tax system.

The Whisky Rebellion set the tone of resistance to taxes upon alcohol which exists to this day. The resistance may be aggressive or passive, a kind of apathy which bespeaks "an almost avowed tolerance of the bootlegger."

Faced with more and more illicit distilleries in Brooklyn, the U.S. Marines in 1869 were sent to destroy them. Citizens of the area beat back the vaunted Marines, whereupon the Army sent a force of some 800 men with fixed bayonets to disperse the mob. The Marines may sing about the Halls of Montezuma and the Shores of Tripoli, but they never boast about Brooklyn.

In 1871 Colonel George Armstrong Custer was ordered to wipe out moonshining in Kentucky. He had as much success with the 'Tucky moonshiners as he had in his famous battle with Sitting Bull five years later.

Long before Prohibition went into effect A&TT agents were tracking down bootlegggers in order to collect the taxes due the government. One of those agents was Jim Nelson, a product himself of the Southern hills. He had the tracking ability of an Indian and led many a raid on stills tucked back in the mountains where the moonshiners, when caught, said they were only making some "corn squeezins" for home use. The life of an A&TT agent in those days wasn't worth a penny. A man working on a case could be murdered and his body hidden so no one could find it, let alone prove that a murder had been committed.

Jim Nelson wasn't going to let that happen to him, and in consequence he managed to accrue about nine notches on his gun. Jim theorized that if you surprised a man his aim wasn't going to be too good. Most of Jim's shots were fired after the moonshiner had fired first. Jim took the first wild shot while turning his body so that it wouldn't be a wide target—his shoulders, body, arm and gun all on a single line—then aim and fire himself. He took such a heavy toll of moonshiners that after a while when a federal raiding party was making its way through the mountains, a moonshiner lookout would call out: "Hallo! Is Jim Nelson with you-all?"

If the answer was yes, the moonshiners called back: "Okay, we puttin' down ouah pieces."

Some of the stills would be found unmanned, the moonshiners having fled along those trails whose destinations were known only to the members of his family. In the beginning the agents simply dismantled the stills. But subsequent raids revealed that the same stills were being soldered together again and put back into operation. Then the agents began cutting the copper materials into strips and piling them up. One agent placed a note atop one such pile which read: "Fix this, you sonsabitches."

Completely wrecking a still in this manner not only ended the possibility of the manufacture of more illicit whisky, but saved lives. Lead poisoning was the invariable result of whisky made in stills which had been pieced together time and again, caused by the metal content mixed with the cooking whisky. Today the Treasury Department constantly warns that moonshine whisky often contains poisonous lead salts and that drinking it may result in death.

Today's liquor industry has mounted a great assault on taxes it has to pay. It admits that all tax hikes will have to be passed along to the consumer—who is already making up a large deficit which comes from the sale of untaxed liquor. For 1962, Americans tossed down over 252 million gallons of whisky; the industry said that one out of every five of those gallons was illicit. The government denied this.

Over and above the value of the dollar is the value of life. Prohibition proved that where the manufacture, transportation and consumption of illicit whisky was involved, crime flourished in many forms. The multi-headed dragon spawned by nontaxed whisky was greatly retarded during World War II with its rationing of sugar. Above all, moonshiners, big and little, require sugar to make their booze. By the 1950's, however, sugar was flowing freely and the government inaugurated the Mandatory Preventive Raw Materials Program in the South, which is still in effect. Dealers are asked to refuse to sell large amounts of sugar to known or suspected moonshiners. Before the program was adopted, dealers were asked to sell the sugar and report the sale right away. Known as the "Sell and Tell" technique, it didn't work very well.

Government enforcers often find it difficult to make headway against the manufacturers of "corn likker" and "white lightning" because of the connivance of local police officials with moonshiners, especially in dry states or counties. One acquaintance of mine, a reporter, visited a Mississippi town and met the sheriff. That officer pointed out the good and bad parts of the town, told the reporter what he could expect to get away with and what he would not be able to get away with, and finally showed him where he could get his regular supply of moonshine.

Moonshine is produced in all sorts of stills. A functioning still, no matter what size, consists of: a boiler, a head, a tube leading from the head to the condenser, another tube which supplies cold water to the condenser, a coil of copper tubing, called the worm, an overflow outlet, and another outlet to drain the distilled product.

The ingredients used are mash—usually a grain—water, sugar and yeast. A still can be small enough to work on a kitchen stove or large enough to require a vast building; agents have found all kinds and sizes. Each proof gallon of nontax-paid spirits defrauds the government of $10.50.

But for the efforts of the agents of the A&TT Division for the calendar year 1961–62, the government might have been defrauded of over $4 million through the manufacture and sale of illicit whisky. For that year agents seized over three million gallons of mash which would have represented an additional 249,869 gallons of moonshine had the seizures not occurred.

Moonshiners must have a fleet of vehicles with which to move whisky; A&TT agents captured over 2,500 trucks and cars. Upward of 6,000 stills were discovered and destroyed, and in all, $2,128,152 in property was captured in connection with the violations. Over 8,500 persons were arrested.

The A&TT's most important case, however, occurred in 1958. Known as the Nollie Garnet Cope case, swift action on the part of agents prevented the distribution of nearly 2,500 gallons of moonshine on the illicit market. Further, a 40-hp boiler, two 1,000 gallon tanks, 31,616 gallons of mash and another 2,460 gallons of booze, seven vehicles and over 300 cases of half-gallon fruit jars, nearly 5,000 pounds of rye, 3,000 pounds of sugar and miscellaneous distilling apparatus were captured.

Cope and Frank S. Davis headed this organization whose operations extended well into the eastern district of South Carolina and into the eastern and middle districts of North Carolina. The huge, unregistered distillery itself was put up near Myrtle Beach, South Carolina.

Actual investigation got under way on August 6 when officers of the A&TT, together with North Carolina ABC officers, followed a tractor trailer from High Point, North Carolina, to the vicinity of Myrtle Beach. The tractor earlier had been identified as the same vehicle observed stopping at a wholesale supply house in North Carolina. The truck halted at a welding shop where men later identified as Grady Lee Estep, the driver, and James C. Minter and William H. McDowell, loaded two steel stills into it. Still holding the vehicle under observation, the officers followed it to a Horry County farm not far from Myrtle Beach. Round-the-clock surveillance of the premises commenced and remained in effect until September 5. During this period, officers were able to identify the men at work in the area and the odor of mash in the air. With this and other evidence, the officers obtained a search warrant. But on September 5, officers on watch saw a trailer being loaded with what appeared to be cases of nontaxed whisky. Officers out along the highway were notified at once and they picked up the tractor trailer and followed it to Elizabeth, North Carolina, where Estep and Eugene Edward Kennedy were arrested after a search disclosed 2,454 gallons of illicit whisky in the trailer.

Officers still at the distillery premises were advised of the seizure of the truck and they then served the search warrant even as the distillery was in operation.

It was discovered that William Howard McDowell was also one of the leaders of this ring, which totaled eight men. Sugar for the operations was secured from Forrest, Mississippi.

Cope and Davis drew four years and $10,000 fines; Robert L. McDowell was sentenced to three years, as was Estep who was also fined $1,000. Robert L. Ellis was given a two-year suspended sentence, ordered on five years' probation and fined $2,000. Eugene E. Kennedy was sentenced to a year and a half and fined $1,000. William H. McDowell drew fifteen months and James C. Minter forty-two months, suspended in lieu of five years' probation to begin at the expiration of a previous sentence of thirty months.

The severity of sentences has deterred many moonshiners. Sentences up to five years are common for major violators. In one unusual case, a still was found in an abandoned Rhode Island textile plant. Many Northern textile plants have moved to the South for economic reasons. This was the first time a traditionally Northern industrial activity had been replaced by one traditionally Southern. The still was a 5,750-gallon twin-column unit, and was captured after it had been in operation only twenty-four days.

Another division of the Treasury Department with which we've worked on numerous occasions is the vaunted United States Secret Service.

Although it now has many duties, the Service was set up in 1865 with William P. Wood as its first chief, to ferret out abuses and offenses against the coin and currency of the land. For a long period the Service was the only general service investigative agency and various departments of the government borrowed its personnel to look into land frauds, lotteries, whisky rings, and to investigate espionage activities during the Spanish-American War and World War I. The Teapot Dome oil scandals and other violations of the public trust came at least partially under the jurisdiction of the Service.

When President McKinley was assassinated in 1901, Secret Service agents were then assigned at once to guard Theodore Roosevelt. Five years later funds were appropriated to provide protection for the President at all times, and in 1913 this protection was extended to the President-elect. Within four years additional protection was granted to the members of the President's immediate family.

The single, most important, most continuing job of the Secret Service, however, is the suppression of counterfeiting and alteration of currency, checks, bonds, stamps, coins and other obligations of the United States and other governments.

From 1935, when 5,500 forgery and counterfeiting convictions were lodged, the incidence of these crimes had climbed by 1958 to 11,000 convictions. These were not all federal convictions. Government convictions for counterfeiting totaled only 817 people from 1945 through 1958.

By 1962, when it was definitely established that organized crime was attempting to move into counterfeiting, 737 persons had been arrested for this offense, and 44 plants confiscated. The 737 arrests represented an increase of 23.9 per cent over the previous year.

There was an increasing amount of forgery involving government checks for 1962. Convictions amounted to 3,414, an increase of 15.1 per cent over 1961. Forged or stolen U.S. bonds accounted for 82 convictions and this too represented an increase of nearly 10 per cent.

While these figures may appear high and on the way to becoming even higher, the fact is that of every eight counterfeit bills made, seven were seized by the Secret Service before they could be passed. The Service has done a remarkable job of keeping ahead of counterfeiters.

One way was through the "Know Your Money" and "Know Your Endorsers" programs advanced by that inveterate cigar smoker, Frank Wilson. His programs contributed immensely to the suppression of counterfeiting and forgery.

The days are gone when crude, difficult-to-render plates produced counterfeit currency which could only be passed in poor light. The counterfeiter has a vast amount of technology at hand. The rapid development of the graphic arts, the high quality of available paper, all make it relatively easy for a man to go into the business of counterfeiting. These factors, plus the wide distribution available to organized crime, make it mandatory for law enforcement officials to be on their toes. The record of the Secret Service has been excellent in this regard.

A case in point, as a result of intensive investigation and surveillance, was the recovery of a million dollars in counterfeit notes in 1962. The recovery represented the largest domestic seizure in the history of the Service. This particular issue was controlled by a group with nation-wide criminal connections. Six types of notes were handled by the ring, which distributed them over the Eastern seaboard.

A new issue of a $20 counterfeit was traced to Cuba. It appeared first in July, 1961, and had come from America. These and occasional worthless $100 notes are taken from Cuban exiles who had converted their pesos into dollars before leaving the island. In 1961, $27,560 in counterfeit notes were confiscated from Cubans.

New Yorkers may remember that in 1961, merchants, bank tellers and anyone who accepted their money, paused and carefully examined $10 bills. Supermarkets had diagrams posted beside cash registers describing how counterfeit $10 bills could be recognized.

The bogus notes appeared in September, and although a dozen people were arrested almost at once, within a month the circulation of the phoney $10 bills had spread as far west as Ohio and Nebraska, as far south as North Carolina and Florida and into Massachusetts, Connecticut, and Rhode Island.

The distribution channels of the criminals helped the rapid dispersion of the issue. However, they get almost as much help from the speed of travel today. Counterfeit notes can actually be in circulation on both sides of the continent in a few hours.

With the government sending out more and more checks to veterans, social security recipients and many others, it is no wonder that check thefts and forgeries are on the increase. In New York a man and a woman admitted stealing and forging 340 checks over a ten-month period. They realized about $17,000 from their efforts, but when they were arrested they possessed only $10 between them. Together they had been nursing a $400-a-week narcotic habit.

Secret Service agents in August, 1961, followed a long trail of twenty-one stolen and forged Canadian Pacific Railway money orders. They went through eight states before they caught the thief, who had got into some additional trouble and was already cooling his hands in an Ontario jail.

The public lost a little over half a million dollars from counterfeiting in 1962, but three and a half million dollars was confiscated before it could be placed in circulation.

That big-gang counterfeiters were seeking a liaison with large narcotic rings was of primary interest to both the Bureau of Narcotics and the Secret Service. But the team work that has existed between the various Bureaus of the Treasury Department could be counted on to thwart any long-range plans of the criminals involved.

# 20 *THE PROSECUTORS*

By the end of the 1950's the Bureau of Narcotics, while still comprising but 2 per cent of the total federal law enforcement officers, accounted for 17.6 per cent of the federal prison population, an increase of 5 per cent over the previous decade.

Below are some examples of the work of the Bureau late in the 1950's and into the sixties.

During 1958, following an extraordinary undercover and surveillance operation by narcotic agents in New York, New Jersey, Pennsylvania and Virginia, a total of 17 kilograms of heroin and 1,347 grams of smoking opium were seized with the arrest of Anthony Napolitano, Anthony Tarlentino, Ignazio L. Orlando, Joseph Lo Piccolo, James Santore and Peter Casella. Subsequently, two other defendants, Vincent Todaro and George J. Nobile, were arrested in possession of over 16 kilograms of smoking opium.

During 1959, Vito Genovese, the number one criminal in organized crime in the United States, and fourteen of his associates were convicted of a conspiracy involving the smuggling of heroin into the United States from Europe. This group was responsible for bringing in at least 100 kilograms of heroin to New York, some of which was distributed to major cities throughout the country.

During 1959, undercover narcotic agents made purchases of large quantities of heroin from Sam Monastersky and Richard Mc-Govern. Investigation disclosed that Philip and Marc Antonio Orlandino were involved, and a later search resulted in a seizure from them of 11 kilograms of heroin. This group had been responsible for distributing heroin in New York and Chicago.

On August 15, 1959, an undercover agent bought one half kilogram of heroin from Carl Fiorito and Theodore De Rose in Chicago. Fiorito is known as a gangland assassin and principal violator of the counterfeit laws. Shortly after the arrests, William Skally, a government witness, was shot and killed in typical underworld fashion.

Following the conviction in 1958 of the infamous Louis Fiano in a federal court at Los Angeles, Anthony Marcella, a notorious trafficker in the Middle West, became Fiano's successor. On March 19, 1959, Marcella was arrested by narcotics agents after an investigation disclosed that he had been dealing in pound quantities of heroin and had sold enormous amounts in Los Angeles and San Francisco.

After a lengthy investigation in 1960, by narcotics agents in co-operation with the French and Lebanese authorities, a major conspiracy involving Mauricio Rosal, the Guatemalan Ambassador to Belgium and the Netherlands, was uncovered. At the time of the arrest almost 50 kilograms of heroin were found in the luggage which Rosal had brought into the country. Subsequent investigation resulted in the seizure of an additional 50 kilograms of heroin. It was later established that this group had been responsible for smuggling more than 100 kilograms of heroin a month into the United States.

Among the more important members arrested in 1960 for their activities in another conspiracy were Giuseppe Cotroni, Carmine Galente, John Ormento, Angelo Tuminaro, Rocco Sancinella and Angelo Loicano. Angelo (Puggy) Loicano had previously been a member of the Gagliano group (Chapter 9) and had served part of a sentence of from five to ten years. These defendants were the principal suppliers of heroin to the United States over a two-year period, during which time it is estimated they smuggled approximately 600 kilograms of heroin annually into the United States, mostly by way of Canada.

In 1960, in Omaha, Nebraska, an undercover narcotics agent made a purchase of evidence from Anthony John Biase which was determined to be part of a large quantity obtained by burglarizing a wholesale drug company. Biase is a well-known Midwest gangster who engaged in diverse organized criminal enterprises. While prosecution was pending, two of Biase's cohorts, Felix Ferina and Anthony Cardarella, attempted to murder a government witness by gunshot.

On several occasions in 1960, an undercover narcotics agent made purchases of heroin from members of a Chicago conspiracy which involved Armando Pennacchio, Michael Carioscia and William Wright. This group had distributed large quantities of narcotic drugs in the Chicago area and were dealing in quarter-kilogram and kilogram lots.

On September 3, 1960, a seizure of 11 kilograms of heroin was made from an organization of traffickers including Frank Borelli and Anthony DeGeorge. Borelli has been under investigation for many years by narcotics agents, and has been a persistent trafficker with far-reaching underworld connections. It has been known that his past activities in the traffic have involved participation with other top-echelon gangsters, and at one time he and four associates had assembled a complete laboratory and chemicals for processing morphine into heroin.

Not a single one of these cases—indeed, not any case cited in this book—could have been successfully brought to trial and convictions secured without vigorous and determined prosecution. For at the end of any criminal investigation stands the prosecutor, the man who must package the facts and present them to the judge and jury; he must hammer home what agents have laboriously gathered at great danger to their lives. This is not always an easy task, for the underworld, unfortunately, reaches into the jury room and sometimes even up to the bench.

James N. Sullivan was a prosecutor who was keenly aware of the minute ramifications of each case he handled. A prodigious worker (weekends were workdays to him) he had a trigger-quick mind. And he was honest. This was one of the many reasons why he was picked to head an additional grand jury investigating a bribery case which involved a former U.S. Commissioner of Internal Revenue and his assistant. He was also considered by the Treasury Department as the man best qualified to probe internal tax frauds and official wrongdoings. The delicacy and danger of such assignments were unlimited; should an inquiry be unsuccessful or should it misfire, change of personnel and the turn of fortune could subject Jim to severe retaliation. Another handicap was that on many of these cases Sullivan would have to be detached from his geographical supervisors, a condition which not only deprived him of advancement but made him extremely vulnerable. Sullivan never balked. He took most of his cases with a light heart.

A mess began immediately when he was assigned to the additional grand jury investigating bribery. Special assistants to the Attorney General, who were also assigned under Jim to the grand jury in Brooklyn, found that the local attorneys didn't always see eye to eye with the men from Washington, although they were on the same team.

The foreman of the jury proved to be eccentric and erratic.

The subject matter before the jury was of intense interest to a House subcommittee, and the administration of the then Bureau of Internal Revenue was trying to cooperate with it.

The zeal of the subcommittee was disconcerting; was it to be denied the information revealed before the grand jury? If so why, and who was responsible? Jim Sullivan walked a tightrope. He could have been cited for contempt by the grand jury or accused of bad faith and noncooperation by the House subcommittee. Bickering, headline-hunting, side-issues dragged in by runover heels, and jealousy sizzled like hot tar during the course of the investigation and hearing. Jim walked his tightrope, tossing alms to the subcommittee and to the grand jury, but all the while nailing down his case. He kept his poise and balance. Throughout the presentation of facts and the parade of witnesses, he held a steady course and finally, overcoming massive difficulties, secured indictments for income tax evasion against the former Commissioner of Internal Revenue and a former District Supervisor. He earned and kept the solid respect of all concerned. In addition to this triumph, Sullivan was the man who, laboring behind the scenes, laid the basis for indictments against criminals involved with a notorious Washington lobbyist.

Max Goldschein was appointed a Special Assistant Attorney General by Tom Clark, now a justice of the U.S. Supreme Court. Max was told to go after the mobs. The meeting between Goldschein and me was the start of a close association and a lasting friendship. Max holds the admiration and affection of the entire Bureau of Narcotics. At that meeting I outlined what I believed to be the greatest threat to the country, the association of criminals known as the Mafia.

A grand jury in Miami, to be attended by a hundred top criminals, from Don Francesco Costello down, was planned. Subpoenas were issued. The men involved in this vast dragnet stood poised. This was the moment many people in federal law enforcement had been waiting for. What was the point of knowing who the Mafiosi were if you couldn't bring them in?

And then we got instructions from higher authorities (not the Department of Justice) that under no circumstances would we be permitted to ask the criminals involved any questions about their finances, since some delicate investigations conducted by another government agency were under way. We had to limit our operations severely, although we could have pulled in at least fifty of the one hundred men to be questioned. Gone were the days of Elmer Irey when we could have pulled these hoods in via the income tax route. Of course, the "delicate investigations" were a dodge to call us off, and it succeeded. It was an angry and a frustrating time and it left a bad taste in the mouth.

We always wanted Max Goldschein to handle our toughest cases. Sometimes we had to wait in line, for he was assigned to prosecute all kinds of federal violations. Sometimes the cases were so steeped in rottenness, Goldschein even had to outwit judges trying the cases. For example, there was a case where local police were being tried on charges of corruption. It was no secret that the judge was very, very sympathetic toward the police department. The indictments were returned against the defendants about five o'clock one afternoon, in spite of the judge. On Goldschein's advice our men were sent out with warrants at once and the crooked cops were brought in to spend the night in jail. They were unable to make bond until the next day. The night in jail kept them from panicking and jumping bond as soon as they were indicted. Max had heard rumors.

Brought before the judge in the morning, the cops, after a night in the cooler to think it over, made the high bail Goldschein asked for. The judge, long on our suspect list, leaned over the bench and took Goldschein to task for the time of the arrests, stating that Max knew very well that they would have to remain in jail overnight when he issued the warrants. "Now, Mr. Goldschein," the judge said with a twisted smile, "that wasn't kosher."

Max glared back at him; he understood the nature of the crack as well as the nature of the judge from whom we tried to keep all our cases. An anti-Semite, by the very nature of his attitude, is anti-law, and this judge was supposed to represent the law, justice. I wish I could say that he is no longer on the bench; unfortunately, he is still there.

One of Goldschein's most important cases came in 1957 when he was assigned by the Department of Justice to make an official inquiry to determine whether there had been a violation of the federal statutes in connection with the disposition of $900,000 in union welfare funds. This was at the time when the large unions of the nation were coming under fire from congressional subcommittees.

Three years earlier, a number of investigations had been started to seek out alleged abuses of the welfare funds by union officials. A House of Representatives subcommittee was investigating in Detroit; a grand jury inquiry probed in St. Louis, and a Senate subcommittee was conducting hearings in Washington, also on the misappropriation of union welfare funds. During the course of its hearings, this subcommittee directed its attention to the Laundry Workers International Union (LWIU).

Composed of 65,000 members in eighty-five locals, the union in 1950 established a national welfare fund to provide limited accident, sickness, hospitalization, surgical and other benefits for its rank and file members. In an agreement with management, the union also agreed to set up a social security department to be managed by a board of trustees. The management was to pay $5 per month per employee, after a specified period of employment, to defray the cost of the program. In addition, a trust fund was set up pursuant to the Labor-Management Relations Act of 1947. It was comprised of six trustees, three from the union and three from management. The Social Security Department had been established to receive contributions from the trust fund.

Sam J. Byers, president of the international union, and Matthew Duley, attorney for the San Francisco Laundry Owners Association, were appointed chairman of the board and secretary-treasurer of the board, respectively, with authority to countersign all checks. These two men, the only members of the board of trustees at the time, selected the Security Mutual Life Insurance Company of Binghamton, New York, to insure all employee benefits except the death benefit, which was self-insured by the Social Security Department.*

The Harlan Insurance Agency of New York, owned by Louis Saperstein, served as the broker for Security Mutual Life. Saperstein had been elected by the (two-man) board of trustees as their agent for $1.00 per year. His precise function was to place the accident, sickness and hospitalization insurance with Security Mutual, and to handle the claims of the union members.

When the Senate subcommittee concluded its inquiry, it reported that there was a discrepancy of $900,000 between the records of the Social Security Department's payments of premiums and the premiums received by the Security Mutual Life Insurance Company which had received monies from Louis Saperstein's Harlan Insurance Agency.†

Further investigation revealed an account in the Merchants National Bank of Chicago in the name of the Laundry Workers International Union, of total deposits from Sept. 14, 1951, to May 6, 1954, of $776,917.37. Eugene C. James, Secretary of the LWIU, alone had the authority to draw upon this account. James was not a member of the board of trustees. Along with Saperstein, he was

---

* The Subcommittee on Welfare and Pension Funds in March and April, 1955, reported that between 1950 and October, 1953, the Social Security Department of the LWIU paid out $3,268,563.09 in premiums for group insurance to the Security Mutual Life Insurance Company to cover its union workers. This money was transmitted to the insurance company through the Harlan Insurance Agency of which Louis Saperstein, a broker, was president. This was done pursuant to a resolution of March, 1951, by the board of trustees.

† This was apparently accomplished by falsely reporting to the insurance company a lesser number of employees than was actually paid for by the Social Security Department.

subpoenaed to appear before the subcommittee. Both refused to testify, claiming constitutional privilege. No books or records were made available to the subcommittee. Also subpoenaed was Sam J. Byers, who did not appear. Instead, a letter from his doctors advised that, since Mr. Byers had a serious heart ailment, the excitement of testifying before the subcommittee could prove fatal.

This was indeed a case for Max Goldschein.

Had there been a violation of federal statutes in the disposition of the $900,000 in welfare funds? Certainly something smelled, especially since the key figures were copping out. We left it to Goldschein to find out what was going on.

Accordingly, he was assigned as counsel for a grand jury convened at the request of the Department of Justice in Chicago, in March, 1957.

A subpoena was issued for Eugene James; he was to bring with him when he appeared before the grand jury the books of the union showing the receipt and disbursement of all monies by him during 1952 through 1956. However, Treasury Department intelligence agents working with Max on the case, had a difficult time locating the evasive secretary-treasurer. One agent who spotted him was almost run over by his Cadillac, when he rushed up to serve the subpoena. When the agent reported the near miss, the entire group became determined to nail James before Monday morning; it was then Friday. On Monday morning James was located in a barber shop. To his surprise and chagrin he was served the subpoena while sitting in the chair, his face lathered up.

The grand jury had already subpoenaed the records of the Laundry Workers International Union and its Social Security Department. They filled an entire room of the U.S. Attorney's office and, though they were painstakingly examined, not once but several times, no information about the $900,000 could be found. On being questioned about the books and records which would show where the money came from and where it went, James said that in August, 1954, his office in the union hall at Chicago had been burglarized. His safe had been cracked and the books and precious records taken. A few days passed and it became apparent that James' testimony was not, to put it mildly, forthright. When his testimony was read back, the Court, Judge Barnes of the "old school," bearded, neat, firm but fair, exceedingly aware of the private rights of the individual and of the public interest and safety as well, was indignant and outraged. He ordered James to answer the next questions without evasion. Max Goldschein returned to the attack, nibbling away:

Who accepted the money? Who spent it? Who kept the books? Who made the entries? Where were the books really kept? What did they look like? Describe the safe. On and on; Goldschein was wearing James down.

The secretary-treasurer testified that after the police had made their examination of the robbed premises, he had sent the safe to the Mosler Safe Company to have them open one compartment the burglar had not been able to crack.

Max Goldschein snapped, "What was in that compartment?"

James took the Fifth Amendment.

The grand jury recessed for two weeks and Goldschein rushed to California to assist a grand jury there in another phase of the investigation of the LWIU. When he returned to Chicago, he was advised by special agent Harold Wallace that the superintendent of the Mosler Safe Company had said he did not have the power to discuss the safe James had left with him. Goldschein ordered a FORTHWITH subpoena *duces tecum* to the company, directing it to bring in all books, papers, canceled checks and other records removed from the safe.

That same afternoon two canvas sacks stamped "Federal Reserve Bank" were handed over to Goldschein. One sack contained contracts, by-laws and correspondence of the union and the other held canceled checks in the amount of $240,000, all signed by Eugene C. James, payable to Eugene C. James and endorsed by Eugene C. James. Goldschein then wanted to know how the Mosler Safe people had come into possession of the canceled checks. James, they said, had been called after they opened the safe, and told to pick up the contents. Although they called twice more, he did not come and they then put the safe in a locker. It was assumed by Goldschein that James didn't pick up the sacks because he didn't want to be in possession of the canceled checks and records while under subpoena. Perhaps he even hoped the safe company would dispose of them.

The balance of the canceled checks were subsequently found and a $900,000 income tax fraud indictment was returned against James, even though he defended himself by claiming the money constituted embezzled funds and therefore was nontaxable. The lower court ruled against this as did the Court of Appeals. James took his case to the Supreme Court. The high court held that from that moment on, stolen funds were taxable. Max Goldschein gave embezzlers another headache: they had to pay taxes on the money they had stolen.

Sometimes a prosecutor will advance his case half-heartedly and then it is up to the Court to see that justice is administered. For in the hand-to-hand combat with the narcotics evil, the toughest enemy is not always the custom-tailored racketeer nor the back-alley punk hovering about a schoolyard. Sometimes our strongest foes can be found in the chambers of justice, the state houses and even higher. The attitudes of these people are criminal. Their indifference encourages the criminal. Sometimes when the evil is finally uncovered, the people react violently, as they did in Houston in 1954.

There, with some members of the police department involved in narcotics traffic and the police chief himself revealed as a user of drugs, the citizens refused to re-elect the administration of Mayor Hofheinz, who had applied the whitewash to this explosive case. Agents Henry Giordano, George White and Fred Douglas made the case in Houston.

Judge Twain Michelsen of San Francisco is nothing like Mayor Hofheinz and in no way like some other justices. He has waged an unrelenting battle against some sluggish officialdom since his earliest days on the bench. He has often written to me in desperation and disgust about the dope situation in San Francisco, a city which the Bureau ranks high as a base for narcotic rings and drug peddlers. Where prosecution for narcotics offenses has been weak, Michelsen has been strong. His twenty-five years on the bench brought him to state this conclusion: "In the absence of legislation that should send dope peddlers to prison for long terms, I am giving the two-count defendants consecutive terms."

Michelsen constantly urged stiffer laws to choke off narcotics traffic. Again and again he appealed to public officials, hoping to arouse them from their lethargy. He knew well the continuing effect of the former rule of people like Tony Parmagini, Mario Balestreri and Jack Sieman. He provided us with one report that led us on a major interstate chase and resulted in the capture and destruction of a powerful drug ring.

When he was finally assigned to the criminal bench, Michelsen called it "a long wished for opportunity to dispose of the cases of convicted narcotics peddlers in the only manner in which I believe they should be handled—rigorously and without compromise. I hope to remain at the Hall of Justice for several years; if so, I feel that many of the 'old-timers' in the illicit narcotics fraternity will have found it uncomfortable to remain in San Francisco."

When the Boggs Act with its stiff penalties was passed in 1951, Michelsen said, "This stiffening of federal laws is a clear reflection of an aroused public conscience." Again he urged California legislators to pass laws no less strong.

But crime in which narcotics were involved continued to mount. Judge Michelsen was particularly offended by the growing toll of youngsters addicted to drugs—youngsters of fourteen and fifteen years. It was a puzzle for him how to treat them. Adult defendants, he noticed with growing horror, were given very short or probationary suspended sentences.

At one point a verbal battle erupted between Michelsen and several state authorities when Joseph Spinoza, who had been tried by Michelsen and recommended for "long time" because of his extensive record of narcotics violations, was transferred from Alcatraz to the county jail for an "adjusted" sentence of ninety days. Michelsen demanded to know how this could have been done without consultation with or even notification to the court. He knew of no legal grounds for the action. State prison officials remained silent before the fury of his condemnation.

Another explosion occurred in 1956 when, on hearing a grand jury decision, Michelsen rejected it to the consternation of many. The jury had indicted Ronald Rodgers, a narcotics parolee, on a new count of furnishing narcotics to an eighteen-year-old girl. Michelsen rejected the decision because not once did the prosecutor bring out the information that the girl was a minor or, perhaps more important, that she had taken the drug without knowing what it was, because Rodgers had never revealed what it was he was giving her. If the judge accepted the jury's decision, Rodgers could have got off with a county jail sentence or, at the most, a year in San Quentin. Michelsen insisted that Rodgers deserved the stiffer penalty of a minimum of five years, mandatory in cases where a person is convicted of furnishing narcotics to a minor. In addition, Michelsen pointed out, Rodgers was still under sentence when brought before the court from the previous charge, parole notwithstanding. The jury asked for clemency because the defendant was only twenty-four years old, but Michelsen answered, "A young rattlesnake is just as dangerous as an old one. These fellows who are selling heroin to your children and mine are just as dangerous as the older ones."

Rodgers was sentenced to ten years to life.

When Michelsen openly accused a state district attorney's office of laxity in suppressing marijuana peddling, still another uproar broke loose. The judge's own investigations had shown a booming dope market in the vicinity of schools and stores patronized by high school students. Further, the judge said that he had received numerous complaints, but the state narcotics authorities and the police department had not themselves acknowledged receipt of complaints and made no investigations even when apprised of the situation. "We have been compelled," Michelsen said angrily, "to put up with the services of a deputy district attorney whose attitude in court is that of a public defender rather than a prosecuting attorney, and who treats our narcotics officers as if they were the criminals to be tried."

For all his firebrand tactics, the powers that be in California agreed that Michelsen, in stiffening the sentences meted out in narcotics cases, had raised a deterrent to narcotic violations, but they found him "otherwise so difficult to deal with" that they wanted him out of the criminal division altogether.

Some time later a defense attorney sought to have Michelsen disqualified from hearing a case. The attorney filed a petition accusing the judge of bias and of possessing a consistently hostile attitude toward narcotics cases. Another petition was filed by another attorney and still another was put forth. All three petitions questioned the defendants' chances for a fair trial if he came up on a narcotics charge. The documents charged that Michelsen was obsessed with the subject of dope. In only six months a court hearing the petitions ruled that Michelsen's contention that the narcotics traffic was loathsome "does not preclude him from trying cases involving narcotic charges."

The motion against Michelsen was denied.

He went on in his furious and sometimes lonely battle to strangle the dope peddlers of San Francisco. I told him after his victory, "May God bless you and keep you in this fight with us."

# 21 ROBERT F. KENNEDY, ATTORNEY GENERAL

When Robert Kennedy was appointed attorney general of the United States, I told the men in the Bureau that the previous attorneys general were sprinters who pulled up at the half-mile post in their efforts to go after the gangs; that Bob Kennedy would go the distance.

His appointment gave inspiration to law enforcement officers who, because of the attitude of many of the men formerly in the post, had become discouraged and had lost the hard, driving will to wipe out crime. It was not that the other attorneys general did not care about the spread of crime; it was just that they were more concerned with other matters. We had known Bob from the days when he and his brother, the late President, worked on the Senate Permanent Subcommittee on Investigations, known popularly as the McClellan Committee. At that time we learned that he was fearless and we supplied him with all of the information he asked for concerning the big criminals. He used it wisely and the underworld had reason to hate and fear him when he became attorney general.

I was reappointed Commissioner of the Bureau of Narcotics on the same day that Robert Kennedy took on his job. The President remarked when he issued me a citation that my appointment was the first one he had made since taking the oath of office.

Almost immediately the new attorney general called the top men of our Bureau together and delivered an inspiring talk. When he was finished, I asked, "What will happen if we bring in the big boys, and the politicians interfere?"

"Commissioner," he said, "you and I will stand together like a rock."

For thirty years the Bureau had been assembing names and identities of the top gangsters in the United States, recording their aliases, family connections, and their criminal specialties. It was a rewarding but frustrating job, somewhat like trying to trace the underground roots of a massive tree. We identified 1,800 of these hoodlums, all associated in a great homogeneous mass of crime. We eliminated the small-time, obscure racketeers and came up with a list of 800 big names in national (and international) crime. We arranged the names by states in a black book we called *Mafia*. Many law enforcement officers have testified before congressional committees and have babbled to the press that no such thing existed. Some men resigned from the Committee on Organized Crime of the International Association of Chiefs of Police in protest, because Chief Edward Allen of Santa Ana, California, and my assistant, Charles Siragusa, were bold enough to speak out against this monstrous organization. For the most part they turned a deaf ear, and when the president of the association claimed there was no such thing in the United States, the Committee on Organized Crime was abolished. In the meantime the Mafia thrived and the agents of the Bureau continued to bring in members who were engaged in narcotic trafficking, but we were at a standstill in our attempts to convince lawmen of the syndicate.

Then Bob Kennedy was appointed attorney general. He had

dealt with many of the hoodlums whose names were in our files when he was the chief counsel of the McClellan Committee. A new day dawned for the Bureau. I had an appointment with Bob Kennedy a few weeks after he took the oath of office, and I brought along my bulky black book, *Mafia*. He scanned the book with intense interest, and called in his assistant in charge of directing the newly organized crime unit. He handed the book to him and instructed him to begin operations immediately against this brotherhood of evil.

Bob Kennedy went all out with the Bureau in our drive against the big international narcotic gangsters. He traveled over the country, calling special meetings with our agents, exhorting them to nail the big traffickers. He would review every case with them personally. He kept the prosecutors on their toes and promised the utmost effort in court to bring about convictions. It was, in a large measure, due to his forceful encouragement of our men that we knocked off such public enemies as Vito Genovese, the number one gangster in the United States, Big John Ormento, Joe Valachi, Carmine Galante, and numerous others.

The attorney general wasn't afraid to admit that there was an association of highly organized gangsters in the country, and he wasn't afraid to term this organization the Mafia when he was asked to testify before the McClellan Committee during the Valachi hearings. "It is a government with an annual income of billions, resting on a base of human suffering and moral corruption," he said. And when he was asked if the syndicate could properly be called the Cosa Nostra or the Mafia, he replied: "It's a matter of semantics. It's the same thing, the mob."

Many former attorneys general (with the exception of Tom Clark, now a Justice of the Supreme Court) would let loose a blast against the underworld and then settle back in their chairs and let it go at that. They seemed to think they had performed their duty merely by calling attention to the problem. Not so with Bob. He followed through. He knew the identity of all the big racketeers in any given district, and in private conference with enforcement officials throughout the country he would go down the line, name by name, and ask what progress had been made. If the atmosphere seemed to be one of status quo, he would light a fire under the fellows who were falling behind. He demanded action and got it. He had a force of special assistants assigned to getting rid of racketeers across the country, and he kept them on their toes by demanding frequent progress reports. In the past two years, at least three underworld conclaves, such as took place at Apalachin, New York, in 1957, have been called off because, as the attorney general put it, "the leaders learned that we had uncovered their well-concealed plans and meeting places."

It was a revelation to me to see what a strong, courageous, and intelligent attorney general could do to spur the forces of law enforcement to root out these evil doers. He had so many important duties I couldn't see how he could devote so much valuable time to this work, what with civil rights and many other problems, yet he never let up. One of these days the country will realize what it owes Bob Kennedy for trying to free the public from the claws and tentacles of these gangsters, racketeers and hoodlums.

It was good to have Bob Kennedy in Washington. His determination to wipe out organized crime has had a significant impact all over the United States. The gangsters are running for their lives.

# 22 A SUMMING UP—THE PAST AND THE FUTURE

On the morning of April 5, 1963, the nation's newspapers carried the details of what has since become known as the "Prettyman Report," a seven-point attack on drug addiction. Former Chief Judge of the U.S. Court of Appeals for the District of Columbia, E. Barret Prettyman, headed the seven-member panel of the President's Advisory Commisssion on Narcotic and Drug Abuse. The Commission was established January 15, 1963 following the first White House Conference on Narcotic and Drug Abuse, held September 27 and 28, 1962.

The Prettyman Report suggested these points to alleviate drug abuses:

1. A federal over-all plan to encourage and steer research into the use of drugs from the laboratory to the community.

2. A special unit of attorneys and agents from the Justice Department and the Narcotics Bureau to find and prosecute illegal traffickers in narcotics and drugs.

3. Tighter regulations to supervise manufacture and distribution

of non-narcotic drugs which have a potential, when used to excess, of creating psychotic or antisocial behavior.

4. Amendments of federal narcotics laws to permit less severe sentences for narcotics users and small-time peddlers. The laws now call for a mandatory sentence of two years for the first offense and five for the second; the latter would remain unchanged.

5. The Department of Health, Education and Welfare would step up efforts to distribute accurate information on drug abuses.

6. A new program of the Narcotics Bureau to provide more modern training and additional information for state and local police.

7. The creation of a joint U.S.–Mexican commission to combat border smuggling.

After the report had been submitted to him, President Kennedy said that the recommendations would be given attention by the federal agencies mentioned, and that they would cooperate with the commission, submitting advice for its final report scheduled for November 1.

On points 1, 3 and 5, I say, Amen. The Bureau of Narcotics for much too long a time has had to fight the peddlers and criminals who have been able to escape prosecution often because of the lack of cooperative effort on the part of other government agencies.

Point 2 sounds remarkably like some units we've had before, like the "Flying Squad" during Prohibition, which failed because of friction; the flying squads usually collided head on with local enforcement authorities, while trying to usurp the prerogatives of those officials responsible for their districts.

If other points in the report are carried out, then less severe sentences, as recommended in point 4, would be feasible. The sentences may have seemed harsh because the Narcotics Bureau has been hamstrung by lack of cooperation, and in order to deter the narcotic criminal and make his conviction forbidding even before he commits his crime, the sentences have been necessarily stiff. I agree with point 6, but will there be enough money provided to make available up-to-date training and teaching available not only to the Bureau, but to the state and local police as well? The recommendations are all well taken, but they require funds with which to be instituted. We have down through the years conducted seminars for state and local police, and to good effect, I believe.*

Point 7 is a formalized recommendation to do what we have always done without actual government agreement or sanction; we have been cooperative with the Mexican police and they certainly have been most cooperative with us.

On the same day the Prettyman Report was making news, the New York Academy of Medicine issued a 70-page document which urged the Bureau of Narcotics to "bow out of the practice of medicine," among other suggestions. The Academy report said that the Bureau was making it difficult for doctors to treat addicts. The fact is that doctors, under our present laws, cannot treat addicts even if they wished to. We do not have in the United States the plan now in operation in England. And we do not have the space to treat addicts; this was an important item missing from the report. Besides, who pays the tab? If the tab is to be paid, more hospitals can be opened; there are very few now, the majority of them private or locally sponsored. The Bureau has been subjected to much criticism for its philosophy, its apparent toughness. In fact, for a condition or point of view which might not have existed had both government and individuals been more concerned with the problems of illegal drug traffic and drug addiction. The Bureau has had to take up the slack, become a Horatio at the bridge. Where were the money, the personnel, the cooperation, the foresight? Now, everyone seems to have it. Our government is of the people; and the type of people who help form a government, an administration, help also to establish its philosophy, its ground rules.

I will not sit by and let the very people to whom I am paying

---

* We have trained over 1,100 local and state officers, or about three times the Bureau's permanent staff.

tribute in this book be maligned by the same persons who often severely limited them in their jobs and who have, if I may be extreme, cost some agents their lives.

Let us share the blame; it cannot rest on the shoulders of a single office which fields but two per cent of the federal law enforcement personnel.

Have the critics of the Bureau been anxious to help the Synanon Foundation? Synanon was founded in 1959 in Santa Monica. Composed of ex-addicts who have kicked the habit via the "cold turkey" route, one which we've seen as the only successful way, Synanon is somewhat like Alcoholics Anonymous. It places great stress on the value of one person being in close touch with another. Ex-addicts are expected to work and contribute to a communal living plan; they are expected to save money with which to return to the world when they feel able. Although a number of citizens in Santa Monica have come to the aid of this group, many, many others, irked by the presence of former criminals and addicts, have hauled the group into the courts.

The new Synanon plant at Westport, Connecticut, has had a similar problem. Synanon has cost the taxpayers very little, if anything. No employer of Synanon members has claimed dissatisfaction. Judges, actors, police and average John Does have felt something for these people. We in the Bureau admire them and wish some of the energy used in the attacks against us could be used in helping them.

The Synanon Foundation should not be confused with the clinic plans of 1919, which some groups have conveniently forgotten. The old clinics called for treatment of the addict while still under the influence of drugs to help him withdraw gradually. Some clinics simply made narcotics available at low cost, as low as two cents per grain. In all, forty-four clinics were opened in the United States. The last one was closed in 1925; most, however, did not run as long. All the clinics were either city or state sponsored, but not necessarily authorized by those governments.

The New York City Department of Health, which cared for

about 8,000 cases of addiction in ten months, said through a spokesman that "We have given the clinic a careful and thorough as well as lengthy trial, and we honestly believe it is unwise to maintain it any longer."

Making narcotics cheap and easily available did not decrease the dope traffic in New York State. In the one-year period when sixteen clinics were in operation, 4,000 ounces of illegal drugs were seized by authorities. Dr. S. Dana Hubbard of the New York City Department of Health said, "The public narcotic clinic is a new thing. In fact, there are only a very few in existence and, if we may judge from our experience, they are not desirable and do not satisfactorily deal with this problem. . . . The clinic has been found to possess all the objectional features characteristic of the so-called 'ambulatory' treatment as practiced by the trafficking physicians."

(In 1962 the Medical Society of the County of New York gave its approval for a pilot project for a narcotic addicts ambulatory treatment plan at a clinic. Sometime later the American Medical Association and the National Research Council opposed the recommendation.)

Touching on one of the problems which still puzzles us so much —the addiction of the young—Dr. Hubbard went on: "Most— in fact, 70 per cent—of the addicts in our clinic are young people (nine per cent, or 743 out of a total of 7,464 were in the 15–19 age group); they have no really serious experiences—surely none sufficient to occasion a desire to escape all of life's responsibilities by recourse to the dreams of narcotic drugs. . . ."

Speaking generally, a spokesman for the Committee on Narcotic Drugs of the American Medical Association said, in part, in a report released in 1921, that "The shallow pretense that drug addiction is a 'disease' which the specialist must be allowed to 'treat,' which pretended treatment consists in supplying its victims with the drug that has caused their physical and moral debauchery . . .has been asserted and urged in volumes of 'literature' by the self-styled 'specialist.' "

And reporting on the clinic at Atlanta, two physicians said, "The only effective treatment for drug addicts is confinement. . .the clinic system was of no benefit to the city."

In Georgia also, Dr. T. F. Abercrombie, Secretary of the Georgia State Board of Health, said, "The narcotic clinic was not beneficial to anyone, and on the contrary drew narcotic peddlers and many undesirables to the city. . .the addicts should be placed in an institution. In addition it was also discovered in Atlanta that many addicts attending the clinic were working in positions hazardous to public safety, such as railroad switchmen and chauffeurs.

At the clinic in New Haven, Connecticut, one addict operated a railroad switch tower during the night shift.

The federal prison at Atlanta reported 13,000 cases of addiction, and at Sing Sing, the number of drug addicts increased from 100 per cent in 1920 to over 900 per cent three years later. The women's workhouse on Welfare Island, New York City, reported that nearly all prostitutes admitted were addicts, and that 60 to 80 per cent of the other inmates were addicts as well.

Louisiana boasted two clinics, one at Shreveport and the other at Alexandria. Both were closed when the following reports were submitted on Shreveport:

It was estimated that 75 per cent of the drug addicts in Texas made their headquarters at Shreveport following the operations of that clinic.

Several prostitutes attended the clinic and plied their trade on the streets of Shreveport. One, nineteen years of age, and another, twenty-three, had never been addicts (in the extreme sense) until they registered at the clinic. Forty per cent of the addicts gave a history of venereal disease, or examination showed its presence.

Evidence showed a continuous traffic in narcotics between clinic and patients and others, and that numerous persons who had never used drugs to a large extent previously, or who had been cured of addiction over several periods, registered at the clinic and started using as high as ten grains daily.

The clinics, some of which Joe Bransky was assigned to close in the South, represented the last widespread effort to come to grips with the *effect* of the narcotics traffic. Perhaps the U.S. Government will lead the way toward a new era in understanding how the dope traffic affects each of us and how important it is to choke off the traffic before it can begin to flow even more heavily through the streets of our cities. Prevention here is worth a million times the cure—the cure no two persons seem to agree on how to administer. Our view is that prevention *is* the cure. Whatever the road, it should be taken at once, for the narcotic traffic dangerously undermines not only the lives of hundreds of thousands of our citizens, but the national security as well.

How?

The record is clear. Communist China, with the greatest land mass in Asia at her disposal, has been flooding her neighboring countries with drugs. Japan, once herself a despoiler of the moral fiber of China during the thirties, has been a major target of the Communists. At the 17th session of the UN-sponsored Commission on Narcotics, the representative of Japan set the number of addicts at 40,000—and they are on the increase. At this meeting the number of American addicts was placed at 45,000, making the Japanese second only to us. There can be no doubt that Japan, one of our bulwarks in the East, is under an insidious narcotics attack.

The Caribbean has long been an important route through which narcotics from Europe could be shunted into America. No one knows yet to what extent Cuba is participating in the effort to undermine the United States with drugs. But certainly, geared as it is for all kinds of warfare, actual and psychological, the Communists may be expected to employ narcotics against America. And if Cuba succeeds in further penetrations of the continent of South America, the illicit drug traffic will be doubled and tripled.

But the greatest threat to America lies within her boundaries.

Crime is close to all of us. We can no longer consider the slums its main habitat; it festers quietly and ruthlessly in the fashionable streets of our country and in many high places of power.

The residents of suburbia have not escaped crime by leaving the cities, as demonstrated in the case of Alvin Beigel.

While New York City slept, federal and local enforcement

officers surrounded a swank apartment building in Queens early on the morning of March 22, 1963. Rumor from the underworld had it that the big operators were moving from Brooklyn to the suburbs where their activities would not be easily observed. Youth workers, police, social workers, federal agents and disgruntled addicts had made life in the Brooklyn slums precarious. The rumor had been traced to Queens and to Beigel, a thirty-eight-year-old salesman who maintained an apartment in Brooklyn as well as in Queens.

The officers did not want to risk throwing the entire building with its hundreds of occupants into an uproar, and therefore had questioned almost none of them about Beigel. It had been ascertained that the salesman kept an apartment in the building, but they didn't know which apartment was his, for there was no listing for him in the lobby register.

The afternoon before the arrest, officers had brushed the handles of his car with a powder that could only be detected with infrared light. When Beigel drove up at three in the morning, parked, and walked into the building, the officers gave him a few minutes to get inside. Then a special team quickly and quietly went into the building and turned the infrared light on the doorknobs. It did not take them long to find the door belonging to Beigel. The salesman admitted agents and police with a shrug; there was nothing he could say, for the entire apartment had been made over into a laboratory for cutting and testing heroin. Police even found a booklet with instructions for these processes. The tenants in the building learned what had happened only when they tuned in their radios or saw the morning papers. The officers had discovered $3,000,000 worth of heroin in Beigel's apartment. Whether the tenants had been awake or asleep, their lives and property were being guarded by people they did not know, people who are their protectors. Unsung, operating under maximum risk conditions, their jobs are never ended.

# APPENDICES

## APPENDIX *I*

Agencies mentioned in *The Protectors*. Please note that eight other operating Bureaus and Offices are also responsible directly to the U.S. Treasury Department.

### The United States Treasury Department

| | |
|---|---|
| I | I |
| I 1789 | I |

| Internal Revenue Service | | | | Secret Service | |
|---|---|---|---|---|---|
| I | | I | I | | I |
| I | 1862 | I | I | 1865 | I |

| Alcohol & Tobacco Tax Division | | | | Narcotics Bureau | |
|---|---|---|---|---|---|
| I | 1933 | I | I | | I |
| I | 1952 | I | I | 1930 | I |

| Coast Guard | | | | Customs | |
|---|---|---|---|---|---|
| I | | I | I | 1789 | I |
| I | 1790 | I | I | 1927 | I |

# APPENDIX II

Throughout *The Protectors* I have avoided using the slang which addicts and traffickers and our agents in undercover roles employ. However, I think a brief glossary may be in order.

A D    a drug addict; A D, so as not to be confused with DA, District Attorney

ACE    a marijuana cigarette; a dollar; a good friend

BAGMAN    pusher, peddler, connection; also swingman

BANG    the sensation caused by intravenous injections of narcotics; a shot

BEE    an addict's habit

BINDLE    a packet of drugs

BINGLE    peddler, bagman, connection

BLACK    opium

BLAST    to smoke marijuana

BLOW    to miss the vein with a shot of narcotics and waste it in the flesh

BOGUE    to be sick from lack of drugs; first stage in withdrawal

BOMB    high potency drugs; not very adulterated

BOSS    same as above

BOY    heroin

BROWN    heroin

BURN    for a pusher to take money for drugs with no intention to deliver

BUST    to arrest; busted, to be arrested

CAP    gelatin capsule filled with a narcotic powder

CHAMP    an addict who will not inform on his fellows

COKE    cocaine

COLD TURKEY    to withdraw from addiction without aid of medicines and usually alone

CONNECTION    peddler, pusher, bagman

COOK      to prepare a narcotic for injection by heating, liquefying

COP      to purchase or steal; in this context, narcotics

DOLOPHINE      a drug used by addicts to help kick the habit without side effects

DYNO      high potency narcotic

FIX      a shot of morphine, heroin or cocaine

GET ON      to take drugs either for the first time or to maintain the habit

GIRL      cocaine because of the sexual sensation when taken

H      heroin

HASH      hashish

JAMMED UP      an overdose of drugs

JOINT      a marijuana cigarette

JOY-POP      to take drugs not out of habit but occasionally for pleasure

JUNK      narcotics

JUNKIE      an addict

MONKEY      an addict's habit

MORPH      morphine

MUD      opium

NAIL      hypodermic needle used for injections; also spike

NOD      to be overcome with drugs to the point where neck and facial muscles lose control and the head swings freely

PIECE      a quantity of narcotics, from $\frac{1}{16}$ of an ounce to an ounce

POT      marijuana

PUSHER      peddler, bagman, swingman

REEFER      marijuana cigarette

SCORE      to meet and purchase drugs from a peddler, pusher

SCRIPT      a prescription for drugs

SHOOTING GALLERY      a place where addicts are given or take narcotics

SMACK      heroin

SNORT      to take heroin or cocaine like snuff

STASH      a hiding place for drugs, a drop

THINGS      capsules, or pieces, of narcotics

TURN ON      to introduce one to drugs, to take drugs

TWISTED      to be high on drugs or sick from lack of them

# APPENDIX III

The following digests taken from the reports of the 17th and 18th sessions of the United Nations Commission on Narcotic Drugs are included here to supply a view of the world's illicit drug traffic. A host of nations are concerned; and they are acting.

Of particular interest is the draft report of the 18th session and its emphasis on traffic in the East.

## Nations Reporting on the Abuse of Drugs (Drug Addiction)
### 1962

"The view was expressed that not enough research has been done on the ætiology of drug addiction, and particularly its social and economic aspects. For example, it had not been determined why some communities were more addiction-prone than others, whether the individual's desire for drugs was innate or acquired, or whether the psychopathic condition of many addicts was congential or the effect of their socio-economic milieu, or even whether addiction was more prevalent among under-privileged and poverty-stricken people than among others. It was mentioned, however, that drug addiction did not necessarily depend on standards of living, since addicts could be found in all sectors of the population, wealthy as well as poor."*

CANADA: Diacetylmorphine the drug to which most addicts were addicted. 3,000 criminal addicts reported. Heavy penalties, but a new concept for treating the addict introduced with the new Narcotics Control Act of 1961.

CUBA: Since the revolution, there had been great improvement regarding *Cannabis* consumption. Education, higher standards of living and stiffer penalties have aided controls.

* Section 135, chapter four, Official Record: 34th Session, Supplement 9.

FEDERAL REPUBLIC OF GERMANY: The total of known addicts was set at 4,334. The figure represents all persons receiving narcotic drugs on medical prescription for more than six weeks.

FRANCE: While addiction raised no social problem in the country where most cases of addiction are of therapeutic origin, the government remained vigilant and exercised strict controls over illicit traffic.

HUNGARY: The few cases of addiction in this country were a result of treatment from serious illness, the Representative said. According to the Permanent Central Opium Board, Hungary ranked high in per capita consumption of ethylmorphine due to the influenza epidemic of 1961, to the preference of Hungarian doctors for ethylmorphine for various disorders, and to the distribution of the drug by wholesalers to hospitals and pharmacies. There were no reported cases of addiction to ethylmorphine.

IRAN: The Representative said that the number of addicts in his country had been reduced 10 per cent and that new hospitals and after-care services were being established to care for addicts.

ITALY: The Observer said that drug addiction was mainly due to therapeutic origin. Drug addiction had come to be considered a social illness, like tuberculosis, and this change of attitude by the public could have very beneficial results. A new center for the treatment of addicts was established with the support of the Ministry of Health, by the Institute of Pharmacology of Rome University.

LIBERIA: The major addiction in his country, the Observer said, was that of *Cannabis* and to a far lesser extent, some other drugs. Taxi drivers were reported most subject to addiction, a fact which had resulted in several accidents. Narcotic drugs were reported smuggled in by seamen on merchant vessels. The Observer expected some increase in addiction as industrialization increases in Africa, and suggested the establishment of governmental agencies.

THE NETHERLANDS: Three government officials working over a year reported to the Representative of this country that, checking a certain population group, they had discovered 428 suspected addicts: 201 males, and 227 females. Of this group, 48 belonged to the medical profession. From this small sampling a general conclusion was reached that addiction might be a greater problem than had been previously thought.

POLAND: Poland reported not more than 200 addicts, mostly of therapeutic origin. Of these, nearly 40 per cent were of the medical and allied professions. This situation was regarded the same as in many other European countries.

THAILAND: The sale and consumption of morphine and diacetylmorphine had replaced the prohibited opium. Laws providing heavier penalties, even up to death, had been instituted. Exemption from penalties was also provided for addicts who presented themselves voluntarily for treatment. Rehabilitation activities on behalf of the addicts have been stepped up.

TURKEY: Turkey commented on its lack of social problems in treating addiction. Consumption and control and manufacture were strictly under government authority.

THE UNITED ARAB REPUBLIC: This Representative expressed fear that the Middle East as a whole might be faced with the threat of increased addiction to "white drugs" because clandestine laboratories, recently discovered, had been producing great amounts of morphine and diacetylmorphine. The main concern, however, was the grave social and economic problems resulting from addiction to hashish and opium which had been transported from Turkey and Lebanon. New legislation, stepped up treatment for addicts, and rehabilitation facilities are expected to bring about reforms.

THE UNITED KINGDOM: The UK reported that the majority of addicts obtained supplies from legitimate sources. Illicit supplies were almost negligible except for *Cannabis*. The UK felt that because of the large number of new drugs the existing situation would be reviewed and an interdepartmental committee on drug addiction established. The UK reasserted its claim that addiction should be regarded as a symptom of mental disorder rather than a form of criminal behavior.

THE UNITED STATES OF AMERICA: The U.S.A. Representative set the present total of addicts at 45,000, a considerable decrease over eighty years ago when there had been 500,000 opium consumers alone. The progress achieved was laid to the system of international and national control established under narcotics treaties.

YUGOSLAVIA: The Representative said that drug addiction did not present any problem, although Yugoslavia was an opium-producing country.

1962: *Salient Points from the*
# COMMISSION ON NARCOTIC DRUGS: REPORT
## OF THE 17th SESSION, MAY–JUNE,
## ECONOMIC AND SOCIAL COUNCIL*
United Nations
(*A Digest*)

United States of America Delegation: H. J. Anslinger; J. T. Cusack, *adviser*; Miss H. E. Dougherty, *alternate*; E. J. Rowell, *adviser*.

### ILLICIT TRAFFIC

1. The Committee on Illicit Traffic consisted of the Representatives of Brazil, Canada, China, France, India, Iran, Japan, Mexico, the Netherlands, Poland, Switzerland, Turkey, the Union of Soviet Socialist Republics, the United Arab Republic, the United Kingdom of Great Britain and Northern Ireland, and the United States of America. In closed session at the Palais des Nations, Geneva, Mr. T. C. Green (United Kingdom) was unanimously elected Chairman.

2. Review of the illicit traffic reaffirmed the conviction of the Commission that only concerted efforts by authorities throughout the world could meet the threat of this evil commerce. The questions considered among the Commission were:

 a. What was the nature of the traffic?
 b. How was it carried on?
 c. By whom is it carried on?
 d. What were the underlying causes for its existence?

* Official Records: 34th Session, Supplement 9.

e. What measures were taken to suppress it?

f. What more was required?

3. The Commission emphasized that the traffic in drugs was a criminal commercial activity *that could rival in magnitude legitimate trade in some essential commodities. Therefore, the problems of production, manufacture, distribution and sale were relevant considerations in the study of illicit narcotics.* * The Commission acknowledged that this particular economy was underground and that the transactions were hidden and the trade statistics incomplete.

4. The Commission noted an account by the Representative of Mexico on the efforts of his government to curb illicit poppy cultivation, *Cannabis* and illicit traffic in general. Substantial results were obtained. The Representative of France again cited the need for closer cooperation among the countries of the Mediterranean to combat illicit drug traffic. Once more he said that efforts should be increased in or near areas of opium production to destroy both poppy cultivation and clandestine laboratories producing morphine base and diacetylmorphine. At the request of the United States the subject of aceticanhydride and acetyl chloride was included in the agenda item and considered in its bearing on the problem of illicit traffic.

5. Statements by a number of Representatives cited the important work played by the International Criminal Police Organization (Interpol) in the fight against the illicit traffic. The Representative of the United States wished to express his government's appreciation of the cooperation extended by Canada, France, Italy, Lebanon, Mexico, Spain, Syria and Turkey.

6. The Commission was disappointed to learn that efforts which had been made to bring about bilateral control of the frontiers comparable to the arrangement between Turkey and Iran, have had little success in the Far East among Burma, Cambodia, Hong Kong, Japan, Macao, the Republic of Vietnam, Singapore and Thailand.

* Italics mine.

7. Opium and the opiates, *Cannabis* and cocaine, maintained their traditional prominence in the illicit drug traffic. There were changes within this pattern, most notably in Thailand where, it was reported, diacetylmorphine replaced opium prohibited in 1959. Indications also existed that the cocaine traffic was spreading throughout Latin America on a more limited scale than opium and opium products, and moving to all parts of the world. Illicit markets included the Mediterranean area, Asia, Canada and the United States of America.

8. Canada, the United States, Hong Kong, and in lesser degree Japan and Thailand, continued as targets for highly organized international traffic in diacetylmorphine. In North America, heavy seizures were reported and routes were traced along supply lines running from Europe from the Near and Middle East and from Asia both to the east and west. Hong Kong, Japan and Thailand were, like the United States and Canada, taking vigorous steps to combat widespread abuse of diacetylmorphine. In Japan, however, it was noted that this particular illicit traffic is increasing.

9. The Commission noted that the opium traffic in the Far East was mostly supplied by the underground production in the Burma-mainland China-Laos-Thailand border areas. From this region, whose limits cannot be precisely defined, came a large proportion of the raw drug which, after preparation or conversion, supplied the addict populations in many parts of the world. It is quite probable that the notorious 666 or 999 brand of morphine originated here.

10. Large seizures of raw opium were reported by countries in the Near, Middle and Far East. The traffic in opiates was closely linked with traffic in raw material. Clandestine manufacture of morphine and diacetylmorphine in Lebanon, Iran, Syria and Turkey was reported.

11. Opium traffic in Europe and Oceania traffic in opium were mainly transit involving merchant ships and crew members. Reported seizures:: France, 3 kg.; Italy, 18 kg.; the Netherlands, 19 kg.; the United Kingdom, 11 kg. A similar traffic took place in

Africa except that some clandestine cultivation for domestic consumption was reported by Tunisia. Madagascar, Mauritius and Zanzibar reported the use of opium on a small scale.

12. There was no substantial opium traffic in either of the American continents. Underground cultivation continued to be reported by Mexico, however, although the government campaign of repression was having considerable effect. The Representative of the United States informed the Commission that in the view of his government, the efforts made by the Mexican authorities deserved praise. Eighty-two hectares of poppy cultivation had been destroyed in only twenty days in a campaign in which new equipment was used. Raw opium seized in the United States in 1961 totaled about 4 kg. and of prepared opium about 8 kg.

13. The Indian government control of opium production was applauded. India, one of the world's major producers, had listed over 200,000 licit opium cultivators. Each cultivator is now licensed and all poppy fields measured by cadastral survey. Cases of narcotic offenses before the courts in 1961 numbered almost 5,000 persons. Seizures of opium amounted to 6,540 kg.; 333 kg. were seized in attempted exportation.

14. Hong Kong reported a total of 16,663 dangerous drug offenses committed in 1961. Some 13,000 people were arrested. Opium was involved in some 7,000 cases and diacetylmorphine in 7,500. Public interest and support, however, had enlisted the populace with the result that the incidence of addiction among the youth of the Colony remained very low. While the illicit traffic continued along the route from Bangkok, it was believed that no large-scale export traffic was taking place.

15. Three witnesses, former inhabitants of Yunnan province in mainland China, had made detailed statements to the United States Treasury Department on the cultivation of opium in Yunnan and its export from there to the Shan State in Burma. One witness had himself been a cultivator, and in 1953 and 1956 he had joined caravans transporting opium to the Shan frontier. There he assisted in its transshipment into trucks for a destination

at Kentung, Burma. He estimated that the total production of the region in 1961 had been around 1,000 tons.

16. The Representative of China* supported the statements of the former cultivator from Yunnan province with reports of his own on traffic from that province to the Shan State of Burma.

17. The Representative of Poland protested the presentation of information concerning the People's Republic of China without a Representative of that country being present. The Representative of Hungary agreed with this view. The Representative of the Union of Soviet Socialist Republics concurred and stated that the People's Republic of China complied completely with the international rules relating to the suppression of the illicit traffic in narcotic drugs.

18. In the Near and Middle East increased trafficking in diacetylmorphine was noted near the borders of Afghanistan and Turkey. The destruction of poppy beds resulted in greater smuggling of opium into Iran. The Representative of the Anti-Narcotics Bureau of the League of Arab States reviewed the situation which was worsening. White drug addiction did not constitute a problem except in Lebanon. The illicit manufacture of diacetylmorphine in the region of Aleppo, Syria, was of growing concern. The use of opium was believed to be spreading to Libya, Tunisia and the Sudan. Jordan and Saudi Arabia had set up special narcotics bureaus. Opium from Turkey and Iran entered Syria and Jordan and was shipped on to Israel and Lebanon, the UAR, Cyprus, Iraq and Kuwait. The Representative of Turkey regretted that spokesmen from the UAR and the Arab League States had thought it possible to attribute the burden of responsibility for opium traffic in the region to his country, and went on to cite the gains made by his country in the control of illicit traffic.

19. Statements by the Representatives of the United States and Canada pointed out the serious effects which the international traffic continued to have on their countries whose addiction rates were set at approximately one person of every 4,000–6,000. Diacetylmorphine accounted for about 95 per cent of the addicts in both countries. In neither country was there clandestine production or manufacture of narcotics. Both were supplied from abroad.

* Nationalist China.

1963: *Salient Points from the*
COMMISSION ON NARCOTIC DRUGS: REPORT
(DRAFT) OF THE 18TH SESSION, APRIL–MAY
ECONOMIC AND SOCIAL COUNCIL
United Nations
(A *Digest*)

United States of America Delegation: H. J. Anslinger, H. L.
Giordano, O. E. Mulliken, J. T. Devive, J. T. Cusack

### ILLICIT TRAFFIC COMMITTEE REPORT

1. The Committee on Illicit Traffic met in closed session at the
Palais des Nations, Geneva, with Representatives from Canada,
China, France, Hungary, India, Iran, Japan, Mexico, Poland, Re-
public of Korea, Switzerland, Turkey, United Arab Republic,
United Kingdom and the United States of America. Mr. R. E.
Curran, Queen's Counsel from Canada, was elected Chairman
unanimously.

2. Observers attending the meeting were from Burma, Greece,
Israel, Italy, Lebanon, the Netherlands, Portugal, Thailand and
the International Criminal Police Organization, Interpol and the
Permanent Anti-Narcotics Bureau of the League of Arab States.

3. It was noted that reporting by governments on the illicit
traffic has improved. . . . The Commission noted, nevertheless,
that more and better reports were needed, and at an earlier date,
to enable it to make a satisfactory study of the traffic each year.

4. According to its decision at the last session, the Commission
gave special attention to the situation of the illicit traffic in the
For East.

5. The Representative of the United Kingdom made a statement describing the situation in Hong Kong. . . . The Colony occupies a small area: 391 square miles of land, and 600 square miles of water in which some 200 islands lie. The population is three and a half million, 98 per cent Chinese. Hong Kong does not produce opium, and the manufactured drugs or raw materials for local illicit manufacture must come from outside. . . . Hong Kong's land frontier of 26 miles length raises no trafficking problem, but the port attracts shipping from all over the world. . . . In 1962, nearly 6,000 ocean-going vessels and over 14,000 other craft came and went in the port. Six hundred and eighteen ships were guarded in 1962; of 56 narcotics seizures (made by the Special Narcotics Section of the Prevention Service) 26 were on board vessels. Six hundred and ten aircraft were also subject to inspection. Enforcement services operate around the clock the whole year long. Between 12,000 and 15,000 narcotics raids are made in a year; 1,300 cases are detected and over 1,000 persons prosecuted each month, and, on the average of 40 seizures are made each day. There were 9,934 seizures in 1962, of which 7,343 were heroin. Three or four thousand heroin peddlers are apprehended every year. . . . Earlier reports have now been confirmed that large quantities of drugs were being air-dropped in the Gulf of Siam— South China Seas areas, and then brought by vessels to Hong Kong. . . . Aircraft used in these operations are reported to be piloted by French nationals resident in Laos.

6. The Representative of the Republic of Korea referred to information given in their Annual Report for 1962. The illicit traffic dealt mainly in raw opium, morphine and heroin supplied by illicit cultivation, and intended for the domestic market. Prosecutions in the cases of narcotic offenses numbered 4,221.

7. The Representative of China stated that the traffic in the Province of Taiwan was not supplied by any illicit cultivation or manufacture, and that all drugs were smuggled into the country, particularly from Hong Kong. About the same number of cases of trafficking had been detected in 1962 as in 1961. These 86 cases were included in the total of 461, involving 536 persons brought to trial during the year. In a case of trafficking at Tai Pei in 1962,

the offender stated that he had dealt with two kilograms of opium which came from the Yunnan border area. The Representative of China thought it important to note that the sample of opium seized in the Republic of Korea, to which the Representative of the United States had referred, had been found on scientific grounds to be of probable mainland Chinese origin.

8. The Representative of Japan made a statement concerning the situation in his country. Owing to strict enforcement measures carried out under the Narcotic Control Law, traffickers had not attempted clandestine manufacture of narcotics in Japan. Abuse of heroin was, however, a serious problem and foreign traffickers engaged in organized smuggling on a considerable scale, operating from Bangkok, Hong Kong and Korea. The quantities of heroin seized in 1962 (8 kg.) was double the 1961 total. The Representative informed the Commission, in a reply to a request for information from the Representative of the United States, that cases of teen-age users and pushers had occurred in Kobe and Osaka and that educational campaigns were being undertaken to prevent youth being victimized by traffickers.

9. The Observer of Thailand referred to the Annual Report of his government and stated that seizures of over six tons of opium in 1962, compared to about four tons in each of the two preceding years, were evidence of continued heavy traffic. Thailand is in the center of South East Asia, geographically, and easily accessible from all directions. There are forty-two possible routes for smuggling from Burma and Laos, but it appeared that Amphur Chiangsan, the Pang Kway district and the Mae Sai district were the three border areas of Thailand used for the largest amount of trafficking toward Bangkok. In 1962 offenses against the Opium Act, mainly smoking or possession, were committed by 2,117 persons of whom 1,673 were convicted. Only one clandestine manufacturing center was discovered in 1962, compared with three in 1961; three packing plants were discovered in Bangkok. The total quantity of heroin (138 kg.) seized in 1962 was more than twice that of 1961, and nine times the total for 1960. There was significant evidence pointing to areas beyond the northern borders of Thailand as the place of origin of "999" morphine.

Pai Lao

10. In commenting on the traffic in South East Asia the Representative of the United States informed the Commission that in the late summer of 1962 reports were received that a huge quantity (40,000 pounds or about 18 tons) of raw opium, in leaf wrappers, was smuggled from the Yunnan region through the Shan state of Burma for sale in Laos and Thailand and for smuggling to the United States. This shipment was reportedly handled by the Kokang Opium Syndicate of Burma. The United States Bureau of Narcotics had requested the Secretariat of the United Nations to determine the origin of a sample of raw opium removed from a seizure made by the Republic of Korea. The Korean authorities, through their delegation in Geneva, associated themselves with the United States' request for a determination of origin. The report of the examination carried out by the United Nations Laboratory stated that the findings "indicate that this seizure very probably originated from mainland China. It is, however, not possible to be more definite in view of the fewness of the authenticated samples from the Chinese mainland."

11. The Representative of Hungary observed that clandestine manufacture, local consumption of white drugs and illicit export all appeared to be consistently on the increase in the Far East. There was evidence also that increasingly effective enforcement measures were being brought into play. However, insinuations about the People's Republic of China were being made with greater frequency, and the suggestion that this country was supplying the illicit traffic in order to finance activities abroad and to purchase strategic materials had to be rejected.

12. The Representative of Poland expressed the view that the term "Yunnan opium" was at best misleading and that its use, while convenient, had gratuitous adverse effects through publicizing the name of a province of the People's Republic of China in connection with information on illicit traffic which was not well-founded. The Representative of Poland also referred to reports by the Representative of the United States of America concerning the cocaine traffic . . . and the alleged involvement of Cuban nationals. While he wished to be understood to sympathize with the United States in its struggle with illicit traffic, he objected strongly to the

emphasis placed on the part played by Cubans and expressed doubt whether nationals of many other countries were not also involved.

13. The Representative of the United States emphasized, in reply to the statements by the Representatives of Hungary and Poland, that his references to Cuba and Communist China in connection with certain cases and seizures which he had cited were intended to bring to the attention of the Commission facts concerning the traffic as it affected the United States of America. There could be no doubt that every effort should be made to pinpoint the source of raw opium and morphine in South East Asia, for the good of peoples throughout the world. All possible locations of the source of supply should be examined, in the Burma-mainland-China-Laos-Thailand border areas where, in particular, Yunnan province of mainland China had been an opium-producing area for centuries past.

14. The Commission took note of data on seizures of opium and opiates in countries of the Americas, observing that situation particularly in respect of the heroin traffic in the United States and Canada, continued to be as serious as in other years. The Representative of the United States of America outlined the problem facing his country and cited significant seizures made in 1962. The total quantity of about 88 kg. was more than twice that seized in 1961. All heroin used in the United States, accounting for over 95 per cent of addiction, was introduced by smuggling, the largest proportion of it originating in Europe and the Far East and entering the country at all frontiers. . . . Illicit imports from France and Italy were made directly into the United States and by way of both Mexico and Canada, and considerable quantities of heroin from the Far East were smuggled through West Coast ports. Two cases of seizures mentioned in detail by the Representative of the United States were illustrative of complexities of the traffic. Chan Way, a well-known seaman-smuggler, was arrested on January 2, 1962, when he transferred a package of 15 grams of heroin to Gee Bing Soon. Sixty-eight grams of heroin were seized from Chan Way, who admitted that he had smuggled it into the United

States from Hong Kong, where he had obtained it from one Wong Chak.

15. The Representative of the United States of America expressed his government's appreciation of the action taken by the government of Italy in arresting Settimo Accardi, an important fugitive from the United States, whose extradition it was hoped would be arranged as soon as possible by the Italian government.

16. The Observer of Burma explained that the presumed area of opium production was divided by the Salween River into areas where cultivation was prohibited, west of the river, and those on the east where, in the Shan state, cultivation was still permitted. Illicit production undoubtedly did occur in Kachin state, but it was mostly for local consumption, particularly in quasi-medical use and in connection with some forms of worship. It was estimated that there were some 45,000 addicts in the Kachin state among a population numbering 525,000. The Representative stated that his government would appreciate receiving from the government of the United States of America further information concerning the report that the Kokang Opium Syndicate of Burma had dealt with a shipment of some 20,000 kg. of opium smuggled from Yunnan through the Shan state in 1962.